Our Life Off the Grid

- An Urban Couple Goes Feral -

J. DAVID COX

Library and Archives Canada Cataloguing in Publication

Cox, J. David, author
Our life off the grid: an urban couple goes feral / J. David Cox.

Issued in print and electronic formats.
ISBN 978-0-9940145-0-4 (pbk.).--ISBN 978-0-9940145-1-1 (mobi). ISBN 978-0-9940145-2-8 (epub)

1. Cox, J. David--Homes and haunts. 2. Davies, Sally J., 1952- --Homes and haunts. 3. Sustainable living--British Columbia. 4. Self-reliant living--British Columbia. I. Title.

GF78.C685 2015 640.28'6 C2015-902902-3
C2015-902903-1

OTG Publishing
Box 53
Surge Narrows, British Columbia
CANADA V0P 1W0
coxdavies@gmail.com

Editor and Book Design: Sally J. Davies
Cover: Simon Davies/Emily Robertson

Picture acknowledgements: Cover and About the Author: Emily Robertson
All other photos by the author or Sally J. Davies unless otherwise noted

For Sally

Camping on lower deck prior to construction

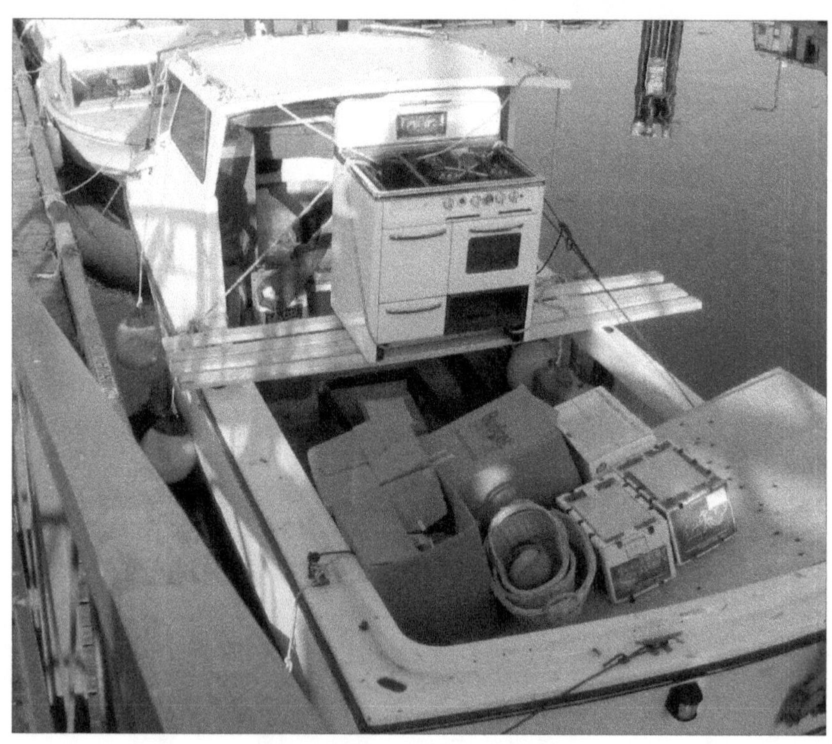

Moving day number nine

Prologue

I was underwater. I was freezing. And I was hurt. One second I was sitting in the boat in the sun, the next I was in the water with the propeller hitting my head as it drove over me at full speed. It struck me like a sledgehammer. Some kind of goo was coming out of my skull as I flailed about, trying to get to the surface. I was starting to think that our move to the wilderness might not be such a good idea after all.

My wife Sally and I were building a small cabin on a sparsely populated and un-serviced island on the British Columbia coast. Around noon on a hot summer day we craved some ice cream so we left our building site for a two mile trip by boat to the local store.

We were scooting along in our small inflatable boat at high speed. Sally was steering the outboard motor and I was sitting up front on the edge of the bow, leaning forward with my arms on my knees, my center of gravity well inboard. I thought I was safe.

However, at the exact moment I straightened up to look at a sun-bathing seal we hit an inexplicably large wave. The momentum of straightening my posture, together with the deceleration of the boat, flung me backwards off the front of the boat. I was upside down in the water under the boat. It was instant. I remember thinking, damn the propeller! Then there was a huge *bang* as it hit me. I remember thinking again, damn, the propeller!

A few seconds later I bobbed to the surface with a view of the boat still moving away from me. I could see Sally's back. That was not a good moment. She seemed so distant. Worse, she was headed the wrong way. I could already feel hot liquid pouring from the top of my head and I wasn't sure that it was only blood. I briefly contemplated the consistency of brain matter. The pain was extreme but not incapacitating. I was conscious but not overly coherent. I remember instinctively calling out, "Oh, my God!"

It occurred to me that "Oh, my God!" was not going to convey the appropriate message to Sally. So I took a deep breath, collected my thoughts, tried to be calm and prepared myself to yell again. This time I had purposefully formed the right words in my head to give her proper directions. And so, at the top of my lungs, I again shouted "Oh, my God!"

This involuntary and repetitive exclamation struck me as mildly amusing at the time. It seemed I was destined to yell prayers instead of instructions. Just as well, I thought, considering the situation. So, I kept quiet and began to swim slowly towards the boat which had finally stopped. It was only a short distance away. It seemed like a mile.

Sally had watched the whole accident unfold in less than a few seconds. I hit the water and the boat was traveling so fast I was behind it in an instant. She didn't have a chance to avoid hitting me. For a brief moment, she was in shock. She quickly stopped the boat in order to get a grasp on the situation. It was the right move. It allowed her to regain her composure and get back to me safely.

As I swam I became more and more aware of my circumstance. I was fully clothed. My glasses were gone. I was injured and bleeding. My immediate rescue was likely, but medical assistance was not readily available. And I was acutely aware of the temperature I was experiencing. I was in very cold water and my body was rapidly cooling.

In the meantime that hot gooey something was pouring from my head and down my face. Sticky warmth covered my head but my body was getting colder. It was very strange and not just a little disconcerting. I started to worry.

Sally restarted the boat and covered the distance back to me within moments. She drifted up neatly with the engine in neutral. After a few futile attempts to get me into the boat, I suggested that I hold on to the rope looped along the side of the boat and that she simply drag me in to the nearest shore as quickly as she could.

Sally took the extra precaution of lashing me to the boat. She looped a rope under my arms and fastened the ends securely. It was a good idea as being dragged through the water increased my heat loss exponentially. It was scary cold. I quickly became so numb I couldn't hold on. I almost passed out.

After what seemed like an hour, but was actually only a few minutes, we ran up on a beach. With Sally's help I was able to roll into the boat. She gave me her shirt to use as a bandage and I held it on the wound to staunch the flow of blood. For the next few hours I could feel what I assumed was a skull fragment as I held it in place. That too, was somewhat disconcerting.

We left the beach and motored another ten minutes to the nearest neighbour who called the Coast Guard. Forty-five minutes later two Coast Guard boats were on the scene and shortly after that a helicopter arrived to take me to the hospital. As the chopper carried me aloft, the Coast Guard staff turned to assist my traumatized and worried wife. They brought her by boat and then by car to join me at the emergency room.

I was very lucky. Not to mention hard-headed. The propeller had sliced through my scalp in two separate places but had not cut into my skull. One blade sliced along the part line of my hair and the second cut almost at right angles near the crown of my head. There was no skull fragment—only a bloodied shirt button and an overly vivid imagination. In retrospect, expecting brain matter to ooze out whenever I moved the makeshift bandage was the worst part of the whole experience.

By dinner time I was stitched up and discharged and Sally and I were catching the ferry back to a nearby island and from there a water taxi to our cabin. A little later, sipping a badly needed medicinal Scotch, I realized I had lost all sense of taste, at least temporarily. I certainly still felt a bit whacked but, all in all, I was pretty much intact and doing fine.

The sun was setting as we sat on the boathouse deck. I held Sally close for a long time and reflected on the day. I was very thankful to be there and grateful for the assistance we had received from the Coast Guard and the Emergency room staff.

"You know, Sal, this wilderness living thing is turning out to be quite an adventure. I am still quite keen but, I must admit, today's little incident with the propeller made me think."

"What do you mean?"

"Maybe I'll get a few extra pairs of glasses. Just in case. Perhaps they make some that float. And how about a freezer? Then we could keep our own ice cream."

She looked at my bandaged head, shook her head and burst out laughing.

"Phew!" I thought. "Looks like she's still onside."

The end of the road on the adjacent island where we transfer supplies from our vehicle to our boat

-1-

Out of the Box

I was fifty and I was bored. I didn't have a red Corvette, I was not sneaking around with secretaries and I had no major hobbies or vices to diligently pursue. Well, there had been a long relationship with golf but it was fraught with tension and frustration. Words were yelled. Clubs were thrown. That love affair was over. And retirement had nothing to attract me. I was thinking of just giving up on dreaming and simply pushing hard for the last few years of work to get a huge bankroll so that I wouldn't have to worry about the cost of old age. It wasn't much of a plan but it was all I could think of.

But, before the big push for financial security, Sally and I realized that our kids were approaching the age at which they were going to be teens, making most of their own decisions—whether we wanted them to or not. And we wanted them to at least have some perspective from which to do this. Growing up in a suburban cul-de-sac was not enough. So we decided to take them out of school for a few months of adventure and learning. We wanted to help them grow up. Traveling, we believed, would assist in that process.

And it assisted me, too. I was shocked by a conversation I had with Sally just as we were about to head out on our big trip with the kids. She told me that we had to leave some money behind for various home expenses. I pointed out that we had paid the house mortgage off, we were going to lock the doors, it was a safe neighborhood and we were insured. I couldn't see the need to put money aside for a house I wasn't living in.

"We have life and health insurance, plus the boat, two cars and the house to insure. There are monthly bills for cable, internet, lawn care, and the alarm and pool service. The window cleaners come twice while we're away and I don't want to lose them. Don't forget the two phone lines plus business line and fax line. And we have four cell phones." She went on and on.

Finally, I interrupted and said, "Okay, okay! I was wrong! What does it add up to?"

"Well," she said, "I figure 1,500 dollars a month should cover everything."

"Are you saying that we have to budget almost 6,000 dollars *not* to live in the house for four months? Does that make any sense? Is that not madness? Do you realize that we have to earn at least 9,000 dollars so that, after taxes, we can leave that kind of money for a house that *we are not living in*?"

I quickly concluded that I had to earn almost 27,000 dollars on an annualized basis *not* to live in my house. And this didn't even include the price of buying and mortgaging the damn thing in the first place! I then tried to calculate what it cost me to actually reside there. To paraphrase MasterCard, it was beyond priceless, it was ridiculous.

That was a very telling moment for me. I immediately understood that I didn't want to spend any more of my life working for a house and chattels. Of course it wasn't a choice I could exercise at the time. Raising a family is a commitment. But part of the deal was that the kids would fledge someday and, I now knew, so would I.

Our big trip with the kids encompassed traveling by recreational vehicle across Canada west to east, flying to Europe for a few weeks and then returning to RV our way back home through the United States. It was a good experience for us all. As we neared the end of our trip we were approaching a junction with Interstate 5 somewhere around Bellingham, Washington. The plan was to turn the motor home right and head north to return to our life in Vancouver, Canada. It was then that I realized I had no desire to go home—none at all. We'd been gone long enough for the general brain-dead numbness caused by running with the rats to subside and I just didn't want any more of it. Home was just not where my heart was.

"You know…it's just as easy for us to go left at Bellingham instead of turning right. We could go to Mexico and kill a few months down there. Waddya all think?"

My teenage son, Ben, usually absorbed in some electronic device, freaked out.

"What? What are you talking about? What about my education? You guys are talking crazy, like, like old hippies!"

My twelve year old daughter, Emily, who always disagreed with her brother on principle, surprisingly supported him this time.

"Hey! Unlike you guys, I have a life! And it's not in Mexico. We have to go home! What kind of irresponsible parents are you? We can't afford to keep traveling! You guys have to go back to work and we have to get back to school!"

Ben and Emily were surprisingly and uncharacteristically passionate about their normal life in the 'burbs and I was left speechless. After all, listening to them describe their lives over the last few years, it had previously sucked. I turned right, as required but, naturally enough, started to wonder who their real father was. I returned to the cul-de-sac. Physically, at least.

But I had left my heart somewhere out on the road. I just couldn't plug back in, at least not like I had before. Then I had an epiphany. I'd run for politics. That had always been something I'd meant to do and could solve everything from my midlife crisis to regular income. And so I gave that a shot at the next federal election, got my butt kicked and decided that maybe I should opt for plan B.

For some strange reason I had also been dreaming about building my own house. I knew it was odd and at first I resisted but, eventually, I admitted to myself that I had this minor obsession and I might as well confess it out loud. I told Sally that I had a future outside of politics—building a house.

"That's nice, sweetie. Maybe someday you can get a hammer or whatever and give it a go."

"Sal, it's not like that. I'm not talking whimsy here. It's more primal, more basic. More like "a man's gotta do kind of thing". I'm talking about designing, building the foundation, construction, wiring, plumbing, finishing the interior…the whole shebang. I am talking about you and me building a house...in the wilderness…from scratch!"

"What do you *mean*, you and me? What do you *mean* wilderness?"

"I can't do it alone. Somebody has to hold the ladder and pass up the nails. Get the band-aids. And we did buy a piece of property a long time ago up the coast. I think we should build there."

"But you don't know how to build a house and I certainly don't. There aren't any services there. What about water and electricity? We have no skills, no experience, no tools, no materials and no money. Aren't there cougars up there? Do you even have any idea where to start?"

"Yes, I do know where to start. I start by getting a job at a company that builds homes and learning all about it. And don't worry about the cougars. If I go all mountain man on ya, I'll be able to handle a few cougars."

After it had become evident to me that I was living to work and no longer working to live, I mentally checked out of the urban rat race. I physically left the city at fifty-six. I took almost six years to actually choose where to go and how to extricate myself from the boiling cauldron of the cul-de-sac and the modern work place. Those years were spent struggling with the transition. What may have appeared to be a sudden leap of faith was not. It was really drawn-out slow motion learning and planning.

A big part of the transition phase for me was working at Linwood Homes, a pre-packaged home specialty company. Sal started by looking into getting her firearms license. Hopefully, it was for the cougars.

Linwood makes cedar homes and house kits and it is an excellent company putting out a great product. It did not hurt that a friend of mine was a major partner in the firm. I learned all that I could in the year and a half I was with them and I was eventually confident that I could, with Sal's help, build a house.

During the time I was at Linwood I also tried to do as much research as possible on life off the grid. I rooted around and actually found my old Whole Earth Catalogue buried in the bookcase. That was a fun but dated read. Solar panels didn't exist in the sixties. So I searched a little further and discovered the modern day equivalent: the Mother Earth News forum on the internet. There were many daily writers and much give and take about living off the grid. Here was an ongoing discussion of the traditional and modern on the cutting edge of simple, healthy living. I was venturing outside the box. But I had company. And I was hooked.

The forum provided a place for people to discuss seeds and fertilizer, chickens and tractors, building, and even old time skills such as quilting, making your own brooms, pickling eggs and dealing with sheep or chicken diseases. There was an article on how to suck the phlegm from the noses and throats of newborn lambs. It seems they can asphyxiate on their own mucous and one is obliged to suck it out of them by going mouth-to-nose. I read it. Clearly, at this point I was straying way too far outside the box.

During this time Sal was working and getting ahead in the corporate world. She went to a lot of meetings, pushed a lot of paper, strove to implement the latest corporate reorganization and continued to put out office fires while wading hip-deep in alligators. Her employment circumstance was aggravated by continual lay-offs and budget cuts. The remaining workload kept piling up on her. She, unfortunately for her health, accepted with diligence and grace the increasing responsibility foisted on her. And, of course, she put out even more energy and effort and worked even longer hours.

One day I noticed that her rosy cheeks were fading. Her normally instant smile was hesitant. She was working way too hard and starting to burn out. She eventually became quite ill and came to the conclusion that she wouldn't recover her health if she continued with her job.

One memorable evening Sally read in our community newspaper that the local secondary school building trades program was in trouble.

"Every year they build a small cabin for a volunteer sponsor. They learn by working on an actual building project. This year the sponsor let them down by backing out at the last minute. You want to build a cabin. I think we should be their sponsor."

"Are you serious? This means we'll be high tailing it out of here within a year...Can you quit? Can you make the leap?"

"Well, I really need to get out of that terrible workplace...and this is what you want, isn't it? I think we should at least take the first step. Why don't you phone the teacher right now?"

"Okay!"

Sally marking locations for house foundation posts

-2-

Our Level Best

"Hi! Do you still need a sponsor for your trade class?" I asked.

"Yeah, are you interested? Great! Let's meet at the school tomorrow morning."

And with that brief phone conversation, the die was cast. I went to Delta Secondary School the next morning and met Dwayne, the building trades teacher, and some of the twenty or so young men who comprised his class. They were a pretty loose group; a bunch of goofy grade eleven and twelve teenage boys. They didn't listen to their teacher much and initially I wasn't very impressed with them. But I wasn't about to miss out on this window of opportunity that Sally had offered. I'd work with this motley crew, or any motley crew. I was just happy to get started on my dream.

"Before we start on this, Dwayne, I should tell you that the cabin I'm planning is nine hundred square feet with a three hundred square foot loft. Is that too big for your class?"

"Nah, we've been building four to six hundred square foot sheds each year but going up a bit in size isn't a problem. We build the main floor here at the school and then dismantle it for transporting to your site. Then I take the kids up there for a week and we erect it on the foundation that you have already put in place. Can that be done?"

"Yes and no. The site is a severe slope so the back of the house will have low concrete posts, but the front and sides will be elevated on logs. I figure they will be about twenty feet high at the very front and, to a large extent are held in place by the floor. So, we'll get it all ready except for the front row of posts. They will have to be done after you get there. Will that work?"

"Oh yeah, no problem. You'll need to transport twenty or so people from the lower mainland, feed and house us for a week and then get us back home, okay?"

"Yeah. By the way, how far will the crew get in a week? I can't imagine getting to lock up."

"We'll get almost to lock up but I can't guarantee we'll finish the roof. We'll get the rafters up anyway. No worries. Maybe we'll even get the strapping on. Just make sure the material is on site. We don't want to have to stop for lack of building supplies."

I showed Dwayne pictures of the site. I showed him the incline of the slope on which we were building by holding a yardstick at the appropriate angle. He was not deterred. We shook hands and I handed him the plans and the first payment for the school to purchase the materials for the main floor.

We are not so wealthy that we can own a home in the city and a second one up the coast. To build on our island property meant putting our house up for sale. So, up it went.

As it turned out, the students don't build much in their first semester. That time was spent ensuring that each kid knew how to use their tools. A few small projects such as building the corbels were undertaken to establish their respective skill levels. Not all of them were A students.

I drove by the school the winter evening the house sold and saw a small, miserable-looking first floor platform sitting in the rain surrounded by slings of lumber. It was not an inspirational thing to do. I didn't tell Sally about my so-called progress visit. I confess to having had a few second thoughts that night, but there was no turning back.

Making a commitment to the school meant we needed to build some infrastructure on site before the students arrived. And in order to do this we needed a place to work. Given that our location was a slope, we were quickly learning that a level surface is a wonderful thing. We decided we had to build a deck. This meant purchasing all the materials from the nearest building supply store, hiring a barge to deliver them and being on site to schlep everything up the beach without a level spot anywhere on which to place it.

All the tools I would need to build the deck would be delivered in advance of building (by me, of course). They would need a safe, weatherproof and secure enclosure. So, step one in the building process was going to be tool storage on site.

I bought a large steel box from the BC Hydro salvage yard and transported it up the coast in my utility trailer by road and ferry to a boat ramp on our neighboring island. It weighed just over four hundred pounds. Sal and I then eased that extremely heavy box off our little trailer straight into our eleven foot inflatable dinghy which we were using as our commuter boat.

When in place, the box looked like the conning tower of a submarine. It filled the boat completely. My steering position was one of stretching out one leg along the top of a pontoon and scrunching the other into a space shared with the outboard engine steering tiller and the gas tank. And, of course, I couldn't see directly ahead, or to either side, actually, as my view was blocked by the steel box. When it was loaded the boat floated a smidge low in the water.

"I think there is room for you, sweetie." I said to Sal. "Just climb on and stand with your feet apart on the bow like Leonardo di Caprio on the Titanic and hold onto the box." A poor choice of imagery, I realized too late.

Sal just looked at me. She didn't move.

"David, it's starting to blow up out there. I don't think you're going to make it. And I sure as hell am not going with you! *You* shouldn't go. And, if you do, you can't take that box. You can't see where you're going and the whole load is way too top heavy. Don't be insane!"

She had a good point, but men, eh? I mean I had struggled like hell to get the thing this far. I needed it. And delivering unwieldy stuff to our property was supposed to be part of the plan. I couldn't wuss out just because of an impending storm and the need to be a contortionist. This was a test!

"I can make it. You coming?"

"No. I'll drive up to the end of the road and wait on the beach. If you get that far, I'll climb on for the last stretch across the channel."

"Okay. Help me tie this thing down."

"Are you mad? If you tie it in, it'll flip you over. When the seas fling it overboard, let the damn thing go! At least you'll be alive and I'll have somewhere to sit!"

"Good thinking." And I headed out.

The seas were two foot swells until I got out of the harbor. Just about then the wind got up and it began to feel like all hell was breaking loose. The boat was definitely top heavy and the top of the box was describing arcs that had to be eight to ten feet in distance from one side to the other. It seemed like I got to the tipping point at every wave. I motored slowly, hugging the shore, with my body straining to keep the huge box in the rolling and rocking boat.

Of course I immediately got soaked by the waves and the spray. But that wasn't the issue. The real problem was that I couldn't turn back. Putting the boat sideways to the seas to turn around would have definitely sent the box over the side and, since I was into it this far, I wanted to make every effort to keep the damn thing. But Sal was right. Tying it in would have been suicide.

Even though the wind was buffeting me and the seas were so high that I disappeared deep within each trough, I seemed to be keeping it all together as I slowly motored up channel to the pick-up point almost ten miles up the coast. It took hours to get there. When I got to Sal she was standing on the shore looking worried. I was shaking like a leaf I was so cold.

"Wow! I never thought I'd see you again. I really thought this cabin madness would be over, settled completely by your early demise at sea. Can we make it over to our place?"

"S-s-sure. P-p-piece of c-c-cake. J-j-jump in!"

As we arrived at our property the waves were breaking on the unwelcoming rocks. Somehow I had to get onto the shore and lift the steel box out of the boat and up the beach.

"So, what's the plan?" Sal asked.

It was time to get a plan. A bit late in the day, perhaps. But I needed a plan and I needed one quick. Otherwise I might look like a fool!

"It's high tide. I'm going to get as close to the beach as I can and then we just tip the sucker over the side of the boat—into the drink! It will sink a few feet and catch up on the rocks below. Tomorrow we'll come back at low tide and it will be high and dry. Then we'll drag it up the shore."

We shoved the box over and it rolled out of the boat amazingly easily. Our inflatable dropped down close to the water on the side it tipped from and, as the box left the boat, we shot the other way like a watermelon seed. There we sat looking at the shore. No box in sight. It was underwater, Davy Jones' locker—literally.

The next day I discovered that dragging the box up the beach was going to be a challenge. It was there to hold our tools and since it had just arrived, ninety percent of our tools had not. We only had a come-along, a block and tackle, and some ropes. But our friends and neighbours, John and Jorgina (Jorge to us), were there to help us get the box up the boulder strewn incline that a Sherman tank could not have negotiated.

We gathered some roundish branches and jammed them under the box. We tied a rope around the box and pulled it with the block and tackle, assisted by the come-along. The box began the laborious inch by inch climb over the boulders and up the steep rocky incline, slowly coming up off the beach. After an hour of pulling and levering, we were halfway done and were about to stop for a rest when my world came undone.

The rope I was pulling on snapped. At the time it failed I was leaning into it like a man on a tug-of-war team. Being on such a severe slope meant that I was hanging practically horizontal over the boulders below. That position changed abruptly when the rope parted and I tumbled backwards down the hill and into the boulder field below. My head hit one of those immoveable objects with what seemed like irresistible force and something had to give. So, I passed out for a sec.

When I came to, Sally and John were at my side.

"You okay?"

"Oh, yeah, just help me up. I'll be fine."

I was assisted to a place where I could lie down on some moss. There was a bit of blood on the back of my head and a bit more on an impact absorbing elbow but after a minute I felt good enough to stand up. After a minute or two of standing, I felt good enough to lie back down again.

But we eventually got back to work and by the end of the day our very own Fort Knocks was in place and secure. If all our building was going to be this difficult, I'd be dead before the foundation was finished.

When the box was eventually filled with the tools I had acquired, we turned our attention to building a deck. Imagine a thirty degree granite slope covered in slick moss. Now imagine an unskilled fifties-plus couple building a strong, level deck on that slope without ever having built anything before. We started with a friend named Gene.

Gene joined us one weekend with a wheelbarrow, a shovel and a willingness to mix concrete. And so we did. Our first batch, mixed in the wheelbarrow, accidentally tipped over. Inadvertently we had just made the first level spot on the property in a place completely useless to our needs. It was a portent of things to come. Of course, before it set up, we inscribed Gene's initials in it. For his kind and generous assistance he is indelibly etched in our memories and on our landscape.

We got more bags of concrete mixed and poured. When the pillars that were going to support the deck were set, we attached the long steel beams we had brought over. With a square steel frame sitting level, we felt a shiver of victory knowing that sixteen or so joists and two hundred and forty square feet of decking were on hand, just waiting for us to complete the project. When finally finished, I called up a contractor friend and told him proudly what we had done.

"Dave," he said weakly, "that's great!"

"Quick, too," I said. "How long would it take you to make a twelve by twenty deck?"

"Unh, well, if it was just me....maybe a whole day. But, if Chris helped, we'd probably be done before lunch. Why?"

Since it had taken Sally and me two weeks, I said, "Never mind, just wondering."

Having a level area from which we could topple off to the rocks and certain trauma below was strangely comforting and gave us an incredible boost in confidence. Of course, it was simply a patch of flat in the middle of hill country but, for the first time since we had been on the property we could stand up straight without our feet slipping out from under us. We were builders.

Somehow we had managed to pick a spot for the house without too much fuss. Not much thinking, either, to be honest. There are a lot of factors to consider when choosing a building site and we knew none of them at the time. Theoretically, one should spend a lot of time thinking about all this beforehand. We hadn't. Only one place looked like it would work so we chose it. I decided to build on solid bedrock, mostly because that was what our property consisted of.

Sal likes sunshine so we propped the site location idea up on that—get up high and orient south. To be fair, I am also keen on a great view and so that meant choosing a spot on the west side of the little finger of land that juts out from the main piece of our property. After that, it was all pure dumb luck. Well, it turned out to be lucky, but there were times when we weren't so sure it wasn't just dumb.

The incline of the rock slope from the shore to our building site turned out to be a relentless challenge to construction. We had to load stuff up the hill the hard way at first, carrying it the same way that the iconic Juan Valdez' mule, Conchita, carried sacks of Columbian coffee beans in the Andes.

The first indication that we were in over our heads was when we started to locate the precise positions for the footings that would hold the posts to support the house and keep it off the ground in a square, level and secure fashion. How do you find such spots when the property slopes away in all directions?

I decided the answer was to hire a local guy, a touted expert. He came out and the first thing he did was to ask to borrow my long tape measure—that was a bad sign. Guys who set foundation points should have a tape measure at the very least, don't you think? Then he walked about the site waving his arms around and said, "About here, will do. This is a good spot…and, oh, I'm sure this one will be okay…close enough, anyway."

I sent him packing and decided to get a team of real experts in so I delegated the chore to Sal and our daughter Emily.

"Sorry, girls, it's gotta be done. It's either carry stuff up the hill or measure—your choice. And we have tons of stuff to move. Here, take this calculator, string, tape measure and orange spray paint and figure out where the posts go. Em, use that geometry you learned at school. Sal, check her math and hold the string tight. It's just triangles—three dimensional triangles. You can do it. Now don't screw up or the house will fall over. See ya later!"

You might think me mad. They sure did! But, honestly, Em has a calculator for a brain and Sal is a stickler for detail and getting things right. I showed them the starting point and they worked off that. And they did well.

"Sweetie, we're done! I'm not one hundred percent sure that we are right, though. We've never done this kind of thing before. We might be off by an eighth of an inch or so but no more than that. Is that good enough for you?"

"How many points did you mark?"

"Like you said, twelve."

"Yeah, well, I've been thinking…I don't know what I'm doing either. The plans call for twelve posts on which to situate the house. That's why I asked for twelve. But we're going to have a deck all around and I have plenty of logs. You seem to have the hang of it. Can you please lay out some more spots for posts in front—say, eight feet out and square to the house. That'll hold up the front deck. Let's do the same sort of thing on the two sides. Leave the rear. I think I'll just add a few more support posts as well. Say eighteen or so in total, why not?"

"Uh, okay, I guess. Is this how things are usually built? I mean, like, just winging it? Is this how other people build cabins?"

"Yup, exactly like this."

"Okay, just checking."

Next up was the boathouse which would double as our temporary accommodations while we built the house. And for that, I needed more materials. I arranged for them to be delivered by a local barge operator.

This delivery was one of our first hints that material handling would play a huge role in our lives. Because our steeply sloped foreshore is strewn with barnacle covered rocks and slippery kelp at low tide, we specified that the barge arrive at high tide. It was going to be quite a chore to get thirty bags of concrete mix, much of the lumber for the boathouse, plus fourteen huge, galvanized steel beams from the high tide mark another thirty or so feet up the beach. Naturally, the barge arrived at low tide. And then the operator proceeded to tell us that he didn't want to be there too long as he had other jobs!

The alternative to unloading right away, made extra difficult by the bad timing, was to convince a seventy year old ex-logger barge operator, who was in a hurry and hard of hearing, to come back when the tide was high. I opted to unload as fast as I could. It seemed the lesser of the two challenges.

I am not so sure it was the right decision, but I was coming to learn that the best laid plans of mice, men, women and builders often go awry and the situation out here in the sticks is always less than ideal. Better to just do it and make the best of it.

Unfortunately, after a couple of loads, the sling on the hoist broke so the materials couldn't even be lifted off the barge. To his credit, this septuagenarian whipped fifty-five pound bags of concrete mix around like they were pillows. He passed heavy, wet, sixteen foot long two by twelve pieces of lumber to me without even breathing hard or straining. Mind you, he did stay on the level surface of the barge while Sally and I struggled up the beach. Still, he was a testament to strength and health. We weren't!

We scrabbled over rocks and kelp. We cut ourselves on the barnacles, crushed our fingers between boards, strained muscles which were unaccustomed to the weight, and worked ourselves into a pair of heaving, sweating, exhausted softies from the city—much to the unconcealed humour of our barge operator.

At one point during the off-loading I paused and, leaning against the gunwales of the barge, gasped for air.

"So," he said to me, "Work in an office?

Loaded funicular cart on its way up to the house

-3-

Let's Twist Again

With the house site determined, the deck completed and the boathouse partially built and somewhat functional, we finally had a good space from which to launch work further afield.

The next step was to build a funicular, like a railroad on a slant, which I envisioned going from the boathouse deck by the water up to the building site. For this I had to bring in my friend, Brian. His contributions to my cabin dream were extensive due to his remarkable energy and almost psychotic determination to get the job done.

A large part of the engineering task was to install steel rails on which the funicular cart would ride up and down. We had to drill through thick steel in order to put the various pieces of track and support legs together like a giant Meccano set. Each rail weighed two hundred and twenty pounds. Each of the eight adjustable legs on which the rails were fastened weighed a hundred pounds. Each foot of each leg was on irregular ground and all of it was on a moss covered incline. And it always seemed to be raining.

Brian did not like the tool I offered for drilling holes in the steel. It was a huge, old and slow Craftsman half inch drill. But he set to work like the fabricating maniac he was.

This old high torque drill has immense turning power and, as long as the drill bit spins, that power is used against the steel and eventually a hole is made. Sometimes the drill bit will catch on a sliver of steel or the operator will accidentally lean so that it catches on the side of the hole. When this happens the drill will keep turning even though the bit has stopped. The operator is then twisted viciously and the result is either a sprained wrist or being thrown off balance. It all happens so quickly that it can hardly be avoided. And it happened to Brian time and time again.

He was working on a slick hillside with virtually no secure footing. The drill caught and spun him completely off his feet and was in the process of rotating him totally when he let go and rolled thirty feet down the hill. Cursing in combinations of colourful expletives, the likes of which I had never even imagined, he clawed his way back to his tenuous perch and jammed the drill back into the hole.

The bit turned for a brief second, caught and flipped Brian back down the hill again as easily as a kid throwing a stone. Brian went back at it despite howls of pain and newly emerging patches of bloody bare skin. It threw him again. He went back. I rushed over.

"Brian, for gawd's sake, give it a rest! I'll do it for awhile. Save yourself!"

He looked at me for a second with the eyes of a demented man and, wresting the drill from me, tried again. The results were exactly the same, but this time he lay defeated at the bottom of the hill in a small pile of mud and let the rain fall on his bleeding and battered body. I finished the hole by being very circumspect and using an exceptionally light grip on the handle. It helped that I weigh almost twice as much as Brian.

"You okay, Bri?"

"I hate that drill."

And so it was that we built the funicular. One torturous hole at a time. We carried the rails up the mossy, rain soaked slope and fastened them to the vertical support poles we had first drilled and cemented in place. It was as if we knew what we were doing. We didn't. We were as stunned and surprised as anyone when the whole apparatus stood strong and solid, straight and beautiful.

Brian and I had designed it and I had salvaged the steel for it and found second hand motors, gears and attachments to make it work. This was a funicular born from scrap. The end result was as good as I could have hoped for. I had an eighty foot inclined railway on which a metal cart rode up the hill from the lower deck pulled by an exceptionally large winch powered by an electric motor.

That funicular saved our lives while almost taking Brian's in the building of it. It carried all the heavy materials up the slope to what would eventually be the house site. The only problem with building a funicular is that you need a funicular with which to carry up the materials needed to build one. But we got it done.

Not all our friends were as committed, or maybe as crazy, as Brian. One weekend some city friends came out to help us. They wore new matching weatherproof outfits and carried plenty of bottled water.

"Right, here we are! Put us to work. What can we do to help?"

"Well, have you ever built anything before?"

"No. But we are willing to learn. Instruct us. By the way, do you have any extra sunscreen? SPF 40? And we forgot our gloves so maybe a chore that is easy on the hands? And where exactly is the loo?"

"Hmmm, the loo is free range. Here's some sunscreen. And I'll get the tools and some gloves. We have to build small square concrete foundations on which to place the vertical support logs for our second deck. I'll need nine such footings. I'll drill into the rock and place a pin in each location and, if you would, please make small square forms into which we can pour the Redi-Mix concrete. Aesthetics are not too important. No one will see the footings but, of course, the frames have to be done right. Waddya think?"

"Great! Do you have plans we can follow? Do you have a Kleenex I can wipe my hands with? And what exactly do you mean by a form?"

It wasn't long after I had cut the pieces, provided everything needed and shown them how to do it, that I heard a shout.

"Hey, Dave, this is impossible! Are we doing it right? Everything keeps sliding down the hill. *We* are sliding down the hill! And do you have more screws? The last bunch fell over the edge."

After about six hours, there were nine little boxes sitting higgledy-piggledy on the side of the hill awaiting concrete. There was a fixed pin of rebar in the centre of each. None of the boxes had been leveled or squared. They just hung there on their pins. Surveying this scene, I had a sense of carnival…like ring toss.

Our friends were not overly pleased at the day's pastime or their efforts. They were sweaty, their new boots and outfits were scuffed and dirty, they didn't think building was fun and they were clearly re-evaluating the entire relationship they had with us. They were polite but, by late afternoon, were more than ready to go back to the resort on the next island where they were staying.

"So, are we done here? Gawd, I need a glass of wine! How long is this house building thing going to take, anyway? Building on a slope is not really a good idea, Dave. Why didn't you choose a level site? And why not get a contractor to do it? What exactly are you trying to prove?"

It was our fault, really. Sal and I had waxed romantic over the past few months about the adventure of it all and they wanted a taste of that. I hadn't really emphasized the difficulty and discomfort. In fact, I had glossed over it, sounding macho and confident instead. It really does sound like a lot of fun when you are sitting in a townhouse in the city drinking wine and dining off fine china. To be fair, seeing things through their eyes, I think I could have been accused of false advertising.

They were very good sports but clearly this was not their thing. Sal and I were grateful for their help and, even more, appreciated their support. It turns out they thought we were pretty crazy, but despite that they came to lend a hand. Now that's friendship.

Unfortunately friends aren't always around to help. I found out that being alone on a remote building site can warp one's perspective somewhat. On one occasion, Sal was in town earning the last bit of a typical living and I was hurting myself in an effort to improve the base from which our further building efforts would evolve.

I happened to pick a hot spell for this work stint and, of course, I got really overheated while I was working. When I get hot I think of global warming and that we are all doomed! It's crazy. I know that. But I was feeling faint. And I started to panic. When in panic mode, call Sal.

"Sal, it's me, Dave. I think we made a huge mistake. Huge! Our building site must be in some kind of freakish microclimate where the heat just builds and builds until every living thing here just explodes! I'm dying! I am gonna blow up! It is *so* hot! We gotta sell…move further north…change our plans …aaarrghh!"

"Oh, you're such a big dork! It's really hot down here, too. We're having a heat wave. It's hot everywhere. Relax. Are you drinking plenty of water?"

"Water? Well, unh…no. Not really. No."

When I work I do tend to get a bit focused and, until I learned better, I wasn't taking breaks or stopping for tea or anything. I'd just go until I dropped. Which, as a rule, wasn't all that long and so progress was somewhat slow.

One of the worst work habits I had, though, was simply not drinking enough water. And Sal knew that. I didn't seem to get it. Admittedly, she told me repeatedly but sometimes my ears filter out what sounds like, blah, blah, blah. It is especially hard to get a handle on such things when you are on the phone in a panic and driven half mad by way of dehydration, a blistering noonday sun and a foundation of Welsh and British genes.

"Drink some water, you big goof! Ya gotta keep hydrated…blah, blah, blah…."

I faded out a few times because of the tone and repetition of the words she was using but I got the gist of it. Blah, blah, blah meant "drink water". So I did.

But I don't think she told me to do it more than once. Honest. So, by the end of the day, I was pretty crazy. I thought I was going to die. I knew that I had to cool off so I threw myself into the ocean. *Oh my gawd!* It was then I knew that I really *was* going to die.

I had taken a burnt and crispy human body and immersed it in a body of water that stays within one or two degrees of fifty Fahrenheit all year long. Glass would have shattered. Some of my systems shut down completely. Others shriveled to nothing. I was imploding with cold! But it got worse.

Even though I had cooled off, I was still sunburned and needing a more relaxing experience than skinny dipping in seawater the temperature of a slushy. I took the inflatable boat and motored around to the little bay at the back of our property to continue my ablutions in the shallows. The sun had warmed the rocky beach and the tide had then come in over it which made the water a more tolerable temperature. Still naked, of course, (what would be the point of getting dressed?) I slipped over the inflated tubes and into chest deep water. It felt weird.

Seems the local oysters were mating and they do that by ejaculating spat into the water. The spat is like Brylcreem. Like lube oil. Like hand lotion. Like some kind of gross goo that covered me like batter. I was freaked.

Of course I flailed about. Of course that caused me to lose my balance and of course I slipped and found myself completely immersed in oyster cum! What a horror show!

I moved to the side of the boat and attempted to get in. It was too deep. I was too slippery. The effort was slapstick porn. There I was naked but for a coating of goo, looking like a walrus mating with a bright red manatee.

Relaxation was out of the question. I was on the edge of panicking all over again. I was covered in a natural jelly and trying to get into a rubber boat. After making a complete fool of myself in the privacy of my own embarrassment, I managed to get close enough to shore to hoist myself back in the boat. And I began retreating. I was halfway back to my building site when I spotted a neighbour heading up the channel in my direction. Great! How does one explain messing about in a red inflatable while nude and covered in white slime?

-4-

Fair Trades

Most weeks I'd show up on the secondary school grounds on Friday afternoon with donuts and cokes. I wanted to get to know Dwayne and the boys a bit better and to monitor their progress. He had some good boys, some bad boys and some real screwballs but they were eventually doing some good work and, within a few months, the floor was set and they were starting on framing the first walls.

In late April the pace at the school had quickened noticeably. I ordered windows and doors and they were test fitted into openings. Roofing was ordered in a fit of optimism.

When May rolled around I scheduled barges, boats, buses, and trucks while ramping up my infrastructure work on site. Logistics began piling up as I made the necessary arrangements to have the disassembled first floor of the house hauled on a large flat bed truck which went by ferry to Vancouver Island. At the marine terminal up island the materials would be transferred to a barge and delivered to our site a week before Dwayne arrived with the students.

I was alone on our site, waiting to receive the delivery of building material. Once the barge arrived it took a couple of hours for the crew to hoist all the piles of lumber, pre-framed walls, slings of windows, doors, roofing and assorted materials ashore. The deck adjacent to the boathouse was piled eight feet high.

Prior to the barge's arrival I had built another deck about eight feet up the slope and off to the side where the guys placed as much as they could. More material was piled on spots of bare rock around the landing area. But even after all that only half my order had been unloaded.

"Dave, there's no more room for the rest of your materials. If you want, we'll carry on down the coast to do a few other deliveries and then we'll return in about thirty hours time to unload the rest. Can you make some room by then?"

"I'll make room. What time are you coming back?"

"Between two and six in the morning, depending on how the rest of the deliveries work out."

After the barge left I began to move building materials up the hill. I put load after load onto the funicular to go the steepest eighty feet from the boathouse deck to the landing near the house foundation. Once the materials reached the top I unloaded them and carried them for sixty or eighty more feet to place them as close as possible to where the house would be built without them getting in the way of the actual construction.

The funicular takes about seven hundred pounds at a time and I loaded and unloaded the cart as many times as I could over the next twenty four hours. It was hard work and I was getting pretty tired when my friend Bill phoned from Vancouver.

"How ya doing, Dave?"

"Not great. The barge will be back in about six to ten hours and I still have tons of material to get up the hill. I'm not sure I can get it done. I'm pretty beat."

"Hang on. I'll be right there!"

"Bill, don't be crazy. You can't make it. You are eight hours away, what with two ferries and all that driving. Not only that, but you won't get to where I can even pick you up until two in the morning and I have to be here for the barge. Stay home. It's impossible."

"Nope, I'll be there." And he hung up.

I didn't give it another thought. I knew that even if he made it onto the last ferry to Vancouver Island from Vancouver he wouldn't make it onto the one coming out from Campbell River. And, if by some fluke he did make both, that would simply leave him in the middle of the forest on the adjacent island in the middle of the night. The logistics of the trip would eventually dawn on him and that would be that. I just kept working.

By four in the morning I had cleared the two decks. However, half walls, some windows, some doors, most large beams and sheets and sheets of plywood were left untouched. I was exhausted. I could hardly stand. I was aching all over and wondering what part of this challenge had attracted me just a few months ago, when I heard a motor boat approaching. Out of the deep, wet grey mist of the early morning, Ed's water taxi came into view. Bill was aboard. He grabbed his bag, leapt ashore and waved goodbye to Ed. Then he greeted me.

"I made it. What needs to be done?"

I looked at him as if he were an apparition. I could not believe my eyes. I could hardly understand how Bill had made it. It was not computing. I was about to speak when we saw the barge approaching and so together we got about the business of helping unload the rest of the building materials over the next few hours. When it was done, we were filthy, wet, exhausted and hungry. I looked at Bill.

"You okay?"

"Yup. Pretty hungry, though. Got anything to eat?"

"Yeah, there's food in the boathouse. Help yourself. Don't do any more work. Just eat and rest. I have to sleep. We'll talk later."

I went to sleep and woke up later that afternoon. Bill was sitting on a chair munching a sandwich. We worked the next day to get the rest of the stuff up the hill. It is hard to imagine that kind of friendship. I'll never forget it.

How do we get fifteen students and their teacher from the lower mainland to a remote location over a hundred miles up the British Columbia coast? How do we bring in enough food to feed twenty or so people for a week and cook with no running water or electricity, not to mention refrigeration? How do we house everyone? Most importantly, who is available to help? We were about to find out.

My neighbour John and I picked up fifteen students in Nanaimo in a school bus and, after taking a ferry to the island adjacent to ours, drove down a dirt logging road deep into the rainforest and emerged at a small waterfront landing where Sally and Jorge were waiting with our small boats.

It was a sunny, blustery day and the water was choppy with whitecaps. The laden vessels transported the boys a couple of miles further into the wilds of Discovery Sound. It was an interesting beginning for the students.

It was beautiful, wild and totally foreign to many of the city kids. Not just a few facial expressions showed awe and fascination. Perhaps a few exhibited a little fear as well.

We arrived at our island location and the class became acquainted with the building site and their accommodations for the next week. Their cabin was minimalist in the extreme. Daniel Boone probably had better digs. They slept in a mattress formation on the floor, like sardines. The three-sided outhouse was seventy-five yards away, overlooking the water.

My son Ben came along for the first few days to "shepherd" the boys and it was like herding cats, only they were louder. But he did well. He was a little older and carried an air of authority that was unmistakable. The boys did as he asked in organizing their sleeping arrangements and work schedule. He was the houseparent for the first three days and was missed when he had to return to his studies at the University of Victoria.

My wife Sally and our friend Perci created a culinary factory from coolers and camp stoves that impressed everyone. Up at six every morning, the cooks didn't quit until nine each night. They made over six hundred meals and snacks that week, all from scratch. Hot cinnamon buns, fruit crumbles, scones, French toast, hams, turkey, stews, lasagna, chili and much, much more. To the boys' (and my) delight the home cooking just kept coming.

Unfortunately it rained torrentially for the first three of the six days the boys were on site. It was slippery and miserable. No work could be done without an element of danger.

Day one was a real trial. There were still tons of materials to get up the hill. The kids passed lumber and assorted building materials in a chain gang strung up the slope and, I am sure, hated every minute of it. I did. Most of the boys tried to work together, but they were not a team. Not yet.

Dwayne had overestimated their ability and, even more disastrously, underestimated the difficulty of the site, especially with it being so wet. To be fair, the weather was something over which he didn't have a lot of control, but to be accurate, he didn't have much control over the boys either. That first day was a bleak experience of accomplishing very little. I was sorry that we were getting off to such a bad start.

Day two was much the same but some of the more skilled fellows started on the last row of foundation posts and then placing and leveling the first floor. The others kept moving boards uphill and dreaming about using their hammers. It was very hard work, especially as the torrential downpour never stopped.

In the meantime, Sally and Perci were working like demons. Breakfast, lunch and snacks were the highlights of the day. Dinners were hearty and filling. Perci even made Kenny, one of the students, a birthday cake. The boys claimed they had never eaten so well. These boys, whose speech was interspersed with words best excluded from this narrative, fell all over themselves complimenting the cooks and being on their best behaviour around them.

The kids ate. And ate. And ate. Sally said she felt like she was feeding a school of piranhas. She and Perci put the food on the table and quickly jumped back so as not to get in the way of the ravaging hordes.

Day three was another tough day for me. Four of the students were very good, extraordinary, in fact. They knew what to do and were doing it very well. The first floor was progressing. Another group was getting tired of moving materials around and were clearly not used to working hard for eight hours, but they were still managing to get some things positioned, stacked and sorted. Some kids ground to a virtual halt at times. Resting was a common state of being. Some, of course, just wanted to quit. I didn't blame them too much. I wanted to, as well. It had been raining since they arrived. The hope of getting all the first floor walls up by day six had begun to fade.

After three days of virtually no progress it was not looking good for getting even the bare bones of the first floor up. I was not pleased. I told Dwayne that he could take some of the useless boys home early. I'd finish up with whoever wanted to stay and we'd try to get it done to a stage where Sally and I could continue.

He was apologetic and later told the boys what I had said. Those at fault seemed appropriately embarrassed. That firm confrontation was a good thing. There was quite a noticeable shift in the collective attitude the next day.

But in the meantime the weather was still holding us back. It was awful. In the early morning hours of day four colossal whomps of thunder woke us as all the buildings shook. We lay in our sleeping bags as a vicious thunder and lightning storm preceded an apocalyptic downpour. It felt like a giant wet blanket had been thrown on our plans.

When the storm passed, kids emerged like half-drowned rats. But that was when the magic happened. They hitched on their tool belts and trudged up the hill to the building site anyway. Progress commenced once again. Something was happening and it was more than just the resumption of construction.

By midday the sun came out and all of the boys were on site, working hard. It was great to see. We got all the foundation posts up and started on fixing the floor in place.

The next day when I saw the kids showing up in clothes still wet from the day before and some with dried mud in their hair, things were starting to feel okay to me. And, best of all, it was starting to feel okay to them, too. When we hauled lumber up the hill with wet moss covered rock underfoot and kid after kid slipped, it was beginning to feel as if a team had arrived. And, when we had the first floor up and some of the walls erected, well, it felt like a victory. It really did.

The last work day was a really good day. Half of the kids worked like a real team…actually, like three or four teams. Dwayne had a group, I had a group, and there were a few who could work on their own as well as any professional. Everyone was tired but every kid who was actually committed to the project put whatever energy he had into the job at hand. It was pretty neat. But it was the end of day six and that was all we had time for. We weren't even close to our goal. Lock up? Not even halfway.

Ours was not an easy project given the size, the challenging site and the weather. But when the first floor was up the levels and tape measures indicated that it was all perfectly square and perfectly level. Amazing! Every kid and every adult was leaning and tipping with fatigue but the structure itself was not. It was just a platform with walls but it was done right.

Almost more important than the technical aspects, the actual structural integrity of the building—and I do not want to underemphasize the importance of that—was the evolution of the crew. They went from a gaggle of irritating teenage kids to a team of workers, and they did it in just six days. It was a wonder.

-5-

Where Do They Come From?

"I talked to the storage guy while I was over on the next island. He wants to be paid at least six months in advance to store all our furniture and stuff."

"That's pretty odd, Sal. I wonder why. Six months is all we'll need in total."

"Well, he didn't seem to think so. He told me that he has people requesting space all the time but he has reserved our unit for us for eighteen months. He made it sound like he was doing us a favour."

"Why did he do that?"

"When I told him we needed to store everything while we build, he suggested we plan for eighteen months because building remote takes longer than people think. In fact, he had an amused smile as he spoke. I assured him that, since we were doing it all ourselves, we could control the pace and we would get it done quicker. It was then his smile got bigger. And then he laughed out loud and said maybe we should plan on two or three years! He did a lot of laughing. I have to say, it wasn't encouraging."

"Well, one thing's for sure. We won't need that unit for eighteen months. He's just plain wrong. Don't worry."

"We have enough food to feed an army!" I said after a day in town as I hoisted yet another cooler up to the boathouse deck. Another large box of dry goods and a few bags of impulse purchases filled the larder to the point of excess and, given our lack of refrigeration, clearly indicated not enough planning and too much impulse. We had way too much food. Or so I thought.

"Sweetie, don't forget that Sue is coming on Tuesday and Don said that he'd come by the following weekend. And Emily will soon be with us for a few days. I think we'll be fine getting through the supplies." Sal said that with a beaming smile that always makes me swoon, shuts me up and suggests that I am fussing too much, all at the same time. I assumed that she was right. She usually is.

We had shopped for the next two weeks of living and working at the site as well as entertaining some guests we expected now that the weather was warming up. We could access the little country store ten miles away by water if we needed to, but we already appeared to have more inventory than the store did, so I relaxed. I shouldn't have.

Early the next morning after breakfast, I dragged out the tools, the generator, the materials I expected to use and I began to try to build some stairs using what seemed to be a random series of instructions from a book on carpentry.

I never really knew exactly where to start on something new so I often started the genset first and plugged in a few tools just to create the right atmosphere. Ambience is everything. But genset racket may also be an unwitting lure for visitors. I think it is. As another consequence of all that noise, I failed to hear the outboard motor of some neighbours from a short way down the coast dropping by to greet us. Once the generator was shut down we all sat down for a nice cup of tea and Sally broke out a few cookies and some fruit. They left just before noon.

On went the generator again and, since I had already used up a lot of my work time with guests, I decided to forgo any further waste of time by skipping the planning and just winging it. Free-form stairs was the vision of the moment. And so things got underway.

Until Linda came into view in her boat and I made the mistake of waving. Linda is a more distant neighbour from another island and tends to interpret a hand waving as an invitation to lunch. Her timing was perfect and we enjoyed her company until she continued on her way an hour or so later.

I started the generator hesitatingly. And I tentatively lifted a hammer and, checking to make sure that no one was approaching, began to hit things—some of them were nails. I experienced that feeling people get when they are sure that washing their car will create a rainstorm.

Just as I was getting my hammering sighted in and could claim more hits than misses, we were hailed from the water once again. More friends floating in to say hello. Nice people. Long time, no see. More tea. More cookies. Lots of nice chitchat. Generator silent. The hammer and nails rested on the lumber in an attractive still life rendition.

That day was a disaster for me, the builder, but it was a major social success. We were genuinely pleased to see everyone and, despite no progress on the stairs, it was a good day.

Sue came up from Victoria the next day. She's great. We love her. Hadn't seen her for months. After picking her up on the adjacent island, catching up with all the news was priority number one. Genset remained cold. Fuel saved. Hammer and nails developed a slight patina of rust.

Day three: Sue's coworkers from the Coast Guard dropped by in their high-powered boat out of Campbell River. Brought cake, needed refreshments. Great guys—wonderful company. And I noticed a spider's web on the generator.

Day four: Sal's former colleagues from Vancouver paddled in by kayak. Nice couple, but hungry. Any problem with an oversupply of food evaporated with the cheese, wine and the lamb chops. They stayed overnight. Everyone went for a nice hike the next day. What fun! I sprayed WD40 on all the tools and looked longingly at the generator. I was sure the paint was beginning to fade.

Day five: Our daughter Emily arrived from town. She unexpectedly brought friends. Surprise! We returned to the building site with two more people than anticipated. Lovely couple. They wanted to work. Sadly, they could not. Did not know which end of the hammer to use. They, too, got hungry. I took them back to their car later that day. Food supply problem emerging.

Day six: Sue left. Emily left. Don arrived. The logistics of picking up and delivering people to their cars parked on the neighboring island took most of the day. Food stocks definitely getting low.

Day seven: Nine visitors to date. Food gone, booze mostly gone—my fault, mostly. First aid kit one hundred percent intact. All bad signs. There are no signs of anything else. No work has been accomplished. If one more guest arrives I will not be responsible for what happens! Desperation enters the equation. So do two more visitors. We serve what we can—little corners of toast and the dregs of the wine supply. Pretend to be Catholic.

Day eight: Hunger begins to set in. We eat a lot of canned rice pudding and wash it down with vodka. Who knew that construction could get so weird?

Day nine: We have to go shopping. No hammering. No nailing. Only shopping. Living remote means shopping is a day-long chore. We returned home in time to admire the tools in the subdued light of the setting sun.

Day eleven: No visitors. Unless you count the gale, the rain and the accompanying high winds. No work either. The smaller nails were being blown about. I stopped caring. Still had vodka.

Day twelve: A good day. No visitors…until 6:00 pm.

Up until that point, things were as they should have been. And I was actually working. But then a guy rowed by just a few yards off shore and I forgot myself.

"Hi!" I said. Then I shut up. I averted my eyes and quickly looked away. But it was too late. Damn. He turned his boat towards the shore. Oh my gawd, I thought. I can't entertain anymore. I'll have to shoot him. I have no choice. No one will blame me...

"I'm John," he said, holding up a plaster cast of a very large foot. "I'm a Sasquatch hunter and I heard that there have been some sightings in your neck of the woods. Can you tell me about anything unusual or odd?"

"Yes, John, I can. Come on up and have a glass of wine. By the way, does anyone know you are here…?"

It turns out that Dr. John Bindernagel is a Sasquatch expert and he was chasing down a lead. We listened to Sasquatch stories until it got late. Dr. John eventually rowed off full of wine, in a small boat in the dark heading south. It was somehow a fitting end to a peculiar first two weeks on site.

-6-

One Nail at a Time

In addition to our furniture and assorted detritus in the storage unit we had accumulated tons of building supplies on site by this point, not to mention the junk and treasures I had been gathering for the last few years from garage sales and salvage yards tucked in amongst it all. Sal often opined that there was more junk than treasure but only time would tell if she was right. For the time being we just put the weird, funky stuff off to one side, hoping that we would use it all. There was a significant pile.

We had nuts, bolts, screws, nails, glues and tools up the wazoo and we were stocked with plenty of food and water for the foreseeable future or at least for the next few weeks. We even had a box of wine and a bottle of Scotch for medicinal purposes such as snake bite and bullet wounds, that kind of thing. We clearly had the stuff. But did we have the right stuff?

Neither Sally nor I had ever built anything and we really had no idea where to start on a dog house, let alone a real house. But that had now been taken care of for us, in a way. The students had managed to get us off to a good start by hurling us ill-equipped into the dark and ever changing circumstance of our own construction and then leaving us like wet, blind newborns on the steps of a potential disaster. There's nothing like terror to motivate survival. Shelter was at the top of our list of necessities.

We did have a level and square platform of nine hundred square feet looming in the air on long log legs at the top of a slope and, in retrospect, the largest hurdle was handled. The fact that we had expected a great deal more from the class was beside the point. We had a good foundation and a solid first floor. The exterior walls were mostly up, but unfinished. They may even have wiggled a bit…but never mind that!

We surveyed the scene, concluded that it was enough of a start for *us* to get started so we took the next step. We ordered how-to books from the library. They were delivered by floatplane to our local post office, in individual green canvas mail bags. A fabulous service and one I'm happy to support with my tax dollars.

Anyway, the easiest and simplest to read were the Sunset do-it-yourself series of skinny, basic books, the precursors to the construction-for-idiots books that we'll hopefully be capable of writing someday.

"Right," I said, rubbing my hands briskly, "Just where do you think we should start, sweetie?"

"Don't you know? What do the books say?"

"Well, all of the simple, how-to books start at the beginning, the foundation. Of course all of the foundations in the books are dug in soft soil on flat land so they wouldn't apply to us anyway. None of them really have a starting point beginning with the rough exterior walls perched on stilts. I think we are part way into chapter four of a twenty-four chapter house building series. But, exactly how do we pick up the pieces from where Dwayne and the boys left off?"

"I dunno. I was cooking. Weren't you watching? What was the last thing you guys did?"

"Last thing done was trying to tie in the perimeter walls. It wasn't completed of course, but they are still standing. That's good. When that was half done with temporary bracing holding it all up, we were pretty exhausted and happy to quit. And then everyone but us went home. I should have paid more attention at that point but I think I fell asleep on my feet.

"Dwayne has also placed some second floor joists as a form of bracing for the first floor walls going up. They were done to help keep things in place but I am pretty sure he was thinking of completing the second floor next. In fact, that large floor-type shelf up there is supposed to be used as a temporary floor for second story stuff, I'm sure. I think we should finish tying in the lower walls and then start on the upper floor joists."

"Right! First we tie in, and then second floor joists it is. You get some joists and I'll find some instructions. By the way, how exactly does this tying in thing work?"

And that is how the house was built. One step followed the next and anyone looking at the current pile of library books could tell what stage we were at.

One of the most interesting and, I admit, frustrating things about building your own house and creating your own infrastructure is that just about everything you do, you do for the first and likely the last time. *Hopefully* the last time.

Sally and I were intending to put up the siding on the exterior of the house. We weren't sure how to go about it but we read up on it and started at a back corner where any initial mistakes wouldn't show too much. After a few hours we had almost finished a short wall. A neighbour, Hugh, dropped by to say hello and he stared long and hard at our initial efforts.

"Siding, eh? Ever done that before?"

"No, never. Why? Are we doing it wrong?"

"Well, 'round here, most folks leave a larger space between each board and then cover that space up with the narrower top piece they refer to as a batten. You don't have a big enough space. No place for expansion. Your siding might get tight and pinch. Maybe break. Want me to show you what I mean?"

And so after that little lesson, we removed what we had done so far and fixed it. Then, doing it for the second time we did it "right" for the first time. We proceeded to work our way around the house, improving as we went, so that the last wall was much better looking and went up faster than the first one.

There were way too many things we needed to get done to ever become competent at any one of them. It was as simple as that. The only chance we had was to get comfortable with being unsure and eventually we came to accept our lack of confidence and carry on anyway. That seemed to be the best way for tackling things as complete neophytes. That, and not getting too upset when we had to redo things and start again.

Despite, and rarely because of, the visitors coming our way, work on the house was slow but progress was made. My recollections of that time are hazy and really just little flashbacks of workaday moments in the sun. I remember getting up, eating breakfast and following Sally to the work site. We would break a few times during the day, argue a bit about what we didn't know (just about everything), crack a few jokes and just plain plug away until dinnertime. When we quit work for the day we'd immerse our sweaty selves in the sea for a nanosecond or two and emerge to a towel, a glass of wine and a bit of a recap of what we had accomplished. I would then read up a bit on what we had to do the following day while Sally made dinner on the camp stove.

Naturally, given our location, we dispensed with formalities and after work we bathed au naturel. This, of course, was fine most of the time but once in a while we were revealed in this innocent state to a gaggle of kayakers paddling around the point en route to what they believed would be an intimate experience with nature. They were right. We turned out to be the wild mammals they were viewing in their natural habitat.

I recall once walking into the water slowly, my middle section danglingly exposed while Sally was just emerging from the sea and jiggling herself up the beach to the solar shower for a quick freshwater rinse. Just as my privates were being featured a few inches above the surface of the water, a kayaker rounded the point and smiled. I felt silly and not just a bit self-conscious so I took the plunge and immersed myself completely and immediately. I spun to watch Sally who, most of the time would have raced for a towel or otherwise acted in a modest and amusingly hysterical fashion.

But it had been a hard and hot day. We were beat. Sal took one look at the lone kayaker and continued with her full frontal shower. I was amazed. Then, the fourteen other paddlers he was leading rounded the point and Sal acquiesced to the dictates of discretion and leapt instantly for her towel hanging in the nearby tree. The group passed by with greetings, waves and not just a few grins.

Afterwards I said, "Sal, it seemed to me as if you were going to be okay with risqué exposure for a minute. The first guy didn't seem to faze you. But when more people came, so did the inhibitions. How do you explain that?"

"I don't know. I was so tired that one kayaker simply wasn't worth the effort of covering up. But somehow fourteen were."

"Given that we don't know any of them, does it matter if you were exposed to one or fourteen?"

"Of course not, there's no *logic* here."

Can she *hear* herself? Why don't I hear this more often?

As time went by we continued to work just as hard as we had at the beginning but we chatted less and went to bed earlier. I never saw the late side of nine o'clock after August. By mid-October, the house had been completed to lock up. The roof was on, doors and windows in. The building was strong, dry and could handle the coming winter. But we couldn't. We were exhausted. I was falling asleep earlier and earlier and was somewhat reluctant to get up again the next morning. Trying to get stiff muscles to get moving took me a long while.

We were still living in the boathouse of course, which also happened to be the space in which we stored our tools, our clothes, our cooking gear; pretty much everything we had for living and working. We had a small antique propane heater for warmth and, now that fall was well underway, we were already using it to capacity. We just couldn't imagine working on the house through the winter without a warm base to return to. And having a hot shower was fast becoming a major goal in my life, not to be satisfied in the boathouse anytime soon. Frankly, I found it hard to imagine ever completing the house at this point. We had to stop.

"So, Sal, it's too cold to live in the boathouse so we can't keep working through the winter. What's the plan?"

"What do the books say?"

"They say we should go to Mexico. Live on the beach. Be hippies. Return in the spring."

"Those Sunset books are great, aren't they? Did they happen to mention how we are going to do that?"

"Yeah, it was very specific. It said to go to a Mexican beach and don't move until March of next year. We can do that. We'll jump in the car and camp all the way down there and all the way back and, while we're there, we just keep on camping. Piece of cake."

"Okay. It's starting to get really cold. I'm having trouble cooking with my gloves on. Let's go."

Months after our Mexican sojourn and exactly eighteen months after filling it (yes, the storage guy was right) we emptied our jam-packed storage locker of our worldly possessions and moved them to our new house. It took nine days.

We'd start off in the morning in our boat and motor ten miles down the coast to the government dock on the adjacent island. We'd then drive our old Ford Explorer with a little utility trailer behind it over to the storage locker. We'd load both vehicles to the gills with boxes and furniture, lamps and appliances.

Then we'd drive it all to the dock. There we'd unload the car and trailer and carry everything down the ramp, along the dock and onto our boat. Once everything was aboard, we'd head back up the coast.

Once at our place we'd get as close to the shore as the tide would allow. I would keep the boat from hitting the rocks and also pass everything to Sally who would take it and scramble up the beach with it. She had to gain at least six feet in elevation so that the rising tide did not envelope our belongings before we had time later on to move them further up to the deck. Once we were unloaded I'd take the boat to the dock on the other side of the peninsula and rush back to help Sally carry everything up to the deck and put it on the funicular.

We could only manage one trip a day because of the time it took. Thank goodness, as it pushed our capacity to work to the limit anyway. We left the heaviest and bulkiest items for the last two days—the couch, the oversized solid walnut sideboard, the vintage range with a cast iron top, and the heavier than lead teak boardroom sized table. For those items, we hired a local guy to help. Sal got a bit of a breather but she had to keep the boat off the rocks and scramble around assisting us.

People visiting would exclaim, "Wow, man, how'd you get all that stuff up here?"

"The hard way—carrying."

"No way!"

"How else do you think?"

"C'mon! You used movers. You must have!"

"Okay. And how do you suppose those movers got here? By way of a moving and storage crew with a boat? And, how would they manage to get that stuff up here? Wouldn't they have to lift and carry, too?"

"Wow! That's crazy. What'd you have to pay those guys?"

Those nine days of moving were not the hardest work we put into building the house—not by a long shot. But we had a deadline to make. Not only was our storage contract ending, Sally had promised to host Book Club. And that date was written in stone.

-7-

Cellular Necrosis

The first real, measurable, positive step I ever took to living remote was to research and then purchase the equipment required to make my cell phone work from an iffy location where the coverage was poor. This was pathetic, of course. Obviously, I was missing the whole concept of getting away from it all.

The young fellow at the cell phone store who convinced me to buy a Yagi antenna and marry it up with a booster was a classic mumbling techie until he found out that my purpose was to live remote.

"Oh man, oh, man! That is so cool. That's what I want to do!"

"You do? Why would a young man invested in technology and still cruising the gene pool, want to live in the forest?"

"Cause I love it there, man. And I hate it here. I grew up in the country and I want to go back!"

"Why don't you?"

"Kids. Wife. Bills."

Seems I was wrong about him cruising the gene pool, but I did understand the trap that he had gotten into. In fact, it was visibly manifested by his little techie room with no windows filled with equipment. It was a cell. He was like an animal in a zoo.

But his good techie advice kept us in communication with the outside world until finally one day it didn't. The signal disappeared. Zero bars of service. When I contacted Rogers Cellular, online, of course, I was informed by my service provider of many years that they had never provided service to the area where I lived.

Chun, of the Rogers' website chat line, wrote: "Your previous years of service were a fluke."

"Well, Chun. I can accept that. I am basically a very lucky person to have had that non-service for so long. Mind you, Rogers never failed to bill me the whole time."

"Pardon?"

"Never mind. What do you propose for a guy who has had his phone service disrupted? Is the system down? Can Rogers realign the tower or something? Am I not paying you people enough?"

"Pardon?"

"Chun! You with me on this? This is simple stuff. My phone does not work. You are there to help. Work with me. Can you fix it? You seem a little spaced out, you know? I'm not feeling the love."

"I am sorry sir. Will there be anything else?"

"No disrespect, Chun, but could you transfer me to your supervisor? I need some help here and I don't think you are up to the task. Forgive me."

"Pardon?"

"Supervisor, Chun! *Supervisor*! *Get me supervisor*!"

"Please call 1-800-Rogers, sir, for supervisor."

"Chun, my phone does not work. That is why I am on the web chat. I told you that. How can I phone the supervisor if I do not have a phone?"

"I am sorry, sir, if you do not have a phone, I cannot help you. You should contact Rogers and subscribe."

In desperation Sal took the phone for a boat ride into the middle of the channel and, lo and behold—reception bars! She retrieved our messages. There was one. Two days without service and only one message. Maybe we can save the money and just cancel.

But, you know what? Chun knows squat! I know that because I managed to get a call out and phoned the Rogers store in town. Told them what happened.

"Sir…uh…I shouldn't say this but the customer service people know squat!"

"Really? I'm shocked. What *is* the world coming to? Think you can do better?"

"Absolutely. No worries. Bring it in, I'll fix you up."

I believed this guy. Three years previously he performed some kind of mobile phone miracle and I was so impressed I went out and bought him a bottle of Scotch. That is not an easy thing for me to give away. He must have been good. I don't remember any part of the actual problem but I do remember the giving away the Scotch part. That is enough of a memory to remain impressed.

It *is* different out here. Hard to explain. You often can't subscribe to something or even get a delivery because the computers don't recognize the postal box number as an address. Of course it isn't a real address so the computers are right. But when you are asked for your address and you say "on a remote island in the middle of Discovery Sound" the dialogue just ends. We have taken to making up an address to keep the computers happy. We live at 3 Shadow Bay Place. Sounds like an upscale neighborhood, don't you think? It usually works, but some postal code listings don't include ours.

"I am sorry sir but your postal code doesn't seem to exist."

"Yeah, I know. You just have to write it in."

"I am sorry sir but my computer won't allow me to do that. Do you live anywhere else?"

"Yeah, of course I do. I was just messing with you. I have a condo in town. And we winter in Rio, of course."

And then I give them my friend John's address in town. They are happy with that and I am sure they are wondering "Duh! Like why does this guy, like, live in a town and, like, try to get stuff delivered to a place that, like, doesn't exist?"

Anyway, like, back to the cell phone battle. It was ugly. Rogers employed the old Chinese art of war strategies; death by a thousand dropped calls, uncountable referrals to others, the "hold-and-listen-to-ads" torture and, of course, the subtle, "Right, I understand the problem. Now, just so I can put you through to the right person to fix this, what is your name again? Your ten digit phone number? Your date of birth, postal code and mother's maiden name?"

I get pretty frustrated with this and when asked my birth date for the umpteenth time, I replied, "January, 1948".

"Unh…sir, I need the day of the month."

"You do? You think it was just a lucky guess that I managed to pick the right postal code, phone number and two parts of my birth date? Do you really think I am a cheater trying to get some advantage over you but you may have *caught me out on the birthday question*?"

"I am sorry, sir, but we are required to."

I was finally put through to a woman who was pretty high up. She came across as confident, arrogant really, but my perspective may have been a little warped by then. She was demanding the oft-repeated security questions before deigning to speak to me. I interrupted.

"Excuse me. Do you have the power to make decisions?"

"Of course!" she snapped. "You are now at *Senior* Customer Care!"

"Wow! Does that mean you are senior to the other fools I have dealt with so far, or does that mean you are a specialist in dealing with geriatrics?"

"What?"

"Never mind. Back to decision making. Can you credit five dollars to my account?"

"Yes, of course. This is the senior…"

"Good, because I want a credit, please. Put seven hundred dollars on my account. Read the file for the rationale. Thanks. It has been great talking with you. Bye!"

"Wait. I can't authorize seven hundred dollars."

"But you are a senior something. You can make decisions. Presumably you can also read. So just read the notes and make the decision. At this stage, I don't care either way. Thanks. Bye."

"That is above my limit!"

"Oh. What is your limit?"

"One hundred dollars."

"One hundred dollars? How *senior* is that? Is there an antiquities level somewhere? Do you have a pre-Neolithic department? Any paleontologists on staff?"

"What?"

"Never mind. Send me as far up the chain as I need to go to get a yes or no on seven hundred. And, while you are at it, could I please have the address of your legal department?"

"I can't give out that information, sir."

"Why not? It's a department within the corporate offices. It *is* findable, presumably. However, if you give me your home address, I'll mail my letter to you and then you can, while protecting their corporate address anonymity, of course, deliver it yourself. How's that?"

"Sir, I have to put you on hold."

"If you put me on hold one more time, I will lose my mind. I'll snap. That wouldn't be good for senior care, now would it?"

"Senior *Customer* Care!"

"Whatever. Unless you can put me through to the president, his or her spouse or the corporate psychologist, I would prefer you do this instead. Make a decision yourself or pass my email address on to someone who can. I am not going to talk on the phone any more. I am off to find the address of your legal department on the internet. Bye."

"Sir, I'll have my manager call you."

"How old is he?"

"Pardon?"

"Never mind. He is senior to you, I assume?"

"Yes."

"Good! Make it so!"

Her manager reached me the next day. Stan. He was impressed that my account with Rogers was older than he was. I said that alone should be enough for me to get my problem resolved. He agreed. That call took less than a minute. I won the battle but it took many hours, spread over six days.

Sal asked if it felt like a victory. No. It felt more like the war in Afghanistan. Is there really a victory for anyone if there are so many casualties?

Another modern wonder is the satellite dish that provides us with our internet access unless the dish is on the fritz. The dish has an arm that holds a device that looks like a ray gun but it's called a horn. The horn points at the dish and transmits and receives the signal. After studying it intently I found that my little mirror-like horn was one-third full of water, distorting incoming and outgoing signals to the point that I was incommunicado except for a few seconds now and then. There was water in the horn, as they say when...well, water is in the horn.

I called the satellite technical service. After an hour of messing with settings and diagnostics over the phone, we conclude the problem is with the horn.

"Do not touch the horn sir. It is a highly technical device that only authorized technicians are able to service. It will void your warranty if you touch it."

"Okay, fine. I live on a remote island. The warranty is over anyway. The service technician will take three weeks to get here if he is in the mood. So what are you saying, I can't take off the plastic cover and fix it?"

"It is highly dangerous sir."

"I just spent the day taking down deadfalls with a chainsaw on a moss-covered slope. Which is more dangerous?"

"I don't know what a deadfall is, sir. And I cannot advise you, sir, but if I was advising you I would suggest you make sure that the power is off should you choose to do something unwise."

Hmm, should I choose to do what, exactly? "Now we're talking. Just how unwise could I get? Imagine the dumbest customer on the planet. What no good could he get up to?"

"Well, a person knowing nothing and trying anyway might try to take the cover off and drain it. Of course it is technically a violation of the warranty that has expired."

"Would the guy be successful?"

"Not likely, but it would definitely determine if the horn was at fault. And draining away the water might work but it is just not the right protocol. Proper protocol requires replacing the unit. I am glad you appreciate the impossibility of doing this work yourself, sir. We cannot be held responsible."

"I understand. Whew! We came mighty close to doing something silly. Thanks. And goodbye."

"Goodbye, sir!"

I didn't consult with my doctor, which seems to always be advised no matter what you are intending to do. I didn't consult legal advisers. I didn't string up orange tape around the site and put up warning signs. No hard hat or safety vest either.

A few minutes with an exacto knife got the cover off and the water drained. The temporary replacement cover consisted of Saran wrap held by an elastic band. A quick fix that lasted years.

Communication is a big deal around here, as you have probably gleaned by now. To aid us in this, Sal and I were given a gift of handheld walkie-talkie two-way radios by our thoughtful city friends, Fran and Sheldon. When Sal hasn't dropped hers in the ocean or forgotten to turn it on, they allow us to be in touch with each other while roaming the property and even out on the water.

Our coastal neighbours thought this was a good idea and they got walkie-talkies too. They were orienting themselves to the new buttons and were doing so by having a conversation. They decided to test the units while sitting in the same room. And because they were using the same channel as we do, we could overhear every word.

Beedle, beedle, went the call tone.

"Hello, Annie here. Robert? Can you hear me?"

"Yes I can. Did my walkie-talkie beedle or did I just hear yours?"

"I dunno. We're in the same room. I can hear everything you say. I think you're too close. It sounds like we are just talking to each other."

"Okay, how about now? I am walking outside on the back porch in my slippers."

"Well, I better go out on the front porch. Think I need slippers?"

Beedle, beedle.

"Is that you, Robert? Can you hear me?"

"Yes, I can."

"Did it beedle?"

"Yes, it did."

"I don't think mine beedled."

"Doesn't need to. You called me."

"Wow! Smart!"

Who needs television, eh?

Author holding a Yagi antenna in an attempt to get cell phone reception

-8-

Wet Behind the Ears

We have a problem. Water is not flowing. Things are not working. There's something wrong in paradise! When I lived in the city water flowed out of a tap. If there was a problem I called a plumber. Out here we maintain our own water system. If there is a problem the only person I can call is Sal.

I have to admit that I spent a lot of time angsting about installing the water system. It's a big deal. An even bigger deal is that our property has a year round stream. We are exceptionally fortunate on that score. Many people rely on streams or wells that run dry by the end of the summer.

I looked at every possible water delivery system available. After careful consideration of every variable, I made the decision to install a ram pump. Then I consulted with my neighbour, John. A very capable and practical man, John laughed at my well thought out proposal.

"You don't need a pump—gravity will do the job. We'll put the water intake in the stream at about two hundred feet in elevation, string out the water line to our houses and Bob's your uncle!"

I was pretty skeptical but in the interest of good neighborly relations I decided to humour John and go along with his plan.

We installed our shared water line which is about a kilometer long. We placed the intake in the stream in a small pool. When setting up the system we made a partial dam to enhance the pool. This, of course, entailed carrying bags of cement, not to mention rolls of water line uphill on a rough trail.

We put the intake under a metal guard to deflect debris, with rocks holding it down. The water line follows the stream, sometimes paralleling it and sometimes actually in it, until it reaches the shore. It then runs along the side of a cliff. John fastened it in place with cedar stakes hammered into crevices in the rock. At his place the line splits and a branch carries on to my house. The water flows thanks to gravity (and John) and we usually have good pressure.

Usually, Sally fixes the water system (thus reaffirming my definition of living in paradise) but this time I thought I'd help. I have no idea what came over me. Maybe we *do* need a television.

Anyway, when the water stops flowing the first thing we do is walk the line and check the connections. And so we did. It is always a gas to push through deep brush but wet and cold winter conditions add a little "je ne sais quoi".

We hopped into the boat and motored to the beach in our bay which is accessible only by water. Remember the cliff face? That's what prevents us getting into our bay by land without mountain climbing gear. We scrambled off the boat over rocks and into the forest to find the valve near the beach. No water.

So, that meant hiking and climbing. More mud, snow and cold. Sal and the dogs were happy. More fun! I, on the other hand, was ready to go home and call it a day. Sal wouldn't let me.

"C'mon! We'll just hike up through the bushes and fix it!" I hate it when she gets all macho like that.

We went halfway up the hill and checked the valve there. It had frozen and split. We (well Sally, actually) pulled it off and replaced it with a temporary connection and up we went to check the rest.

The stream was engorged. It was a torrent. White water was flowing like the semi-waterfall it is, dropping steeply. The stream bed was strewn with deadfall, bushes and boulders. Getting up the hill was mostly just a hike but, being a smidge portly (especially when wearing what felt like ten layers of clothes) I tended to use all fours at times. Even Sal had to climb now and then when it got steep *and* muddy.

She went first. She went fast. And she called down from the top, "All right, sweetie?"

I finally got to the top. The water was so high and the debris so thick we couldn't reach the water intake but we could see another valve a little way downstream that was squirting like a geyser so we knew that water was getting into the line—and getting out almost immediately. We replaced the broken valve with another connection. Water was now in the line and the line was intact.

So we went back down to the beach, opened the valve there and waited with anticipation to see the water come gushing forth. And…we waited.

Still no water. This is not easily explained but here goes. The water is coming in through the pick-up and all the holes in the line are now fixed. We opened the valve at the bottom of the hill to let the air out as the water displaced it. Therefore, we should get water flowing, right?

Wrong! Not if there is still some freezing in the pipe. And that is what we were thinking. We figured that there was something frozen (ice probably…duh) in one of the dips and valleys that the line creates as it wends its way down the hill. So the water that was now in the pipe has to melt the ice lump until it gets small enough to be dislodged and flow through. We were comforted by the fact that we have about ten days of water in our storage cistern before making a cup of tea becomes a challenge.

I woke up to Sally's cheery "Good morning! You'll never guess the good news."

"You're going to stop being so cheery and let me go back to sleep?"

"No, silly, the water is flowing! I just filled up the cistern and came to tell you!"

Normally, the second coming of Christ would be insufficient to make me want to get out of bed early. And, even then, I'd still be groggy and grouchy. But, I confess that the water flowing again made me instantly happy.

"Woo hoo!"

Turns out we must have been right. Who would of thought? The water line must have been blocked by ice and the water pressure eventually melted it and pushed it through and voila! Oooh, I love it when things work logically. It is so rare.

Logs we have gathered will be winched up the slope

-9-

Quest for Fire…wood

We've been picking at our woodpile these past weeks. No big fires in the woodstove, our only source of heat, just a few small ones in the morning to take the chill off. But each little piece reduces the pile and today, when I go to bring wood inside, I notice that the first of our twelve rows of stacked firewood is two-thirds gone.

"Sheesh, Sal. The wood pile is dwindling already! We were so happy to have that woodshed full and now, in a blink, we are almost down to eleven rows. I'd say we have used close to five percent of the pile already and we have yet to have a fire all day."

"All the more reason to make plans to go south. It seems everyone around here, when they are talking about getting away from the winter for a bit, throws out the line, "and we'll save some wood"!"

That's pretty funny. Spend time and money traveling and the first goal of the trip is saving the woodpile! But it's kinda true. You see, you can't buy the wood. There is no one to go and get the wood for you. Firewood is all about working hard and very little else, except a little bit of danger and a lot of sore muscles.

It's quite a process. First we watch for logs going by on the tide. A log makes a break from the confines of a boom and, not being nimble of foot, simply goes with the flow, or the current in this case. There is, however, a high and a low tide and a log can easily get caught up on a beach on a falling tide. Of course, the tide continues to rise and fall and, though the log makes sporadic attempts at freeing itself, it is usually caught and trapped somewhere along the path to freedom and life becomes a beach.

December and January bring the highest tides of the year, often supplemented by forceful storms. If a log is ever to get free again, this is the time for it. In fact, this time of year can bring a virtual carpet of loose logs to the inner channels and some choice logs amongst them. This is our opportunity to hunt and gather our year's wood. Nothing like a polar bear boat ride to ring in the New Year.

Purists don't approve of burning logs that have been in salt water because the salt gradually eats away at the metal interior of wood stoves. The alternative to pulling logs out of the sea is to find a tree on our property that has been blown down by the wind or to cut down a tree. We would then have to cut the branches off the trunk with a chainsaw. Then we would cut the trunk into rounds. Then we would have to move heavy rounds of wood out of the forest through impossible terrain to the shore with no machinery to help us. Once at the shore we would lift the rounds into the boat and out at the other end. This doesn't include getting them up to the house, splitting and stacking them. No thanks! We are willing to sacrifice a little metal to save a lot of work.

When we see a log out on the water we get out the binoculars. Is it floating high in the water? If so, it's not waterlogged. Is it less than ten inches in diameter? Anything larger is harder for us to handle. Does it have a lot of knots? Knots make it difficult to split and sometimes it's just not worth the effort. What kind of wood is it? If it's fir we're happy. Hemlock is good, too. Cedar is good for kindling as it burns fast and hot. However a good cedar log is prized and we wouldn't cut one up for kindling if it could be used for lumber. If all the questions are answered satisfactorily we rush to the boat armed with lengths of rope attached to log dogs (not to be confused with Portuguese Water Dogs, although our two often come as well) and head out to salvage it.

Once we get the log back to our beach we tie it up with all the others we've collected. Once we have eight or so logs, it's time to get them up above high tide. While the tide is out I cut the logs into ten foot lengths with the chainsaw. This sounds easy but the logs end up all higgledy-piggledy on the shore and I am cutting at awkward angles while slipping and slithering over kelp covered rocks. I'm sure this is all very normal for real woods people but I still have a city streak in me so it's hard. Poor me.

To get the logs up the hill we have rigged up a highline. This is a one hundred and twenty-five foot steel cable suspended between a ring drilled into rock down at the beach and the top of a steel tripod on the ridge near our house. A pulley is attached to a gas motor powered winch. It runs along the cable and hanging from it is a block and tackle, a configuration of ropes and pulleys to provide a mechanical advantage when lifting a log off the ground.

One of the hardest parts of the job for Sally is setting the chokes. These are heavy nylon belts which, once the logs are cut up, she has to wrap around each one. She attaches a loop in the end of the choke to a hook hanging from the block and tackle and pulls the log up until it is clear of the ground.

Each log length weighs between two hundred and four hundred pounds. Sal weighs one hundred and twenty pounds so her heft in relation to the log's weight has to be in the right ratio. The block and tackle gives her a four to one advantage so her weight is just enough to lift a log. Most times the weights are balanced or, sometimes by mistake (mine), the log has the advantage. This is where the fun begins. Sal will pull and pull and the log will slowly lift. Part of it is still on the ground or in the water and so, by pulling it up by one end, she gets a bit of a weight advantage, in the initial pulls anyway. And she needs all the help she can get.

When we were pulling up logs for the first time I guess my estimating was not dialed in as accurately as it should have been. Sal started with a particularly heavy hemlock. I guess it was about five to ten percent more than she could pull.

After she pulled in the slack on the rope I could see the rope tightening and the choked end of the log lifting a bit. I watch from on high to make sure things work out. And I watched as the log lifted higher. The higher it went, the more weight was transferred to the lifting rope and the block and tackle. At one point, before the log was raised high enough to clear the entanglement of other logs and debris, it seemed that a standoff had been reached. Sally was pulling with all she had and the log was not budging.

When that happens, Sal gets pretty stubborn. She *is* going to lift that log. She is the one in control. She knows that she is the Bull of the Woods! Gawd help anyone or any log that won't do as it is told!

She reaches as high on the rope as she can and lifts her entire weight off the ground. The log moves upwards slightly. Not releasing the rope at all, she begins to bounce the log and herself to some sort of jolly jumper rhythm and, with each log bounce up, she tries to pull the rope down. This little bit of applied mechanics adds another five pounds or so to her weight and the log moves up an inch or so at a time.

She keeps up this church bell ringer style strategy while she and the log slowly rotate on the spot. Sometimes she is hanging just a foot off the ground and sometimes, after a half-rotation, she is hanging a few feet off the ground because of the slope. Swinging with a five hundred pound log pressed into her face, she is suspended by a rope and holding her entire weight in her hands and arms. With a bit more bouncing she can usually rotate back to solid ground.

When the log is as high as she can get it, she has to get on her feet again (slipping slowly down the rope sometimes) and then tie off the end of the rope to somewhere on the log so that it stays in place. She wraps the excess rope, ties it to the log and then, wildly circling her arm over her head to indicate that I should start pulling the log up, she moves to safety. I am grinning from ear to ear.

Usually we pull the log segments up to a narrow ledge above the beach to let them dry out. We end up with a pile of thirty or so arranged like pickup sticks. One time Sal was nimbly dancing across them as she tugged a log to and fro trying to get it to settle down into the right place. I stood at the winch controls and watched the activity from the top of the ridge. It looked to me like an accident waiting to happen.

"Sal! I don't think scrambling over the pile is a good idea. There are four or five tons of unstable logs perched halfway up a steep hill and you are dancing on top of them like a Chinese acrobat. What would WorkSafe say?"

"Don't worry! It's not hard. I've got my balance. And they are lodged in pretty good. I'll be fine."

We've been together for forty years and if there is one thing that separates us it is her no fear attitude. Sal laughs at danger and piles scorn on warnings. Worse, she takes umbrage at being told what to do, even if the message is delivered with tact and sensitivity. In other words, when it comes to safety she thinks like a sixteen year old boy on a skateboard in front of a gaggle of girls.

I am a bit more careful by nature. But I've learned not to warn her directly. I do not instruct and I do not criticize. I am also cautious about what I say. But this was too much.

"Damn it, Sal. Get the hell off that pile! Stay uphill of the logs at all times and be safe for once! You are freaking me out! If you don't get off that pile, I am coming down to drag you off!"

That little outburst surprised even me. Those could have been fighting words. I was hung out on a very thin chauvinistic limb. The smell of danger in the air was palpable. My foot had been put down firmly and it usually ends up in my mouth when that happens—especially when telling Sal how to do something she has been doing well for a long time. I cringed at my indiscretion.

"Okay, sweetie, I'll play it safe."

And she got off the pile and completed the job taking the necessary care for her own safety. I was in shock! I had no idea what just happened. Everywhere I looked there was danger. I had looked left and looked right and leaped blindly into the fray. And it worked out. It's so easy to make a mistake out here and then someone can get hurt. It could've been me, given my outburst, but of course logging is also a dangerous pastime. Telling Sal what to do? Suicidal!

To get a log up the hill, Sal gives me the signal when it is ready, as would the whistle punk she is acting like, and I start the winch. The winch slowly pulls the log uphill to the top of the ridge. Once the log arrives I disconnect it, roll it out of the way and send the block and tackle back down the highline to Sal for another. We have to bring up about sixty lengths each year. Though we do most of it ourselves we try to include young, strong people when they are around to help. When they do they are gobsmacked.

"Oh my gawd! All that wood has to be found, towed, tied up, sorted, cut and hauled—just to get it into position to buck, carry, chop and stack! I can't believe it!"

"Yes. And Sally and I consider ourselves lucky to be able to find the logs floating by. Can you imagine having to go foraging about the woods for suitable trees, chopping them down, limbing them and then dragging them to the water? That's what the old-timers had to do. And then they had to build their house, farm their land, catch fish, find work and raise children. We just quit at the end of the day and drink wine. Those old homesteaders were tough!"

"*This* is tough," they say.

Once the logs are up on the ridge behind the house I buck them into rounds. Of course, this seasonal event typically comes about when I am already walking around slightly crooked from an uncooperative muscle group in the lower back region. It seems to be the way of things. Cutting rounds and splitting is made more difficult if you are using most of your breath to scream out in pain. And, during these primal outbursts, Sal is reluctant to get too close to help. Oh well, it keeps the wolves at bay.

Sal doesn't have the weight, power or sense of rhythm that is required to split big rounds. It is one of my few abilities—I can swing an axe with just the right tempo, like a Motown Temptation. Doo wop! Split! Another round in pieces. I've got the rhythm. I'm going to work on the lyrics.

A spine with an invisible screw driver stuck between vertebrae, however, limits one's moves and so I was hot water bottling as fast as I could a few seasons back. Just when I was wondering how I was going to get all the wood split, the answer miraculously appeared. Sal received a gift at book club. One of the other members was interested in sharing her visiting volunteer workers. Seems we were going to have two strapping young Dutch men come to visit and I would be introducing them to the splitting maul. Perhaps, after that, I would be introducing them to the hot water bottle.

I love the enthusiasm with which a newly arrived guest will attack a pile of wood needing splitting. There is a lumberjack inside everyone, it seems. They pick up the maul and start whacking. Wood flies in all directions. For a few minutes, anyway. Then they slow down. After a bit, they stop, get some water and look around for a face saving way out.

Of course, I usually try to make it easier for them to quit, "Hey, man! Looking a bit bagged, aren't ya? Y'all might want to rest up for later when you may be called on to lift a few cans of beer and your knife and fork!"

It's funny, really. You come out here and enjoy getting into shape, developing skills and getting stronger. It is definitely a good thing. At the same time, you realize that you *have* to get stronger. It is not an option. There is no choice. Get weaker and you have to go back to the city and buy a condo. Get cable. I don't want to do that.

It's a subtle lesson, though. Of course we all know that we are dependent on our health but, in modern times that has a more general meaning. There is usually only a minimal standard of functioning one requires from oneself in the city. You need to be able to sit on the couch and talk on the cell phone and make deals and reservations at the sushi bar. Maybe drive a car with GPS and cameras so as to minimize the effort.

Out here, things are different. When you are healthy and going like a train it's great, but you are stopped in your tracks when one of the wheels comes off. Out here, you can be as nutty as a fruitcake and dysfunctional in oh so many ways and you can still get along if you have a strong back.

So, not wanting to take any chances, my first real concession to getting on in years (not counting prescription meds) was to buy a small five ton splitter. Works great. Instead of splitting all the rounds by hand we now haul them by wheelbarrow an extra fifty feet or so to the deck adjacent to the woodshed. The little Chinese one toothed wonder splits them easier than a mother does a pie. I modified the splitter by attaching longer legs so it is at table height and eliminated the safety feature that made it impossible to turn it on with one hand. The manufacturer incorporated this for liability reasons but not having a hand free to guide the wood is also unsafe. It would be especially aggravating to hurt one's self *because* of the safety feature!

However, I love it when a mechanical purchase from China actually works. I have tried to avoid Chinese machines because they are bad for the planet given the Chinese record on pollution, bad for our economy by taking manufacturing offshore, and my experience has been that they don't always work well. And, if they do, they often don't last. Too bad, really, as the one thing they do work for is my budget.

Speaking of budget, I just checked Craigslist to see what a cord of wood goes for in the city. I was surprised to find out that it is anywhere from three to five hundred dollars. We need three cords every year so on average our labour is worth about twelve hundred dollars, given that the wood is free. So if it takes us one hundred person hours to get our wood in, we are "making" more than minimum wage. Cool!

The author operating winch as it pulls logs up from the shore

-10-

The Road Less Traveled

Ever wonder where all the hippies went? All the flower children? All the back-to-the-landers? I did.

Was it just a phase? Was it a fad? Well, part of the answer to that question is that some of the young people in the Seventies found their gene puddle a long way from the city and stayed on the land they migrated to. These hippies became homesteaders. It wasn't easy. Not in the least. But some persevered. So, for them, it was not a fad but a way of life consciously chosen and worked at. And it worked out for them.

Sally and I immersed our toes just enough in the Seventies to buy the property we now have. When we visited post-purchase and the reality of homesteading became apparent we retreated to the city. We could clearly see that making a living on the land was way too hard for the likes of us.

Other than old hippies, the balance of the off-the-gridders out here are old fishermen and loggers, early retirees, later-in-life urban escapees, cottagers who commit to more time than just the summer and a few whack jobs who simply don't want to be anywhere else due to the high concentration of so-called normal people. We have also greeted a few young people coming back to the islands to follow the same path as their hippie parents or grandparents.

But back to the old flower children. They are fascinating. They have kept, to a large degree, anyway, their ideals, their beliefs, and their politics. Their libraries stock Ken Kesey, Carlos Castanada and Rachel Carson. They have added much needed and varied skills to our area and have created full and enriched lives complete with many different vocations and healthy families.

Of course, they had to make a few changes to the original idyllic plan promoted by the Whole Earth Catalog, but it is still pretty earthy. They call the whole earth Gaia these days and it allows for engaging in the commercial world now and then, employing hot running water, refrigerators (for some) and keeping to a single spouse, for the most part.

The old hippies are now clean, skilled, hard working and occasionally able to buy new. Still voting Green, but out of necessity driving SUVs and running generators, outboards and maybe an ATV, although still making every effort to limit the use of petroleum. Still walking and talking off the grid but employing computers and cell phones while doing it. And they still think globally and act locally. They compost, of course, and there are still the essential organics, recycled items and funky decor but, all in all, it is an integrated lifestyle that proves healthy and fulfilling with much less of the stress, materialism and debt found in suburbia.

But it ain't all bliss, even here. The hippie life did not, generally, provide much for old age. Hippies did not often have the opportunity to contribute much, as a rule, to pension plans or RRSPs. They did not, as a rule, make enough money to save any of it. Hippiedom was largely hardscrabble. And now that they are getting older, it is getting even harder to scrabble.

And that won't likely ever get easier. As a generalization, most would be like fish out of water if they had to live in the city or an urban setting. Living in a small box does not work for people who have lived in the great outdoors most of their lives. I don't think they can go back. They are not equipped financially or psychologically.

I can say this, I think, because I have come to much the same place myself, albeit from the opposite direction—from city to country. I do not have the desire or the need to return to the city, but I don't think I have the option to do so either. It is hard to get on a moving merry-go-round.

Which is fine. For me, it is like not having to join the war in Syria or live in Toronto. But I am reminded of the old adage turned on its head: "When God opens one door, He closes another". The gates to the city are closed to me now that I have entered the garden.

Back in the Seventies there was a fork in the road. Some chose the left one and went as far as they could with it. They found the garden. Others chose the right and found the party. They drank the Kool-Aid and ate the caviar. Some of the lucky ones (and I count myself amongst them) went down one road and then backtracked and tried the other. All in all, everything considered, weighing the two, well…I think the left one seems to have a bit more going for it. It is definitely the road less traveled.

Community means something extra when you're on the road less traveled.

A neighbour called. Needed to use our vehicle. So, it's gone for a day or two. A guest called hoping to be picked up from the next island. We checked around and found other friends coming out to the island the same day and so our guest will be picked up by them and delivered to the dock at the end of the road where we'll meet them with our boat.

Yesterday, John and Jorge picked up some supplies in town for us. The best neighbours in the world, by a huge margin, are these two. John drops off movies that he has brought over to the island, even before he watches them! He also shares books, but he usually reads them first. After these many years I know that I could ask for just about anything. Of course, in an effort to be good neighbours ourselves, we try to ask for little and only in a pinch. Weird, how that works, eh?

Doing for others is a way of life out here. What has become so ingrained in our daily lives here is, however, foreign to many, especially to those who live in the city. We, at least, just didn't do any of this as city dwellers. In the suburbs, if everyone on our block needed a loaf of bread, thirty cars would leave thirty driveways and arrive at the store. Everyone would say hi to one another and then thirty cars would be driven back. Here, calling around to see if we can pick up a few things for others while we are shopping only makes sense. And everyone does it.

Mind you, it is done, primarily, for those located fairly close by. And the protocol is to offer first before someone has to ask. Actually, asking is not so good. Waiting for an offer and then accepting is the proper protocol. Should someone be going to town and they do not offer to pick up something, it is assumed that they have way too much to do and no face is lost. And, once in awhile, if something is more pressing than a loaf of bread, it is okay to ask if someone is going to town. But such an imposition must be reserved for really necessary things such as a part for the boat motor.

Other unwritten rules include the favour being limited to, at the most, a *few* items from the same shop. Preferably one that the shopper will be at anyway. It would be considered very bad form to say, "Would you mind picking me up some chocolate fudge from that new shop just out of town and I need a few spare sparkplugs from the auto parts dealer as well. A newspaper would be nice. Do you think ice cream would melt or do you have a cooler?"

This is much better. "If you're catching the ferry, would you mind dropping off my overdue movies at the gas station on the way?" Or, "Oh, you're going to the hardware store? Thanks for asking. I need a half inch drill bit. Thanks, nothing else. That's it."

Of course, in a pinch, anything goes. So, this time, there went my car.

Commerce is different on the road less traveled.

"Need a small compressor?"

"Umm, not really…why?"

"Well, you know that big old creosote timber you got tied up on the beach? I'd like to have it. Like to trade this small compressor for it."

"Oh, you don't need to give me anything. But let me think. Do I really need the timber? Nah…probably not. Got enough projects to keep me busy. Go ahead, take it."

"Well, I think you need a small compressor so I'll bring it over for you. Can't just take a guy's wood, can I? Wouldn't be right! Just wanna go measure that timber now that I'm here."

"But I don't even have any air tools. Why would I need a compressor?"

"Well, I got air tools. You can always use mine. Anyway, everyone needs a compressor."

And so it is around here. Rural economy. Unstructured business. Illogical deal making that is well, kinda logical in the micro context in which we now live.

People almost always make an effort to pay back and keep the books even but often they don't use money with which to do it. Since there is no real monetary type currency with which to measure, we have to use an ad hoc currency, as it were. I call it in kind. Which I interpret as you just have to *kinda* keep it even.

Even if the item or service being requested is of more significance or no significance to you, you'll be paid something that is deemed fairish. In some way, at some time, probably, although memory, or lack thereof, is a significant factor in the whole thing. All in all, it's pretty good.

And there is little or no negotiation. You either go for it or you don't. And, anyway, it is not like someone can say, "Oh, you think the timber is worth more than a small compressor? Okay, I'll make it one and half small compressors or even a medium sized compressor." He can't do that. He's got what he's got. To try and fine tune the deal is considered gauche. It's also impossible.

Sometimes it seems really out of whack. Especially if you think like I did in the city. Out here in the country I might rewrite a contract for someone or successfully get an insurance settlement for a neighbour for whom such work is like learning a foreign language. "I've got two salmon here for you and a few jars of Jane's strawberry jam coming next week. Hope that squares us?"

"Yeah, of course. Great. Thanks!"

When I worked in the city and did a contract or service or mediation or negotiation, I would charge for that service. I'd get paid an amount commensurate to the result and I was always okay with that. Whatever it was, it was sufficient for us to live our lives. But, out here, that same compensation method can't possibly work. For what I might charge a significant sum for in the city, I might get a few salmon or maybe a piece of old logging equipment in the country. Or just the knowledge that I have a favour I can call in.

It is not that the service isn't appreciated; it is just that service out here is reciprocated in kind, not money. Well, sometimes it is reciprocated in small compressors, lumber, salmon, prawns, crab and the like. Filthy lucre? Not so much. But can't that be unfair? Not really.

Say I needed to have a tree topped, something I'm not comfortable doing. My neighbour comes over, has lunch, climbs the tree and tops it. Then he comes down, has a beer and leaves. Eight months later I write his submission for a small construction contract, something he isn't comfortable doing. So, now we are square and no money was involved.

If I had to have a tree topped in the city, it might cost me five hundred dollars. If he had to hire me at city rates to write his contract submission, I might charge five hundred dollars. But neither of us lives in the city so the question is really hypothetical. He does tree tops. I do contracts. That's all there is to it.

Like the tree falling in the woods when no one is around to hear it making a noise (or not), it's a question of philosophy, really. When work gets done in the forest and there is no accountant or paperwork, how does one measure the value? Answer: in community, not money. It's the Wilderness Free Trade Agreement.

-11-

Earthquake on Aisle Seven

We were at the supermarket when the *little* one hit. There was an old guy in front of me attempting to get out his credit card while trying to answer the cashier's question about his loyalty points. Nothing was happening very quickly.

"Wow! Did you feel that?" the cashier asked.

This was way too much stimulus for our guy. He was dealing with his wallet, the credit card machine, his personal identification number, customer loyalty points. Then another question. He was simply stunned. He looked up at her, "Huh?"

"We had an earthquake! Just now! Didn't you feel it?"

"Huh?"

I was somewhat amused by this bumbling old fool who was surely a little older than me. I was totally justified in my condescension towards him until I realized that we had just experienced an earthquake and I hadn't noticed it either.

Well maybe I did. Kinda. I did feel a bit of a shift in the space-time continuum but, of course, at my age and not doing my yoga regularly, I just wrote it off as another woozy moment. I get that now and then. Feels a bit like an earthquake now that I think about it…but now I had to rise to his defense.

"Hey! At our age, the floor moves all the time. It's called getting old."

The poor old git finally managed to enter his PIN and get his food into his ecologically correct green cloth bag. He left in a confused state. It was Sal's and my turn to face the cashier

"Wow! Did you guys feel it?"

"Yes!" I left out the part about being simply confused as to what was happening—wooziness, balance, sugar deficit or, as a distant possibility, an earthquake. I was still processing. And I felt the cashier was only on a need to know basis anyway.

Sally, who suffers from intermittent vertigo, innocently asked her "What are you talking about?" She hadn't noticed a 6.4 on the Richter scale either.

"We just had an earthquake! The whole building moved. It was incredible. Didn't you feel it?"

Sal looked at her blankly. Then she looked at me.

"Hey, you should be pretty familiar by now with what the earth moving feels like sweetie pie." I leaned forward and offered up a slight leer and a twisted smile.

Sal and the cashier looked at me, assessed the possibility and burst out laughing.

Small towns have a way about them. People are generally a bit more curious about others and typically have the time to engage when going through a minor transaction. Short, personal conversations ensue. People connect. I'm not going to be invited to a wedding by our friendly cashier, but I'll be sure to hear about it the next time I'm in. Coming from the big city where a lot of daily interactions take place in a more professional and less friendly way, we notice on our town trips that everyone is much more casual and laid back.

That's a good thing because sometimes we are stressed to the max. We get up early to prepare for our tri-weekly trips to town. Sally collects all the garbage and recycling into plastic bags (ironic in itself, don't you think?) and in winter we dress in layers (about five for me, a gazillion for Sally).

I gather up the Rubbermaid totes (not a plug, but life off the grid would be impossible without them) and coolers, loading them onto the funicular cart along with the garbage, recycling and a couple of backpacks and send the whole schmozzle down to the beach.

I trek to the dock to get the boat and Sal gathers the gear at the water's edge. Once I pull the boat into the beach Sal throws everything in and we head off. A short while later we are at the community dock on the adjacent island. We tie up the boat and carry everything up the ramp and along a rough trail to deposit it on the side of a dirt road. I hike up the steep slope for about a hundred and fifty yards to the parking lot and drive our vintage SUV down the slope to the trail's end and we load up the gear. After a twenty minute drive along the dirt logging road we reach pavement and follow that for another twenty minutes. We drop off garbage at our "Garbage Club" dumpster and then hit the recycling centre. It's then a quick leap to the ferry terminal to await its arrival. So far our journey has taken an hour and fifteen minutes.

After we had been loaded onto the ferry and the departure time came and went, I asked one of the workers why we weren't leaving.

"Weather. It's pretty rough just around the point. Hard to get into the berth at Campbell River. But we'll leave in a minute. Soon as the captain works up his courage!"

I laughed at the obvious joke and went back to the car.

Sure enough, we left within minutes. Rounding the point, we experienced all hell breaking loose. The ferry pitched and rocked and then it tipped and rolled for the fifteen minutes it took to cross the Straight. Sea water sprayed over the hood of our car that was parked first in line at the bow. Sal got out to take a photo but it was too rough and wet. However, once on the Campbell River side, the captain berthed that boat as gently as if he was placing a robin's egg back in a nest. Not a bump. Bloody brilliant he was!

Once in town we started our chores. First stop was the paint store for, you guessed it, paint. Then another stop for engine oil and muffin tins. Next is a big box grocery store to get chicken for the dogs and then the candy store (Sal has a serious fudge habit).

Off to the big box hardware store to pick up the six items out of our list of ten that they'll have, on average. Eight out of ten items is a marvel. All ten? Never gonna happen.

"Sorry, sir, we don't have nails just now. Out of hammers, too. But a shipment is due tomorrow. Can you pop back into the store tomorrow?" (No, but maybe you can "pop over" to a remote island?)

Then at the doctor's office:

"Sorry. The doctor isn't available after all. I can fit you in tomorrow at the same time." (Unh…doesn't "appointment" mean the same thing to a doctor as it does to the rest of us?)

Another store:

"Yes, sir, we carry those. I'll have them in by Thursday at the latest." (May as well make it a Thursday sometime next month.)

For every place that is a disappointment there is someone who goes above and beyond.

"I need a piece of glass cut, please. Thirty-three inches by thirty-six inches, single pane, normal thickness."

"No problem, sir. It'll be ready tomorrow."

"Okay, but I can't get back in tomorrow. I live remote and only get in every few weeks. Could you hold it for me?"

"Oh, hell, come back in an hour. I'll cut it myself at lunch instead of putting it in the system. How's that?"

And that kind of consideration shows up a lot. If someone knows it's a long trek you've made, often they'll try to make it work for you. This is small town living at its best.

We blitz in for a quick lunch at the Ideal Café, a greasy spoon diner that caters to loggers and looks like a movie set. Probably the best roadside cafe I have ever been to. The waitresses all wear really tight jeans or short skirts, know everyone, and rush about doing everything at top speed. The food is great. Tea is served in those leaky stainless steel pots that waste everyone's time and patience and spill water over everything. Classic.

After eating we race off to Andrew Sheret for plumbing stuff. Sal gets that while I hit the propeller shop. Then off to Western Equipment for a mallet handle, log dogs, a quick perusal of pulleys and on to the bank. Next we head up to the Japanese food store for some gyoza, yakisoba and tuna. After Katie's Rice Box we buy some firebricks at Quality Stoves to reline the woodstove. The drugstore is next and then I go to the nearby liquor store and Sal heads over to Save-On for the big grocery shop.

I then divert to Lordco (gas line fittings) and, while waiting to help Sal load the totes of groceries into the truck, decant the Scotch into a large plastic bottle so that I can return the glass bottle now, rather than carry it over to the island and back. The liquor store staff is more than a bit curious to see me back so soon with empties.

"Never mind, I'm green! The planet is going to hell! Causes me to drink heavily, being green, ya know, but at least I'm recycling my empty bottles!"

Sal then goes off to get her hair cut by Kat, I go to the marine store and Staples and then we swing by Woofy's, our second to last stop on the way to the ferry. There the store clerk mentions that the ferries have stopped running. We quickly finish up and race to the ferry terminal to check it out.

"Well, he may try to get in one more run," says the woman at the ticket booth, referring to the captain. "He missed the last run but he's pretty good. If he can do it, he will. If you have more shopping go ahead and do it but phone me in twenty minutes. I'll know by then if he's going to try again."

We rush out to buy Sally a replacement pair of rubber boots, an important item in our lives. When I call the ferry terminal I get the word.

"Yes! He's making another run. Better get back here!" And so we did. As we pull up to the booth I ask for tickets for two adults.

"No dogs today?"

I am stunned. How does she remember this stuff? We rarely have the dogs with us.

Our Pathfinder is one of the smaller sport utility vehicles. We pack it so solidly this trip that, by the time we leave the last store, Sally has a huge cardboard box of groceries on her lap and a case of frozen dog food at her feet. Her seat has been moved forward so that some of the boxes could be loaded on the floor behind her. Once in line Sal somehow manages to pour us tea from our thermos and then burrows her way out from under the cargo to cross the ferry terminal to talk to someone she knows.

As it turned out we were lucky to make it onto that ferry as it ended up being the last run of the day. Other neighbours weren't so lucky and had to spend the night in town.

Once across the channel and off the ferry on our neighboring island we head to the pharmacy where the pharmacist not only knows me, she knows my prescriptions by heart and who my doctor is. Prior to moving to the country I went to the same pharmacy in Vancouver for fifteen years. No one knew me there and I didn't know them either.

Next is the combined gas station/movie store to get some new rentals. I don't know why we bother. They have a penchant for Bruce Willis movies and really dumb, dumber and dumbest comedies. *And* we've watched most of them. But we look anyway.

By now it's dusk and we are still at least forty minutes from the boat so we head off. We see a few deer as we travel the logging road. As it is getting dark, I drive down the steep hill to the beach to let Sal out at the trail to the dock. Then I drive across the beach to the water where Sal will bring in the boat. I unload from the truck as Sal places carefully by weight, the three hundred pounds of groceries, dog food, and miscellaneous purchases and gear in the boat. When it's properly loaded she heads over to the dock to wait for me. I take the truck back up the hill and park.

The wind has been blowing up since we've been away and the seas are choppy. We head across the channel in the dark and as we get close to the other side we can see the dogs running to the shore, as they recognize the sound of our motor.

The tide is running hard with a two knot current going past our place and the wind at my back is about twenty miles per hour. As I approach the shore the waves are making the bow describe three foot arcs. Sal leaps onto a slippery rock and turns to grab something from the boat as I attempt to hold it off the rocks by using the throttle and alternating between forward and reverse gears. We miss. I am swept away by wind and current.

"I'll bring the boat around again, Sal! You may have just enough time to grab one item at a time!"

And that is what we do. I take the boat in as close as I dare and drift down past Sal who is precariously perched on the rocks. As the bow goes by, she grabs what she can. One hand is for safety, the other for a full cooler or heavy tote. As I circle around, I take a minute to move the other items to the very front of the bow for her to reach. As well the boat needs a bit of a pump out each time I go around because the waves are breaking over the stern. I am soaked by the time we get everything off. Sal has a cut on her ankle.

I take the boat around to the dock and come back to help Sal get everything from the shore up to the waterfront deck and then loaded onto the funicular cart. I send the cart up to the house where we unload everything and carry it into the house. Start the fire. Sal begins to put things away. I pour tea and then wine and Sal puts on the oven to warm up a dinner that she has pre-cooked.

The fridge is full and the freezer is jammed. We have everything we need for projects and repairs. The cupboards are definitely *not* bare. Whew!

With a bit of luck we'll be good for a few weeks.

Fiddich and Megan

-12-

Eau d'Otter

I had promised Sal a dog, any dog, whichever one she wanted. When our new home was no longer a building site it was time to fulfill that promise. Sally's birthday was coming up so I contacted the British Columbia Portuguese Water Dog Association as this was Sally's choice. I spoke with the woman in charge regarding PWDs and who gets them.

"I understand you have dogs for sale and that they cost about two thousand dollars. Could you put me on the waiting list for one?"

"Well, I have to interview you first. You can't have a dog just like that, you know. Why do you want one?"

"Well, to be honest, I don't. But my wife does and I want my wife. Ergo, dog."

"Hmm…well, there are no puppies due for at least six months."

"Thank goodness! A reprieve! Wahoo! Will you put me on the list? Maybe at the bottom?"

"I'm not so sure you're going to make a good dog owner…"

"I probably won't. I'll be good to the dog and treat it with grudging respect and all. You know, food, water and the odd pat on the head. But Sal will be the Mother Teresa of dogs. She will love her dog to bits. In fact, part of my reluctance is that I'll come fifth in the love line up after my son, my daughter and the dog. Yes, I can add. But Sal will leave space number four open, just in case. Trust me, I'm fifth in a group of four."

"Well, I still have to interview you both."

"Okay, but by the way, do you ever have any discount dogs? Maybe one that has a kink in its tail or is pigeon-toed or cross-eyed or something? One ear, perhaps? Just a bit scratched or dented?"

"*Absolutely not!* I am definitely wondering about you. Our dogs are pedigreed and blah, blah, blah, blah and you'll be lucky if we allow one into your care. Your wife better be as great as you say she is or you don't stand a chance!"

"Oh. Sorry. Forgive me. I'm just a guy trying to make his wife happy and I'll do whatever it takes, even if that means acting like I want a dog. Honest, I can pull that off. You'll see."

"I doubt that but, say…have you ever thought about getting an adult dog? The puppy stage is a difficult one and it requires even more patience, tolerance and love than what I'm hearing from you. Perhaps you'd consider an older dog?"

"That depends…how long do PWDs live?"

"About fourteen years."

"Got a thirteen year old?"

I waited a day before I phoned back.

When we arrived at the kennel a few days later I got out of the car first and was greeted by a very stocky Standard Poodle-type dog with no hesitation or malice in his approach. Good looking dog. I put out my hand in that open, palm side down, vulnerable way of greeting dogs that basically invited him to bite me. And he did!

I wasn't sure that I had been bitten at first. I looked at my hand and there were definitely little dents in the skin but it was more a taste than a bite. PWDs are a "mouthy" breed, I later found out, and they often touch their teeth to a hand to get the "feel" of a person.

I looked at him. He looked at me. And I wondered whether I should proceed any further. Still no real threat was being made but, on the other hand, no ground was being given either. He seemed to be saying, "Had enough? Or do you need me to tell you again?"

I stood there undecided until his owner showed up.

"Bogart! Come here!" He did as he was told and Sal and I went to shake hands and undergo the interrogation that would or would not result in our being judged worthy. Bogart was the reigning sire at the kennel and had a vested interest in who came and went. Obviously, I thought, his vote had already been cast. Judging from the scowl on the owner's face, she was leaning in the same direction.

So, as I always do when meeting strangers, I let Sal go first. I call it putting our best face forward. People allow her into their space much more readily than they do me and I then get to follow quietly behind. This was definitely one of those times.

We went through the heavy grilling and, of course, I sat back and Sally answered just about everything. It was not hard to do that since the breeder barely acknowledged my presence, possibly due to our previous phone calls. I got the distinct impression that she preferred dogs to people and females over males of both species. I have experienced that kind of initial cool reception before from women. Could it be me?

While we underwent the judging process, we were introduced to numerous dogs. I remained, for the most part mute, although I confess to tentatively offering up a bit of light charm in the form of self-deprecating humour. To get anywhere with women like that, I have to deprecate like hell. It is not that hard, actually, as I have plenty of material.

But I also noticed that I was not the only mute one. None of the dogs barked. Well, not that I could hear, anyway. Occasionally I would see a dog make a barking-like head gesture but no sound resulted and the dog went about its business of ball chasing, so I wasn't sure.

Seems they had been debarked. Some show dog breeders debark their dogs by having their larynx lasered. It is illegal in some countries. Not Canada. It didn't seem like a very nice thing to do but, of course, I levied no criticism of the breeder lest she rip me a new orifice and sent us home dogless. But I didn't like it. Neither did Sally.

We were introduced to Megan-the-mute and a love bond formed between her and Sal faster than five minute epoxy. Megan was four and was a champion specimen of a PWD with awards and ribbons to prove it. She had spent her adult life warding off all advances, remaining chaste and a nonparticipant in the PWD breeding program. I suspect she is a lesbian (not that there is anything wrong with that!) but obviously she would be a disappointment to a breeder and Bogart, the resident stud.

"If you'd like, you can take Megan for a while, say a month, and see if you get along. If you do, we'll make it work. If you don't, she can come back here. And, remember this—she will always have a home here. Don't ever think of getting rid of Megan if your life circumstances should require it. Bring her back!"

It was pretty clear that the breeder loved her dogs, larynx removing notwithstanding. They are fed well, treated well and shown as much love and attention as anyone can sanely do with a large number of dogs. But being a breeder is not the same thing as being a dog owner. Dog owners make a dog a member of the family. My worst fear.

We had not gone more than ten minutes down the road with Megan in the back seat when Sally decided that Meg must surely be lonely back there and climbed into the backseat with her so that more snuggling licking and hugging could take place. Megan even did some of that as well. Forty years ago it took me a lot longer than ten minutes to get Sal snuggling and hugging in the back seat, I can assure you.

About an hour into our trip home Sally said to me (from the backseat) with authority in her voice that was not to be dismissed, "We aren't going to take Megan back! This is working out just fine"

And so the trial period ended.

Meg did well her first year. So did I. Sal was ecstatic. Even our kids took to Meg knowing full well that she was a kid replacement. It's a good statement about your kids when they can love and accept the new dog that Sal inadvertently called Emily, our daughter's name, at least half the time. Of course, she evened that out when Em came to visit by calling *her* Meg.

We went to see the breeder one day, just to check in. It seemed only fair to show her that we had turned out to be worthy owners and, to be honest, Sally was just a bit proud of how happy and healthy Meg was. It was time to show off.

When we arrived, we went through the ritual of talking dog, oohing and aahing over the latest batch of puppies. Then the dogs were let out and I noticed Fiddich, and not just because he was named after the Scotch.

This guy was about fourteen months old and easily as big as Meg. It was hard to tell because his feet hardly touched the ground. I swear this dog had the same air time as a gazelle. He leaped and bounded and jumped and flew from one place to the next. He was a veritable rust colored ball of energy that rarely and barely touched the ground. Honest, I have had kites that spent less time in the air.

In a moment of weakness I said to the breeder, "Geez, he needs some space, that boy. If you ever want to let him go on vacation, we'll take him for a week or so. You know, like parole?"

Sal stared at me. "What?"

The breeder looked at me. "Are you saying you want another dog?"

"No, no, *no*! You women! Everything has a double meaning for you. No, no, no! I just said that we'd give this poor bastard a chance to be free, that's all. A chance to fly, a chance to feel alive, a chance to explode on this planet like he obviously wants to. Then we'll bring him back. No more dogs!"

And so it came to pass that Fiddich joined the family. What can I say? He flew and leapt and jumped and landed in our life. I had very little to do with it.

Our dogs had been restless for a few nights. Seems there is a wolf pack nearby and a whole lot of howling is going on. Our poor, mostly mute mutts can't really participate in the choir of the wild but they try, rasping out a few dog whispers and the occasional half bark from Fiddich. It is just as well. The wolves call to hear the domestic dogs reply which they then lure to the pack with a female in heat and then have their guest for lunch. Literally. Since they can't hear our dogs, they don't come out this way.

Generally the dogs sleep outside in their kennel. When it is cold or snowy, we (Sal) keep the dogs in. And when there are wolves around we don't take any chances. So the dogs have been in these past few nights and even for good portions of the day. Some might call this being humane.

Sadly, I have to report that Meg has abused this privilege of extended hospitality. She is like fish or visitors who begin to smell after three days. Malodorous in the extreme. It seems that Meg has discovered the mother lode of all otter latrines and has reveled in it. The smell is more than skin deep. Dogs like that sort of thing—eau d'otter. I don't.

So, what we have here is a failure to relate on basic standards of hygiene. Communication is clear but polarized. Meg thinks she is irresistible. I think she is revolting. And Sal is trying to mediate this. It isn't easy. A cigar can be just a cigar but sometimes a dog is an otter's anus.

Yesterday Sal washed the dogs and I dried them off. After drying, Meg smelled worse. So, back into the tub she went. She still emerged stinky, but not because we didn't have enough Pert Plus shampoo. She had been "Perted" generously. So, weakened in my resolve by Pert and oh! de poop stench, I relented. She came into the house smelling like a pulp mill in August.

Sal took the dogs swimming in the ocean this morning. Megan was the black creature from the lagoon. She *still* stinks. You might think that I should simply adjust. I can adjust to freezing temperatures, no water, isolation and, most of the time, to the inane nonsense spouted by some CBC announcers, but this is asking too much. Tomorrow we're expecting a howling gale. I am going to lash Megan to an exposed tree. I'll let you know how it goes.

Fiddich and I were left alone yesterday. Sally had taken Megan with her to stink up the post office. Sal was standing in for the regular postmistress for the day. They wouldn't be back until dinnertime.

It was cold and clear and inviting and so I went outside for awhile. Sal likes the dogs to play fetch every day and so I went out to do that. "C'mon, Fid, let's play fetch!"

Fetch is crazy. I don't believe in fetch. I think the whole concept is overblown. I don't believe fetch is either necessary or important for me or for the dog. It's just dopey.

If you have a dog that is stuck in an apartment or even a backyard, then, maybe a little fetch is in order. I'll grant you that. Dogs need to move and run. I get that. But, if you have a dog whose backyard is the great outdoors, unfenced, unrestricted and virtually infinite (if he does a little swimming which, call me crazy, Portuguese water dogs should be able to handle) then he or she is the captain of their own ship, so to speak. They can go anywhere, do anything and they don't need me or a ball with which to do it.

But…Sal likes it…and, well, it was a nice day…and the dog seems…never mind. I went to play fetch.

We play fetch on our peninsula mostly. It is over fifteen acres. Plenty of room and lots of elevation changes. Bushes, trees, gullies, mud. A perfect place for a dog.

I throw the ball. Fid brings it back. It's a simple concept made just a bit more challenging by the topography, but that is what constitutes the spice of life for a dog.

"Go for it, big boy!"

And off he goes sniffing and charging around. Nine times out of ten, he brings me the ball. It is the tenth time when it gets interesting.

Upon that occasion when Fid fails to solve the hidden riddle of the far flung ball, an impasse and a dilemma is created. For me, anyway. We can't play fetch without the ball and I do not have a better nose for it than does my companion. Can I even recall in which direction I last threw it?

I must find the ball. It is an expensive, non-chewable, specially constructed ball-with-ears (don't ask) that Sally values even more highly than do the dogs. It is their favorite ball. So, I go looking. The longer it takes, the more desperate I get. The more desperate I get, the happier Fid seems. I think he knows that this is the tenth time. It is my turn.

Go for it, big boy, he's thinking. I'm waiting...

While I am ferreting my way around, sniffing and charging through the bush, Fid sits primly and watches. I admit that he looks pretty happy. And I am looking for the ball. He is just waiting. Maybe he is grinning. Occasionally he looks like he might offer a bit of encouragement but he rarely does. He never helps.

Ten percent of the time, I am fetching for him. This never feels right to me. So why not quit? Go in and have some tea? It's only a ball.

Well, I confess to feeling not just a little pressure. Sally likes me to play fetch with the dogs but she doesn't want it to end badly. Not having the ball at the end of the play is ending badly. Should that be the case I am in way more trouble than I would have been if I hadn't gone for a fetch in the first place. I start to panic. I can't think clearly. I am getting hot. I start to pant. I sniff for water.

I am telling you that I think fetch is crazy and when the roles get reversed, it is even crazier. Thank gawd, we found the damn ball! And yes, once I found it and calmed down, I threw it for Fid again a few times (it adds an element of danger) but I stopped short of losing it again. The ball is still ours. We live to fetch another day.

With Megan fetch is simple. She loves to play, even though her back legs are getting kinda wobbly and it is not like our property is a gentle flat meadow. This place is pretty vertical and anything thrown basically goes downhill. And she goes after it with gusto. So far, pretty normal.

But if she wants to play fetch and we don't, she plays fetch by herself. Bear in mind that we live on a really steep slope. The front deck of our house is eighteen feet off the sloping rock below and the terrain dives more abruptly after that. Anything thrown (or dropped) from the deck will travel pretty far. And Meg knows this. So she will get her toy, be it ball, bone or stick, and push it over the edge of the deck herself. She'll watch it fall and roll down the hill and then she'll run off, tail a-wagging, and get it. If we say, "Meg, you do it! You do it!" she'll repeat the process until she is played out. That's not all bad. And, it gets better.

As she ages, she is getting tired more quickly. Now she plays fetch for awhile by herself and then, after the panting gets heavy, she just sends Fid! That's right. She drops the toy over the edge of the deck and then we all look at each other for a second as if no one knows what to do...and that is Fid's cue to run to the rescue. He retrieves the toy! Repeat as necessary.

We can play fetch without getting out of our chairs and without putting down our wine glasses. Does it get any better than that?

-13-

Playing with Fire

Sal and I have lived remote for some time now. Ten years at this writing. We are committed to this lifestyle, partly because we have no other place to live but also because, even if we did, we would choose to be nowhere else. And that kind of commitment to our lifestyle and location means a commitment to our personal relationship as well.

Because of our lifestyle we are living more closely and intimately than ever before. We may have thought we were married before, but now we are *really* married.

We have been together for over forty years. How we have managed all this time, I'll never know. One of us, it seems, can be a bit difficult. But living together when we were in the city was mitigated somewhat by each of us having full-time jobs and rich and supportive social lives, not to mention children. Combining all that with our other obligations resulted in not having much exclusive time for the two of us for the greater part of thirty years.

Living full time together at our remote home, however, is quite a different scenario. Not only am I always here, I am always here in a smaller space than our previous home. Admittedly, I am inclined to hover at times, especially when Sal is cooking. It can be a bit disconcerting for her and she occasionally shouts, "Looming!" and waves a cooking utensil menacingly at me.

But this kind of closeness is okay for me. Sally is a delightful person and nature has a way of pairing the yins and the yangs, so we get along pretty well. Still, I understand the problem of this type of change. It can be a difficult adjustment from virtually no time together to full time together.

Some couples have creative coping mechanisms. I know of one pair who has lived in adjacent but separate cabins for years and enjoy the occasional meal together. Sometimes they include their respective dates. Another couple lives in cabins over one thousand miles apart. She goes north when he goes south and vice versa. He has a small fleet of old, restored farm tractors, despite the fact there are no roads on his island, and she has a collection of golfing instructors.

But, for many others, increased closeness is a good thing for the marriage. It's kind of a second chance at getting things right. Our minds are mostly free of rat race related stresses, our kids are grown, obligations have lessened and there's a new appreciation of life and our partners. It's a honeymoon all over again.

Well not exactly *always* a honeymoon. We often have lots of chores to do and we need to work together sometimes. Sal is the best partner in the world but, sadly, we don't actually work well together.

She insists on knowing what we are doing in advance of doing it. I prefer to discover what we end up with. Fundamentally different. She reads the instructions…I mean, seriously? I sometimes glance at them just to make sure that I already know what they say.

Sal also cleans up a lot. But she tends to clean up while I am still in the middle of the job. Admittedly, I am disinclined to finish anything, so undertaking a cleanup after a week of inactivity makes some degree of sense. I understand that. But I really need all the stuff lying around to remind me of what stage I am at in the project. If everything is put away, it looks pretty much finished to me. And, anyway, it took a lot of effort to spread that stuff all over the place. I just don't want to get it all out again.

We are also both natural managers. Sal's also a very good worker but it's the dueling manager thing that makes life difficult.

"Sal, grab that board, please, and go up the ladder and hold one end near that log!"

"Why? Why am I doing that? Shouldn't we miter the end first?"

"Well, that would be a good idea if we were going to have mitered ends but these are butt joints. Please. Just go up the ladder."

"I don't really want butt joints. I prefer mitered joints."

"Now is not the right time to tell me that."

"Why?"

"Because they have been cut to length and are now too short to miter."

"So, you already screwed up?"

"Would you please pass me the chainsaw and then stretch out between the two saw horses for a sec?"

Actually, Sal is pretty good to work with. She thinks so, anyway. She enjoys working in the outdoors. And, even if the work is hard going, she knows how to find a way to have some fun.

That is a beautiful thing. I admire it. Can't do it, but I admire it. Especially when she takes a break to have fun when she is working on her *own* job. She'll stop to toss the stick for the dogs, for instance. And she'll be happy. She'll smile. It's a lovely thing to see.

Sometimes, however, when she takes a break to play with the dogs or watch an eagle soar or a butterfly fly and I happen to be on the roof balancing a board waiting for her to refocus on the job at hand, it just seems so wrong.

"Uh, Sal, I have the board here. I am ready for you to put in the nail…you know, like we planned?"

"Just a sec, sweetie, Megan lost her ball. I'm just going to get it. I won't be a minute."

Working together is both a delight and a challenge. I've discovered that Sal has promoted herself and she is now my supervisor. I now report to her. It's like reporting to Lucille Ball.

I've decided to appoint myself a supervisor as well. So now we have too many supervisors on site and not enough willing workers. Labour problems seem to plague us.

This is an amazing problem when you think about it. There *are* only the two of us. And we are great partners in most things.

"What are you doing?" Sal says, sounding, to me, somewhat accusatory.

"Just cutting a log" I say defensively.

"Did you measure it?"

"No. Thought I'd wing it…looks about forty-eight inches."

"What? You have to measure!"

"Well, of course I measured it, didn't I? It's exactly forty-six and seven eights."

"Well, you didn't tell me!"

"No. True. I didn't think you needed to know."

"Well, I can't help it if I don't know what's going on, can I? Why are you being so difficult?"

"That's the kind of guy I am—difficult. Now, if you don't mind, I am going to cut the log now, you micromanager!"

"I am *not* a micromanager! And anyway, you're the one who isn't communicating."

And so it goes for a few minutes and then things are good again and we go along nicely for another hour or so before another petty tyrant issue erupts. I can't honestly say that I am any less guilty than she.

I sometimes—actually, often—don't know what I am doing and having questions asked of me is vexing. I tend towards the terse and snappy at such times. Mea culpa.

Sal has a good attitude and is willing to do what needs to be done. But as I mentioned, she does like to have an overview of the job and an idea of what is going to happen before it actually does. She likes plans, lists and proper preparation. Those are totally foreign concepts to me.

I tend towards winging it. I like to think of it as being creative. Sometimes I call it "organic". And I prefer the "just do as I say" type of worker—the kind who can also read my mind. So, that prerequisite is, for sure, not really fair to Sal. She has trouble reading my mind and, of course, there is no plan in there to read, anyway. Hell, there is barely a mind! Even if she could read it, there would be way too many pages with incomprehensible scribbling all over them, given my inclination to being a sketch-on-a-napkin type guy.

When you think about it, it is a bloody marvel we ever get anything done. But it is always interesting and really, I do love working with Sal. Unfortunately it's not mutual.

"I've got this idea for a huge project and I really need you to work with me."

"Sorry, I'm going to be away then."

"You don't know what it is or when we are going to do it!"

"Whenever, whatever. I'm pretty sure I'm booked."

"See, you *can* read my mind, after all."

So, because of the labour disputes, Sal and I don't usually work together. She does her thing. I do mine. It's better that way. I love her and all. And I am pretty sure that she loves me. "I'm here, aren't I?" she says whenever I seem insecure. But our thinking is different. Our pace is different. Our view of things is different. And of course what is worse, we both think we are the boss. And, it would seem, I am wrong about that.

It makes no difference what the job is, one of us always knows better. The problem is that we each think it is ourselves. That person also thinks the other is there to assist, hold things in place, fetch things and make tea.

We were installing steel cross braces for the new, lower funicular. The apparatus that I designed, bought stuff for, and had done all the work on to date. One might assume that this chore would be mine to supervise given that Sal hadn't even looked closely at it. Don't assume. It seems Sal knows a great deal more about funiculars and metal fabrication than one would suspect. Or so she claims.

Oh, I am only kidding. Mostly. The truth is that even though we don't work well together we *have* to now and then and, when we do, we do just fine. Well, fine enough to get the job done, anyway. The real issue is that neither of us knows much of anything and the enveloping pall of fear and ignorance when we start causes doubts and confusion. This is not an optimal work environment when we are confused and insecure. Well, for Sal anyway. I am, of course, blessed with the male ego. The male ego abhors a vacuum. So, it fills it in with bluster.

For this work on the funicular I was using my half-inch heavy-duty Milwaukee drill. It's lighter and faster than the old Craftsman. One minute I was drilling through steel, the next I was smelling smoke coming from the suddenly noisy innards of the drill. It sounded like a bearing rattling and screeching. *Something* had gone wonky inside and the drill was of no use despite my immediate but ineffective tampering with a hammer and copious amounts of WD40.

So I turned to drill number two to finish the job. We managed to get two cross braces on, despite the circumstances. But we had five or six more to do and a few other pieces to attach as well. We'll be drilling through thick steel at least a couple of dozen times over the course of a few more days. And then we have to countersink the bolt holes after the holes are drilled.

I sure hope Sal knows what she is doing. The way things are going I'll *want* to be fetching and making tea!

Sal and I had another chore that required us to work together. We headed out early one morning at high tide to position her small boat at the base of the makeshift ramp we had built for getting the boat out of the water. The previous day we had pulled two skinny logs into position. They were now parallel to each other at a gentle angle covering the gap between the beach and the waterfront deck. This makeshift marine ways would allow us to pull the boat up the logs and onto the deck for some much needed maintenance. However, the tide was a bit too high to start manhandling the little vessel. We'd just get water in our boots. We know about these things. We seem to always get water in our boots.

Water *in* the boots contradicts the purpose of the damn boots in the first place, but we seem to do it all too often and then have to walk around finishing whatever chore we have started—usually the remainder of it on dry land—with water swishing around our feet. How stupid is that? But, I digress…

After breakfast we went back to haul the boat out. The tide had dropped a foot or two and the boat was just about perfectly situated for a pull.

"Sal, I'll get the winch set up. You go down to the boat and push the stern over so the boat comes straight up."

"That log has floated in and it's blocking the ramp. Shouldn't I move it out of the way first?"

"No. Not necessary. The log will act as a roller. Just position the boat."

"I'm not comfortable leaving the log there. I think I should move it. Plus, I don't know what the plan is. Do we have a plan?"

"The plan is simple," I say, raising my voice slightly. "Rope is attached from winch to boat. Winch pulls rope. Rope pulls boat. Boat slides up ramp. Got it? Winch—rope—boat—ramp—comprendo?"

"No need to yell. But I'm not sure that it will be okay. I'm worried. I want to check out stuff, or something."

"Sal, trust me. I got this. Just get the stern straightened and do as you are told!"

"What? What did you say?"

"I said, get the stern straightened and then get a *hold*!"

She bought it. Oooh that was close! I had been playing with fire.

As the boat slowly came up the ramp, Sal clucked and shrieked and called "halt" a couple of times for no reason but we eventually got the boat up without too much fuss or muss. Really, the ramp worked like a charm.

"So", I said smugly, "that went well. Compliments all round, I'd say. Mind you, I think it should be *you* giving the compliments. So?"

"Yeah, great job! You did good…this time."

I had already partially turned away and didn't quite catch it, "What? What did you say?"

"I said you did a good job and everything was *fine*!"

Communication is the secret of a good marriage.

Sally had just returned from kayaking. These last few years, she and two neighbours have gone on a day long paddle to some remote, desolate location and then come back. They do about fifteen miles, give or take. It usually requires eight hours or so. They might stop once or twice. Lunch, pee break or two, maybe tea. Then home.

Today is sunny, bright and windy in a way one might describe as blustery. The seas are a bit choppy. Nice day for a sail. Kayaking? Not so much. But they don't care. They just paddle. And paddle. And paddle. And then come home.

"So, how was your day?"

"Great!"

"What did you do?"

"Paddled, silly. That's what kayaking is."

"So…you left home paddling and then paddled around until it was time to paddle home?"

"Yeah, what's your point?"

"No point (which *is* my point, actually). Glad you're home. Glad it was good."

I really don't have anywhere to go in the conversation. Not with her. No common ground there. She's from Venus. I'm from Mars. She paddles. I don't.

But we don't have to understand each other to be together. *Obviously.* You'd think it would help but I think, now that I muse on it, that complete understanding would be dull. I might know what she was going to do next! As it is, I have no clue. I still don't get paddling…like…just for paddling's sake?

There may be a clue in hiking. Another activity I don't get. Maybe if I understood hiking for hiking's sake I might understand kayaking. Sal can hike and hike and hike and then come back and call it a great day. We're a mystery, we are.

"What did you do?" she says.

"Not much. Thought. Planned. Wrote. Read. Measured a few things. Ate my sandwich. Thanks, by the way. It was good."

"What did you plan and think about?"

"The new ramp. Went and measured it again. Planned it out again. Walked around. Looked at the rocks. Checked materials. Made a change or two…in my head…just getting a feel for it."

"Don't you just get a ramp, drag it up and that's that?"

"No. Pretty complicated, this is. A smidge of rocket science involved. Winches, ropes, concrete, drilling bolt-holes, that sort of thing. Needs some planning, it does."

"Didn't John just drag his up and that was it?"

"Well, yeah, but…"

"So, you want tea?"

"Yeah, tea would be good."

There is a lot of love and acceptance in that conversation. If it qualifies as a conversation at all. She paddles. I think. Then we have tea together. It's weird, but nice. And it works for us.

-14-

Where the Wild Things Are

The morning started well. Great, actually. We were out on the deck as a school of Pacific white-sided dolphins paraded north. There were close to a hundred of them and they were leaping and swooshing at a rapid rate, jumping into the air in groups. They were close in—so close you could see their eyes. It was a veritable march of dolphins.

Then, after watching them roll on up the channel we went about our morning business. Sal and I boated over to unload supplies left in our car which was parked on the adjacent island and came back to our shore for further schlepping of them up to the house. Then Sal headed off around the tip of the peninsula to tie the boat up at the dock. Just as she was out of sight I heard her on the walkie-talkie.

"Wow, David! Dolphins are just flying by! All around the boat! Holy…"

I grabbed my walkie-talkie. "Where are you?"

"I'm just around the point and *oh my gawd! Oh my gawd! Orcas! Wow...you should see this—oh my gawd! They're chasing the dolphins...no...no...wait...*"

I wait. Nothing. I wait. More nothing. "Sal? Sal? What's going on?"

"Uh…John and Jorge are coming out. There are tons of orcas…I think they've trapped a bunch of dolphins in our bay…*oh my gawd! They're hunting! You gotta see this!*" Then more silence.

Crackle…pssst…static…crackle. The walkie-talkie came to life again.

"Dave, this is Robert. I'm getting my boat! I'll pick you up as I go by!"

Robert picked me up a few minutes later and we scooted into the bay. We looked around in amazement. There were half a dozen orcas surrounding us. They were swimming back and forth at the mouth of our bay. We looked further into the bay where there were a few more orcas closer in. We looked past them to see thirty or more dolphins herded up in the shallows near the beach. They were clearly panicked.

For the next hour or so we all watched from our small boats, drifting with our motors off, as the dolphins feinted and swerved in an effort to get to open water and the whales dove under our boats and swooped in for the kill.

The trapped dolphins swerved around in retreat and headed for the shallows as the orcas swam at them in successive waves. Now and then we would see a dolphin escape by boosting itself across a shallow rock shelf on the far side of the bay. But we never saw the ones that were being caught. The actual eating of dolphins was taking place underwater out of view.

What we know for sure is that the number of dolphins corralled at the head of our bay was diminishing. We watched until the whales eventually had their fill and swam away. The surviving dolphins hung around a bit longer and then took off once they determined the coast was clear.

Eating on the run, eh? Sheesh.

That evening we were enjoying refreshments with John and Jorge. We relived the spectacle that had taken place in our bay earlier that day. The conversation moved to the pair of ravens who live nearby and how they had managed to infiltrate John's prawn bait box so he had to construct a stronger one. The ravens had also left a twenty-five cent coin on their feeding platform over at his house. John and Jorge had suspected Sal and me of planting the quarter, but no, we convinced them it wasn't our doing. We spoke of the otters who had stolen two-thirds of his cabin's insulation in trade for a lot of poop. And we spoke of the pair of eagles who had just returned to their lofty perch by our house.

But by then, of course, I was aching to tell a story and so like the fool I am (think Charlie Brown trying to kick the football that Lucy holds for him), I began. It was going to be a long one about China many years ago. I was into the middle of it in no time.

But we have a tradition in my house—stories must be broken into segments. Sally determines when. They don't have natural chapters so somehow, in some way, Sally finds a way to interrupt the story when she feels it needs a break.

"...and then, just as the Chinese police arrived and the naked girls ran off into the woods to hide, the pressure in the old steel boiler in the back room got too great to stay..."

Time! Sally would stand up and start walking around the room. "More cheese, anyone? How about some more wine, or maybe tea?"

What would Jesus do?

But this time the story was interrupted by the dogs. I immediately suspected that Sally had recently trained them to do this, but they were actually alerting us to something outside. Naturally, I attempted to continue but, like every other time, the story was halted by the diverted attention of my audience and so I gave up and we all went outside to see what was going on. Turns out the dogs were on to something.

There was the pod of six or so orcas swooshing by, right near the shore. One large male was very prominent with his huge black dorsal fin coursing along. They looked great. It was worth the interruption and, as soon as they saw that they had done their job to alert us, the dogs settled down.

And so, as usual, I wrapped up the story in a few quick sentences. No one seemed to mind the short version.

The next day Sally headed up to the post office and the community centre to socialize and pick up mail and a few dozen eggs at the same time. It was mid afternoon as she headed home in her little Miata-like speed boat, just zipping through the summer air. Good day to be out and about!

Up ahead she saw what looked like typical flotsam generated by the high tide. At first glance she expected it might be a log. It had branches sticking out of it. Probably a windfall, she thought, as she altered course to pass safely by.

But whatever it was seemed to be moving against the current. In fact, this windfall seemed to be making headway against the wind and waves. Sal slowed the boat and looked a little closer.

It was a deer. It appeared that the buck had disembarked from the neighboring island and had been traversing the channel—not very quickly—and was swimming the last few hundred feet to our island's shore when Sal hove into view. The buck seemed to pick up a bit of speed as Sal got closer. Not easy when you are swimming with hooves and skinny legs, I am sure.

Sal stopped the boat immediately so as to relieve the poor animal of any unnecessary stress and sat there watching as he continued swimming. He seemed to sense he had a bit more time after all, and moved with calm deliberation a little way down the coast to find an accessible place to land. Finding the right depth and lunging out of the water, he emerged onto the shore, looked at Sal one last time and then headed inland.

Sal started her outboard, and resumed her journey home. She arrived with a wide grin across her face and a brief but nice story to tell about passing the buck while getting the mail. As I mentioned, it can be good just getting out and about.

Wow! The chemistry in our house changed overnight. Our friend Lina had come to stay for a few days, so instead of watching a shoot 'em up last night we watched *The Time Traveler's Wife*. And then they (les femmes) picked the tearjerker *Remember Me* for tonight. I'm getting nauseous, cinematically speaking.

"Geez, couldn't you two find something that had some cars blowing up? Or maybe some guy morphing into a monster or something? How about a sci-fi thing with spaceships? You know, good movies?"

They looked at me, said nothing, and walked past me as if I wasn't there.

Oh well, today I had a *real* monster from the deep. John stopped by after his prawning efforts and tossed one of his traps ashore.

"Hey! You guys may want to have a look at this!"

In the trap was a beautiful reddish coral colored octopus about the size of a very large grapefruit with attendant tentacles. He (or she? hard to tell) was in the trap and chock full of prawns. He had feasted before John pulled him up in the trap which he had been unable to leave due to his new found girth. We opened the access door and managed to release him, gently dumping him out through this larger opening. We placed him on the steel grids that comprise our sea stairs from the water to the high tide line.

We were pretty sure he'd slip through a space and skedaddle off. That's what octopuses do. As a rule.

Not this one. He just seemed to get stuck. We think he was just way too full of prawns to get through a space that he would normally easily pass through. So now we had to coax him.

"Oh no, don't let him die!" Sally sounded a little worried.

So, we poured seawater over him as we pushed and prodded and tried to herd the octopus' many tentacles back into the sea about fifteen feet away. He was a reluctant puss.

I tried lifting and pulling him first by one tentacle then by gathering a bunch of tentacles together but the suckers on his remaining arms clung to the rocks so strongly that I thought I might tear him in half. So, the brute force technique was abandoned. We were going to try psychology instead.

"Think! Think like an octopus…what would you do?"

We put a really large bowl full of water beside him thinking that his natural instincts would pull him into the water and then I could fling him back into the ocean. He headed up hill away from the water instead.

"I thought octopi were supposed to be smart!" shrieked Sal.

Lina stood there transfixed, looking like the land locked Swiss she is. I happened to realize I was wearing my house slippers at the time. Marine biologists we were not!

An opportunity! Puss passed over some kelp. No firm ground to stick his suckers to. I swept him up and rolled him downhill towards the water as Sal poured water over him. It is hard to imagine an octopus losing his sense of dignity but, as much as it is possible, rolling down the rocks must have been mortifying for him. He looked a little redder in the face. Wherever the face is. I'm sure it was embarrassing—especially being man-handled by a man in slippers. He eventually sorted himself out and slipped into deeper water.

There are wolves around again. We don't see the wolves but we do hear them. They are up island from us right now and we can hear them faintly on windless nights or get news of them from our neighbours.

The latest news is pretty neat. One neighbour has a wildlife camera sitting in a tree near her home. Her house is on the route of the wildlife highway, the place where animals can most easily pass from one island to another. Lately she has caught a few wolves on film. But the most interesting part is that she also has two large dogs. *Very* large dogs, Mastiff-Rottweilers. Probably close to a hundred and fifty pounds each. It seems that the alpha male of the local wolf pack dwarfs them.

"He seemed twice as big as one of our dogs. He was black. And he was huge!" she said. That is a big wolf.

And they are an effective, flourishing pack. They know their business. Last summer, a couple of other neighbours were anchored in a little bay up the channel taking a lunch break from their busy day of log salvaging. While sitting in the boat, they heard a big splash behind them, not far away. They turned to see a deer swimming hard for the far shore. It had just launched itself into the bay. The reason became obvious pretty quickly. The wolf pack was right behind it.

Some members of the pack jumped in the water to continue the chase and others immediately started circling around the bay by land. They silently and quickly moved away and waited in the bush to see where the deer would decide to leave the water. As soon as the tired deer got to the beach they were on her. They then dispatched the hapless doe and enjoyed her al fresco on the spot. There you are having your tea and cookies and a deer is turned into lunch before your very eyes!

"Yikes! You better get out here. It's the wolves again! They are making the hairs on the back of my neck stand on end!"

Once I am horizontal, it usually takes the power of a billion nuclear explosions (aka the sun rising) to get me up out of bed, but Sal looked pretty excited and I could hear the howling through the walls. It seemed very close.

We stood listening while in our bathrobes standing together at midnight on the deck with the stars brightly hung overhead and a brisk southeast wind in our face. Romantic in a Transylvanian kind of way, don't you think?

Fiddich and Meg were hysterical. Running up and down the ridge, doing their best to join in with the sing-along but, without larynxes, it is hard for them to make much of a contribution. So they just struck a pose with muzzles pointed to the sky and Fid grated out a Louis Armstrong impersonation of a howl now and then. Meg, of course, just pantomimed it. So it was up to me to answer properly.

"HHHhhhhhhoooooooooooooowwwwwwwooooooooooooooooooo, HHHhhhhhhhoooooooooooooowowowwowowwooooooooooooooooooo."

Everything fell silent. The wolves shut right the hell up and Meg and Fid looked at me like I had just said something in completely bad taste. "That was all wrong!" They were embarrassed for me. Sal just muttered something about old dogs.

Another try— this time with feeling!

"HHHHHHhhhhhhoooowwwwwoooooooowoowowooowowoowoooo."

Meg and Fid were thrust back into the game. Sal looked away from me and back to the sky. And the wolves set off a blood curdling chorus once again. My first faux pas de lupine had been forgiven. I wonder what I said.

The wolves were letting it all hang out and they were just across the bay, less than a quarter mile away. There seemed to be a half dozen voices but they have the ability to make a couple sound like a choir so there is no telling just how many there were. But it seemed like a lot. It was actually a little scary.

The call of the wild at our back door. Very cool.

Sally installing the wind turbine

-15-

Energized

There is a sense of freedom that alternative energy provides that can't really be described adequately in conventional ways. It is more than being independent of a faceless, inhuman utilities company. Or government. It is more like a measurable manifestation of personal growth.

Independence, coupled with a bit of competence and a familiarity with one's personal life support systems, actually feels like an extension of one's self. As if you have grown stronger, somehow. It's odd. I am older, stupider and definitely poorer but, somehow, I feel stronger, more able and more competent simply because I put another area of my living requirements under my own control.

I can fix my own power generating system. I can add to it. I can change it. It does not send me mail or phone me. There ain't a smart meter reporting on me, either. I can care for my system as I do myself—hopefully a bit better. It is this sense of becoming more capable, and gaining these kinds of abilities and skills, that I am talking about.

There's something else as well. Having an alternative energy system feels organic. Crazy, eh? I mean, I have a steel tower for the wind turbine and wires and batteries and generators and solar panels and who knows what technology and yet it feels organic. And this is why. The energy that powers it comes from the sun and the wind. And the more solar panels I add, the more organic it feels. It just feels natural to me in a way that being on the grid never can.

We try to do all this independent, personal growth stuff in other ways too, of course. Gardening, fishing, hunting (some day, maybe), fixing things instead of buying new replacements, building, cooking from scratch and all that. Hell, we even try to eat the hundred mile diet and do it with slow food. But there is nothing quite so satisfyingly lovely to me as generating our own electricity. You might want to try it someday.

Putting together an alternative energy system is not as easy as it looks. And it looks hard because it is. And it is also expensive. And it can be very confusing. If there is one statement to operate from, it would be this: don't believe what you read. Your case will be different. And don't think that you can do just part of it. To do it right, the system has to be balanced and all the parts have to be simpatico right from the start.

Part of the reason for the difficulty is that much of it is counterintuitive. That which you think you need, you don't. That which you dismiss as not so important is really, really important and much of what you need is never mentioned by the salespeople because few of them actually live off the grid. And, even when they do, each system should really be tailored to your needs rather than what they happen to sell. I know that sounds like a bit of crap. But it isn't.

For instance, one of the things the experts tell you to do is to add up your home's consumption rates for your appliances, lights and everything that uses electricity, and then add a percentage for future demands. If you do that, you might find yourself looking at ten or more kilowatts of power and requiring a generator to provide it.

This formula might work if you use everything electrical in your house all at the same time. I don't know anyone who does that. I initially followed the advice of a knowledgeable and well-meaning friend and bought a generator that ended up being far too large for my real life requirements. Big mistake. I now have a much smaller generator and save a lot of fuel.

"But what about solar energy?" you ask. The reality is that at my latitude solar panels are great in the summer, good enough in the shoulder seasons and often inadequate in the winter. In the winter I have to use the genset to supplement them. Over time I hope to increase the number of solar panels to keep this to an absolute minimum.

"Okay, but there's wind power," you say knowledgeably. "How about adding a wind turbine to supplement the solar panels in the winter?"

A brilliant thought, especially as that's exactly what I came up with. So I bought a small wind turbine. I started the project on a day off when Sal was away. I read up on the wiring for it. Reading how to do things is an important way to use down time. Otherwise I might die. I have huge holes in my skill sets. In fact, I am missing whole sets.

There were dire warnings every page or so in the turbine installation manual. Warning! Failure to fasten tab A to slot B may cause irreparable damage to the turbine or severe personal injury! Danger! Inadequate hangers may cause tower failure! Attention! Follow instructions precisely or your warranty may be void and your bowels torn out through your throat! And on and on until it felt like I was trying to follow instructions for a homemade improvised explosive device. It's a lousy forty-eight volts!

"Yes, well, forty-eight volts across the heart and you are a dead turbine owner," warns my friend, Bill.

So, I read. I examine the parts and I get confused. So, I have some tea. And read some more. Sally would express even more confusion than me. No stupid ego to get in *her* way and so I'd lay on the manly bravado.

"Hey! How hard can it be? We'll just be careful with tab A and get on with it, my little sugarplum."

She'd look relieved and I'd have to step up and do what I said I would do. Being macho is like daring yourself by proxy.

Pretending that I know what I am doing keeps us moving forward. Macho may be stupid (and it is) but it helps lead the way. I just don't quite know where we are going. Thankfully, neither does Sally. If we went with caution we'd never have gotten to where we are today.

But I *do* read the instructions on things electrical. I have to. And I hate it. It's like reading Chinese. I'm sure hieroglyphics are easier. But electrical speak is completely unintelligible to me. First, you have to be a native Geek speaker. Secondly, you have to think this stuff is really neat. And thirdly, you have to get comfortable electrocuting yourself. I have a long way to go. I am just partly into the geek phase. I'm at a place called "dorkism".

So, I go to the electrical panel and examine it. This wire goes here…and that one goes there…and so what the *#!%$ does that mean? I get most of it. But there are gaps. Gaps that can cause a spark to jump. I may have once known how to fill those gaps but I don't know now. So I just look at it.

You know what I see? I see a jumble of wires of all different colors. Then I look at the diagram and you know what I see? I see straight black lines on white paper neatly going from one weird electrical symbol to another weird symbol. To my way of thinking, the two are not even remotely similar.

Never mind. Tomorrow I'll say, "Hey, Sal, what do you say we wire up that old turbine, eh?" She'll say, "Well, if you think so…" And the next step will be taken.

The turbine we purchased was (you'll notice the past tense here) a four hundred watt Air-X wind turbine which, according to the instruction pamphlet that came with it, was to be raised on schedule forty pipe fifty feet in the air. Yeah, right.

Turns out schedule forty doesn't work. Too flimsy. I know this because I tried it. We pulled the tower up part way when it folded in the middle, narrowly missing our dear friend and neighbour Jorge, smashing the turbine to the ground and putting a dent in my pride and wallet at the same time. I was not happy that we had such a close call. So not happy, in fact, I procrastinated for a year before buying another turbine and trying again.

This time, we used an old ham radio tower, thanks to John, who presumably didn't want to put his lovely partner at risk again when it came time to help us erect it. The tower is triangular in shape and comes in ten foot lengths. I bolted two lengths together and, after mounting them on a hinged steel plate, pulled up twenty feet of tower. I had three more sections to pull up and attach. Each section weighs about seventy pounds and is awkward as hell.

The plan was to have a rigger (Sally) standing atop the existing tower and the rigger's assistant (me) hoisting the sections up using a gin pole, an ingenious device. It is a temporary extension of the tower attached to the side of the existing structure with a pulley on the end of it. We used it to pull up and place the next section. The gin pole then moves up with each section as it is placed.

Even though I am large enough to be accused of being in two places at once, it is not true. I can only be in one place, albeit spread out generously. Sal had to be the one at the top. For one thing, my feet wouldn't fit into the footholds on the tower. *And* I was able to pull each tower section up using the block and tackle system we rigged, and she wasn't strong enough to do that. Plus I could belay her weight so that, if she fell, I could catch her with the rope. Had it been reversed and I fell, she'd simply zip up to the top of the tower as I came down.

Once I lifted a tower section to a level just above the tower that was in place, Sal wrestled it so that the connecting bolt holes lined up. Then she had to insert the bolts and tighten nuts on them. It was more than a little tricky.

"My knees are shaking," she said, somewhat weakly.

"It's good to get that fear out of the way now at twenty feet. By the time you're up at fifty feet, you'll be relaxed enough to pose on one foot like you do in yoga. Anyway, after thirty feet the fall will kill you, so from then on, it doesn't matter."

Her response was unprintable. Seems she is somewhat reluctant to explore her inner Sherpa. Her intermittent knee knocking increased until she was suggesting that the vibrations were going to loosen the bolts already in place. So during the placing of the next three sections she would come down to compose herself, and ascend when it felt right. She was up and down like a yoyo.

Sal took forever putting the bolts in place but I knew why. Her hands were shaking as much as her knees were knocking. Usually whenever Sally is doing something along construction lines that she is not happy about, I crack jokes to help her out. They are rarely funny. They are not really intended to be. They are meant to be mildly annoying so that she gets mad and yells expletives at me. I laugh and she gets to vent her frustration and it helps her to relax. It's construction site therapy. She participates well as a rule. I have heard some dandies.

Not this time. This time wasn't merely just frustrating or difficult. It was past unpleasant and awkward. This time it was scary. For both of us. I kept my jokes to a minimum—one. The response I got from it told me that this was not the time for any more stupid jokes. So I shut up. We worked in silence until it was done.

Once the sections were up, I had planned to slip a fitting over the top of the tower which the turbine would be affixed to. But I am faced with the curse of the measuring tape in the hands of an idiot. Me. I measured the lower end of the tower section—nine and one-half inches. And then John fabricated the fitting for me. It was perfect—just a tad over nine and one-half inches. Just big enough to fit snugly over the top of the tower. Or, so I thought.

Unfortunately the tower sections are tapered a smidgen so that each one fits inside the section below it. I should have known that. I hadn't measured the proper end. Obviously I should have measured the top end which is just a little bit larger. Damn.

So, I bashed for awhile (*persuaded* is the fitting term in the workman's vernacular) but it remained resolute. So I decided to fabricate an adapter piece. I ripped some steel strips and drilled out bolt holes. Then the hard part. I had to explain the modifications to Sally.

"Now you see, sweetie, this fitting didn't quite fit so..."

"Doesn't fit? Didn't you measure it? I'm not going to work with something that doesn't fit at the top of that tower!"

"Now, sweetie pie, I have an answer for this. All you have to do is..."

"Me! All I have to do! Forty-five feet in the air and I have to do what? Are you crazy?"

"I am sensing a bad attitude, here, Sal. It is just..."

"Bad attitude! You say I have a bad attitude and you expect me to climb..."

There was not a breath of wind all that day. This, in the beginning, was a good thing as Sal was up there next to knife sharp turbine blades and a sudden gust would have cut off her nose! Well, that's not really true, but that's what I told her. Helped keep her amused at the top of a forty-five foot tower while she put the last piece in place.

Putting the actual turbine on the top required Sal to stand on a small platform hooked onto the very top of the tower. With a personal safety line attached, her body above her knees is now above the top of the tower so she can affix the turbine on its mount. The cables securing the tower are below her. The only thing protruding from the top of the tower where she is standing is a metal pole on which the turbine sits and it is at belly button level. That means that she is standing in the sky with nothing in front of her but space and looking forward to heaving a turbine up onto the pole. She did it with aplomb.

I, for one, was glad to see the end of *that* chore. Standing on the ground with one's thumb in a dark and awkward place is frustrating and tiresome. I got a bit of a crick in my neck. I asked Sal for a massage.

The tower chore had been all consuming for a number of days. Crazy, really. The brochure said that, with the manufacturer's special kit (which of course we didn't have), the whole thing could be up in as little as two hours. Fact or fiction? You decide.

One thing about off the grid power is that batteries are needed to store the energy produced, be it from solar, wind or generator. The more and better batteries I have, the more juice I can store which means I don't have to run the generator so often.

Having too few batteries means not being able to store the energy for future use when it is being produced, so good storage capacity is really important. Of course, having too many batteries is not only expensive but, if the generating source is not big enough (say, too few panels, small wind turbine, puny battery charger) then the capacity is never utilized. This is not good either. The batteries don't like it. I can't emphasize enough how keeping your batteries happy is critical and how balancing the system aids in all this.

Batteries occasionally need to be replaced. Fortunately I have a friend in the battery business. He keeps an eye out for good batteries that have been used a bit but are still virtually one hundred percent. This happens in industrial applications now and then.

I needed four more batteries to add to the eight I had to get the right balance. I called my battery friend. I was in luck. He had sixteen good batteries he was holding for guys like me. So, I told the folks up here about the other twelve.

"Yeah, please. I need some. Could you put me down for a couple?"

In the end I ordered all sixteen. But these puppies are not your basic car battery. They are three times the size and each one weighs one hundred and fifty pounds. Sixteen of them weigh over a ton.

By a miracle of cooperation, kindness and professionalism all sixteen batteries got to the terminal in Vancouver where a trucker picked them up and dropped them off at the barge landing just north of Campbell River.

The barge guys loaded them aboard and went to various ports of call over the course of a few days before delivering them to our government dock.

Elapsed time: five days. Cost: a few hundred dollars. Efficiency and ease: priceless.

Once on the dock, it was every man or woman for themselves. Sal and I hauled the four we had ordered into our boat and took them to our dock. There we transferred them from our bigger boat into Sally's little boat. The next challenge was to get them up the hill to the house. The winch and highline had worked well for bringing up logs to the ridge behind the house so it was time to employ it once again to bring up the batteries.

In addition to the four batteries coming up there were eight old ones to go down to take back to town to dispose of. The plan was to float the little boat under the highline at high tide. High tide was at noon that day.

We planned to use the big swatch of fishing net I had scavenged a year or so ago to bundle the batteries up and haul them up the hill using the winch. The hard part was going to be the two of us on Sal's tiny boat balancing like ballerinas while we loaded the net with a hundred and fifty pounds of lead and acid. I was looking forward to that.

With the batteries, the outboard and Sal, her little Whaler was carrying over nine hundred pounds. At the best of times there is only about six inches of freeboard. With this load she did not have a lot of space between the water and the gunwale as she made her way carefully into the lagoon. At this point I decided I didn't want to add my weight to the load.

The lift was carried out successfully and we ferried the batteries by wheelbarrow, one at a time, from the ridge to the battery shed. The scary part for me is when I add the new batteries to the ones that have already been in service for the last year. When I do that, I am basically adding two hundred amps to four hundred amps and making a potential arc of death if I do something wrong. I hate that.

So, I checked and checked and then I checked some more. I was ready to attach the final battery cable to the inverter and marry up the whole system. When it was time to drop the cable on the battery terminal, I was pretty confident. But I checked again.

As I was finally getting close to the terminal with the potentially lethal connection in hand, Sal walked by and yelled, "*Zap*!"

It is always a funny joke. We love that one. Whenever one of us is doing electrical work and concentrating hard on *not* dying, the other waits until the moment of truth and yells “zap”! Good fun. Ha ha ha.

In a few more years she’ll be yelling “contact!” instead, as she applies the paddles to my heart.

-16-

Uplifting

The funicular that Brian and I built makes schlepping things up and down the hill much easier; in fact, it makes it possible.

But unfortunately it is still not easy enough. This past year I began Funicular Part II, the lower section. This additional funicular will begin way down in the ocean at the low tide mark and go up to the lower deck to meet the first funicular that goes from there up to the house. With the tide fully out the distance to be covered is seventy feet. This second funicular will also act as a marine ways to pull the boat out of the ocean and up to the deck on a specially designed (by me, of course) cart.

The new funicular will be operated by a handheld wireless remote controller. I am hoping to be able to drive the boat to the lower tracks, summon the cart, drive the boat onto it and, a minute or so later, step off onto the boathouse deck. You have to admire my optimism.

I have already encountered some major challenges in this project but none quite as formidable as the wiring diagram. My Siemens motor controller came with instructions for programming written in German. Enter my friend Bill, the same Bill who had come from Vancouver in the middle of the night to help unload the materials for the house. He is an extremely knowledgeable techie and he programmed it for me.

"I didn't know you spoke German, Bill."

He looked at me blankly, "I don't. All computer programs speak a similar language and that is all you really need to know."

Yeah, right. Sounds like Geek to me. But it works great.

Bill wanted me to integrate the electrical system of Funicular Part II with the electrical system of the original Funicular Part I. After four years I have barely mastered how to turn it off and on. I told Bill I was not going to be able to combine the two systems, especially as he lived a hundred miles away.

"Never mind, I have it in my head. I'll draw it up and I'll print out a diagram for you. Anyone can follow a diagram."

Yeah, right. The diagram came yesterday. It looks like the communications system for a NASA space station and the labels, names and abbreviations are as close to Cyrillic as one is likely to find outside of Russia. I don't have a hope.

Sally took one look at it.

"Please don't go anywhere near our working funicular! We *need* that thing. If we try to do this, everything will get totally screwed up! Gimme that paper!"

Normally, I would argue a bit. Put up a small macho protest like "If Bill says I can do it, I can do it". But not this time. I wouldn't have fooled anyone. It took me several moments just to figure out which side of the diagram was up. By then, Sally had snatched it away. Some projects go even more slowly than others.

Okay, so I won't be combining the two systems. At least that's clear. All I have to do now is wire in small twenty-four gauge wires from the receiver into the Siemens motor controller, the inverter and the transformer. All this so that the hand held remote control will run the winch that the new motor powers.

The circuitry for this is quite simple, really. A bunch of wires in, a bunch of wires out and relays and switches thrown about willy-nilly to make sure it all happens in sequence. I understand that it is a piece of cake. For someone. Not me.

The fellow who sold the motor to me explained it all in the few short minutes it took to put the motor in the back of the car. Of course it sounded like Swahili but he seemed to know what he was talking about.

"So, do you know what you just said?" I asked.

"Um, yeah, I do."

"Good. Give me your phone number and email. I'll send questions with diagrams. Please say everything again when I do that, but say it in writing, and not in a foreign language!"

"I was speaking English!"

And that is the way it is out here. You conceive of something basically simple, in concept anyway, such as a marine ways. There have been marine ways since there have been boats. Shouldn't be too hard to build, right? Of course, we modern guys don't have minions to heave and pull the lines so we have to make do with minicomputers, electric motors and remote control devices. I think minions are better. Easier, for sure.

And machinery isn't easy to install. The remote control devices—industrial quality, don't you know—didn't come with instructions. There are thirteen wires coming out of the receiver. Dangling. *No instructions*. So, where do they go? I contacted the supplier.

"Yeah, geez, isn't that a crazy thing? They don't have instructions. I've been through this before. You can call Kang in Langley. It's his company that makes them. Problem is he doesn't speak English too well and just gets mad when we ask him questions."

"I'll call him. I really need to know where these wires go."

"Good luck! The mill guys just bought seventeen of them. They already had a dozen or so. So they *do* work and the guys like them, but I have no idea how to wire them in."

"I'll try Kang. If that fails, will the mill guys show me?"

"I'll ask them."

So I get through to Mr. Kang.

"Mr. Kang? I bought a pair of your 760XLs. They seem great. But I am not an electrician. Do you have a wiring diagram?"

"Oooh…sebun sisty essers. You must buy from surprier. No direct sales! Rank you."

"No…no…hold on! I already *have* them. I am just confused over the wiring. Can you help?"

"So sorry. No direct sales. You call surprier. I have phone number."

Mr. Kang was already getting agitated. I could hear his thoughts. What is wrong with these people? I don't speak English. They should talk to the guy I sell through. That is why I have a supplier. If I could speak English I could sell direct!

So, due to my gift of clairvoyance, I sympathized with Kang and was, in any event, not getting anywhere and just making him angry. I could determine the wiring diagram of a Korean's cerebral cortex in Langley easier than I could the product he sold and so I bid him adieu. In French, of course. Why not? He was already ticked.

"Au revoir, Mr. Kang. Bon chance en Canada, eh? Ecrivez instrucciones (instrucciones is Spanish but it was all I had at the time) s'il vous plait. Bon pour economics, sais vous?"

"No direct sales!" he said in salutation.

I think we understood each other. We parted amicably.

Sadly, it is little obstacles like this one that hold up my progress. If I was just better educated, skilled, equipped and multilingual, I could get on with things. Physical energy would also help but we have to be realistic. This chore is going to require teaching myself to weld, figuring out the wiring of a remote control device and its attendant attachments and applying all this to galvanized rails that have to be installed on a barnacle and seaweed covered irregular rocky beach when the tide is out. You will understand if it takes a while. I've been snacking on high energy chia seeds to help with the energy part. And I've taken out a few books on welding for Sally. We'll see how that goes.

Enter my son Ben and his partner Katie. With both of them chock full of turkey from our Thanksgiving dinner the day before and a big Sally breakfast this morning, we set out in the rain and began to position the rails. They are angle steel, hot-dipped galvanized and measure five inches by five inches. The steel is about three-eighths of an inch thick. They are cut from dismantled transmission line towers. They are very heavy, unwieldy and we are working on a steep, rocky, irregular slope. Not easy.

The first step is to get the steel rails to the lower deck. The four of us wrestle and drag them over from where they have been laying in wait for this special day. Once there we drill holes in them to accept the fasteners. We use our friend Bob Buxton's great invention, the Badger. It's a mini drill press that fastens a drill to a piece of steel and provides the force needed for the drill bit to get through it—brilliant! Maneuvering the beams to a conventional drill press would have been impossible.

We then slid the beams off the deck and placed them onto the horizontal supports that Sally and I had previously cemented into place. After that we fastened on the rails. It was a bit of a challenge but Ben and

Katie were equal to the task. I lagged a smidge behind but was useful as a humorist, supervisor, life coach on various topics which were, surprisingly, not of much interest to them at the time, and, of course, I was the one who had the basic overall vision for the project. Don't underestimate us visionaries. It all worked out. I think we were all pleasantly surprised.

Katie is beautiful, funny and intelligent and both Sally and I are hugely fond of her. But she is also as strong as a bull. I like this trait in a woman a lot more than I ever thought I would. Katie has a really "great set o' pipes for a chick" as they say around here. She and Ben provided the bulk of the brute power and the job went easily as a result.

I thought I'd provide a nice reward for Katie and Ben in the afternoon by way of a little more life coaching but, oddly, they both chose to go out with Sally in the rain to visit our neighbours instead. Katie mentioned something about drinking heavily. I guess that means we will be having a little talk later about that, too. I do enjoy evenings with the "kids".

I always love it when Ben and Katie come to visit but this time was special. I had really needed their help to get me moving on the lower funicular project. Ben and I got on it again first thing the next morning.

"We're going to need all that stuff down on the beach. There are two saw horses and a sheet of plywood under the boatshed you can use to make a temporary table. I'll get the rest of the tools."

If there was a response, it was a grunt as he turned to get that first chore done. There were no questions as to "Why are we doing this? What's the plan? What thickness of plywood? Do I really need that tool? Shouldn't we get some whatchamacallits? Have you read the instructions?" And other such things my usual helper would ask, while throwing a stick for the dogs and wondering aloud if she should get a hat and the occasional comment of, "Hey, look! Was that a jay?"

Working with men is so much easier. Yes, I know that is sexist. But it is true. Well, it is true for men working with men, anyway. Working with women *may* be so much easier if the person expressing such an opinion is of the female persuasion. Who knows? It is a completely different work culture. I think both genders have weird gender-based languages and habits peculiar to themselves. Sally's are *definitely* peculiar.

For one thing men don't talk as much, but when they do it is pertinent to the job at hand. "Seen the hammer?" Women seem to talk the whole time they are working together and when they do, it has nothing whatsoever to do with the job at hand. "Did you hear? Sarah had that mole removed."

C'mon, you know it's true!

Anyway, Ben and I got to work and, of course, we worked on the lowest portion of the track system while the tide was out and that section was out of the water. And we did well. We had been at it for a bit when Sal called and offered tea and turkey sandwiches. My son is a good worker but there is little that will get between him and a turkey sandwich. The tools were still rattling on the ground as he raced up the steps to claim his prize. So we took a break.

He's also good at taking breaks. I don't blame him. He doesn't have to work with the tide every day and he is not aware of the speed at which it can claim your work area. *And* any tools left too low on the beach. I put off the decision to head back to work until I thought we had no choice and, leaving him with half a turkey sandwich still to devour, I went back at it. He followed and we barely got the final bolts on before the water washed over the lower section. In fact, we got the last two bolts on under water. Cut it pretty close but we got it done.

I hadn't worked with him in a few years but we didn't miss a beat. Complete harmony. The conversation would consist of, "Got a bolt?" and I would hand him one. Five minutes later…"Which hole's next?" And I'd point. A few minutes later…"Got another bolt?"

It was a gift.

-17-

Summer Whine

I'm not really antisocial. I like people just fine, especially from a distance. It's just that we'd had *enough already* with people in our personal space. It had been a busy summer.

But I knew I had to get a better attitude. Twenty or so neighbours were going to be dropping by for burgers and beer. Lots of smiling, chitchat and socializing in store. Woo hoo!

Local folks. Good eggs. This group was involved in our latest community project. Builders, mostly, and partners of builders. Of course, the timing couldn't possibly have been worse. I was just cobbling together a log run and tinkering and adjusting as I went. I could hear the guys already.

"Oh! I see you're building a log run. Something like old Jimmy's, except he used old growth twelve by twelve cedar timbers with one inch galvanized bolts on cement columns. Ya think those scrap boards of yours will last?"

Should be good.

I was not one hundred percent sure all twenty would show up. They've all had a busy summer, too. Our island is like a leper colony from October until March and then we are remembered by the multitudes. People start calling in April for a possible visit in August.

"Hey, Dave, long time no see. We gotta get together, man! Hey! My relatives from Scotland are coming again this summer. Grandma and all the cousins. It would be such fun to show them your cabin. Can you fit us in sometime in August?"

"Who is this?"

"Dave, it's me! Charlie! Howzit goin'?"

Truth is—it's mostly left in Sal's court. Oh, I occasionally suggest a visit or issue an invitation but she has the calendar and the pen. It's better that I just refer such matters to her and then go along with them—whatever they are. Grumbling the whole time, of course.

Weekend guests left yesterday. It was a good visit. Really good. Guests arrive today. In-laws. They're great, too. Other friends called. They wanted in, too. Had to turn them down. "Sorry, no room at the inn. 'Tis the season."

It's funny, really. All our guests are good. Some "gooder" than others but they are all fun. But there definitely is a way to be a guest. And it is different from what you'd think. In fact, it is different from what I would have thought prior to being a remote host.

Visiting off the grid means a shift in thinking including, but not limited to, packing lightly and properly, bringing any special personal requirements and, well…the list could go on forever.

Proper off grid visiting requires an awareness of what living off the grid means and who really has that if they haven't experienced it? It's like going to a different culture of sorts, and guests regularly, like any foreigner visiting a different land, put their foot in it. Let me give you an example.

We know that when guests come they have to catch ferries and make connections and so we anticipate that and make scheduling commitments to accommodate them. We usually have a list of things to do to get ready in advance of their visit, from a day spent shopping in town to laundry and cleaning and baking and arranging for activities. This is not unusual for hosts but, out here, we do have logistical challenges. Of course we can't always anticipate correctly, but we really want to. Guests simply don't know that there is so much preparation, planning and organizing.

One beloved family member made two promises to visit and each time decided at the last minute *not* to. Which is fine. Life happens. But a bit irritating after having made two unnecessary shopping trips to town. She didn't know. Still doesn't. Probably never will.

Another comes out and says casually just before Sal is about to serve a giant paella made from food gathered from the wild, "Oh, seafood? I never eat seafood. Or white bread. Got anything gluten-free?"

Usually it is a much smaller, trifling matter. If a guest is arriving on the twelve thirty ferry then it is to be expected that they will arrive at the pickup point about an hour or so later. And so it is arranged. I leave by boat a half hour in advance of their arrival at the dock on the adjacent island. I am now incommunicado. But, should they decide to stop for lunch or sightsee along the way, there is no way to let me know and so I sit at the dock, waiting. Not knowing, just worrying. There is no phone service there. If they are really considerate and call Sal at home she can usually get me on the walkie-talkie or VHF and pass on a message. But something as simple as stopping for lunch can be inconsiderate. Who knew?

And so it goes. Some guests leave the lights on. Some try and download movies on our limited satellite service. None of those things work here like they do in the city. Out here the repercussions of simply not knowing can be annoying, at the very least. Download a long video and the satellite service may shut down for a twenty-four hour period. That sort of thing.

Some guests "get it" right from the start and behave better than I do. Well, in a social context, they all behave better than I do. But I am talking about off the grid behaviours here. Some are really great—they even take their garbage home with them! This is truly the mark of the outstanding off the grid guest. Even an offer to do so gets major points.

The truth is there are no easy answers to this. Some of the people most loved are complete doofuses once they leave the norms of the city. They ignore the "wear sensible shoes" advice and appear in flip flops to navigate uneven, rocky, slippery, terrain. But they are still friends, they are still worth it and their visit is still to be cherished.

Part of the fun of guests is you get to complain to your neighbours about what you have been through and they like to up the ante with *their* horror stories.

After giving a mini-seminar on producing electricity off the grid, in an attempt to educate a visiting school group from Hong Kong, we emphasized that any appliance with a heating element sucks the power out of an off-grid system in no time. Following the talk Sally was appalled to hear the whine of a hair dryer in our loft—the culprit was the teacher!

Randal easily topped that. He was convinced he had a significant problem at his guesthouse. Despite his best efforts and plenty of sun on the solar panels there was just no power available and he was going crazy trying to figure out what the problem was. It all made sense when he eventually discovered the curling iron in a guest room that had been left on 24/7.

Of course some guests are always a treat. That was the case when friends Trevor and Judy arrived. We've known them for almost forty years. It was great to see them. They had a hard slog covering the one hundred and thirty miles from Vancouver to our island by sailboat—against the wind. But, as any yachtie knows, the wind is against you, or "on your nose" about ninety percent of the time. Doesn't matter which way you are going either. It's like a maritime version of Murphy's Law. It's why power boats were invented.

Trev is quite a guy. Like many of my friends he wants to help me do something, get a little dirty and get a chore done. Aargh, aargh, aargh! I love these guys. I am not one of them, but I love them. I much prefer to write about them, supervise them, or fetch them beers. This getting dirty and sweaty got old for me a long time ago. Back when I was sixteen, actually. I haven't been keen on that kind of fun since then. I don't mind the beer part. But, after that, some of us guys have different interests.

Of course, living out here means I have no choice, really. I have to do that stuff. Well, at least the stuff I can't palm off on Sal. So I have my share of scars and I have to clean the dirt from under my nails all the time. I get sweaty. I am a cream puff but the chores still have to get done. It helps when friends come all keen and all.

"So, what can we do? We love to get things done. What chores would you be doing if we weren't here—let's get at 'em!"

I am thinking that I really should exploit this lunacy while I have the chance, but it is hard to take advantage of people you love. I hesitate for a few seconds.

"Well, there's that old snag that's threatening to fall on my highline and I'd like to get it down. But it's dangerous. All twisted and hollow. This is the tree of death and I am not keen."

"Wahoo! Let's get on 'er!"

It is nice to have that support. So, I get out the ropes to lash this puppy to another tree so that it doesn't kill me as it falls.

"Nah", says Trev, "Just a cut here and one there and we'll jump out of the way. No problem."

Sheesh. I forgot about the macho part. Working alone, I can be frightened on my own time but working with "quite-a-guy" means getting at 'er and doing so *now*!

So we forgo the safety lashings and I am cutting into the widow maker with Trev off to one side encouraging me.

"Looking good. It's gonna work, for sure."

At this point I am stretched over a small gully, using my chainsaw on the pillar of treachery with one hand, holding myself from falling with the other, and thinking, just how did I get myself into this?

"You're doing great. Just be a bit careful now…"

"Fine time to get all safety conscious on me now, Trev!"

"Let's tie a rope on it and give 'er. We should be able to pull it now!"

So, I stop and we lasso it. And pull. The tree breaks off and topples…kinda. It's now hung up on some other trees. I am about to deal with that when Sal shrieks and beckons forcefully.

"Look!" she says with her hands clutched together up by her collar bone in a similar pose to the one struck by Judy standing beside her. They are both staring down. I rush over to look and on the deck there is a mouse in the final throes of death by poisoning. They are transfixed.

"Cute little guy," says Judy.

"Do something!" says Sally.

I pick up the splitting maul which is leaning nearby and drive it deeply…into the earth just off the deck making a spontaneous mouse grave. With a flick of the wrist the mouse is in the hole. The girls shriek. I split the mouse in two with the maul to save it from being buried alive and from any more suffering. Then I leave them. They are shocked.

It is a brutal world. Karma is king. And I am about to wrestle the hung tree from the skies and see how this karma thing is working for me today. I wished the mouse had waited until later.

We push and pull and the tree comes down perfectly. Trev is ecstatic. So am I. But I am now wondering about the "quite a guy" credentials. I got a lot of support. Verbally. I won't be so easily charmed next time. So, we head off to the next chore—steel cutting. Lots of sparks. Lots of hot metal bits flying around. To cut through this thick steel plate, you have to be "quite a guy". I hand the mini grinder to Trev and leave.

Half an hour later, he is done. Happy.

"What else you got?"

He really is quite a guy!

Most guests are good company at first. The good ones can carry that magic over until the next day and the really good ones leave long before the question comes up. Being a good guest is challenging work and a life skill rarely taught and even more rarely learned. I should know—I never get invited anywhere. My wife says my reputation precedes me and all our potential hosts have warned each other. But I think they've just lost our phone number. Regardless of the reason, I blame myself. I didn't know the rules.

So, despite a lack of recent (or any) experience, I have compiled a list of rarely published ideal guest behaviours culled from the stories of those neighbours civilized enough to have friends who visit. If you follow this advice to the letter, you'll be guaranteed seasonal invitations for years to come.

1. This tip is foolproof. Never accept an invitation, but send a good bottle of wine by way of an apology. Trust me, the invitations will continue as long as the wine shows up and you don't.

2. If you do accept an invitation do not try to change the dates offered. It's either all systems go, or not at all. The logistics involved in getting guests to cabins can rival space shuttle

launchings and, what seems like a minor adjustment to you, may involve water taxis, shuffling furniture, rescheduling of others and numerous phone calls and unnecessary worrying. Go, stay, or die, but do not change the schedule.

3. Do not ask your hosts about wild animals. They don't know. The definition of "wild" is that no one knows where the animals are or what they are going to do. Take comfort in the fact that most people are singularly unappetizing except to grizzlies and, to a bear, they prefer German tourists delivered by tour bus.

4. Understand that all outhouses are unpleasant and that is why wild animals whimsically choose different spots over thousands of acres on which to relieve themselves. It is man's folly that we choose to make one place loathsome and then complain about it. Use the privy, wander off into the bushes or shut your system down. There is no other choice.

5. Further on *that* topic, if you have inhibited bowels, no one needs to know. Ever.

6. You can never bring too much wine. You can, however, consume too much wine. Know the difference.

7. Take long walks and stay healthy. Hosts like a break but broken guests are annoying.

8. If you enjoy an expressive and uninhibited sex life leave it at home. There is no room in nature for such activities. It disturbs the wildlife and attracts bugs.

9. If you snore, insist on sleeping outside and downwind.

10. Guests should not bring guests. It upsets the natural order of things.

Rachel, Roger and the Author modeling their island hats

Sally dressed for winter boating

-18-

Neighbours in the Hood

We have some very interesting neighbours, Jack and Liz. We're quite close to this couple in some ways, but it's been a pretty one-sided relationship as they're more like freeloader acquaintances. They come over to our house for dinner all the time but never get it together to invite us back. When I think about it, it's obvious that they are keeping us at arm's length.

They will come and engage with us for the purpose of getting food, or possibly for their entertainment. However, their real lives, their family lives, their intimate lives, are kept very private. They never discuss anything personal with us and we don't even know precisely where their home is. Jack and Liz are ravens.

Ravens mate for life and, from what little we know about our neighbours, I can report that they do seem to be monogamous. Of course, I don't cover the distances they do and it is unlikely I would know the signs if one of them *was* stepping out. But Jack spends a lot of time mooching around here and Liz just doesn't seem the type. She's a bit nervous, a little fearful and quite a homebody.

I know what you're thinking. You can't tell them apart. They all look the same! But here's the weird part—they don't. Jack's billing and cooing partner, Liz, is slimmer and, if it is possible, blacker. Certainly her mood is darker and more aloof. She deigns to shriek her displeasure when we have incurred it and is always complaining or harassing Jack about something but, generally, she keeps her distance unless he is with her.

Jack is larger and sports an elegant ruff about his throat. He struts up and down the deck like a model on a runway. He is a smidgen on the macho side and way cool. He does seem to keep others out of the picture. He has carved out his domain and he does not tolerate incursions. Not even by the eagles. Not by a flock of crows. Not by anyone. Nobody messes with Jack.

Jack and Liz have been together for as long as we have been here and most likely longer. That's pushing ten years. That has to tell you something about their relationship, eh? And I have not even mentioned the children! This couple may be very private but they evidently *do* get it on, at least around February or March.

By late spring we have little Lizs and Jacks all over. Every year. And, just for the record: all the babies look like Jack and/or Liz. The newbie fledglings always take after their mother verbally. You can hear their cries for miles and, should you miss them, they'll repeat the refrain constantly during the day while sitting as close to us as they dare in a nearby tree.

So, one can conclude something from the arrival of progeny. Well, at least that no other species was involved. Yes, I think Jack and Liz are pretty straight ravens.

Seals, on the other hand? Don't get me started! I have never seen a greater percentage of deadbeat dads than those in the seal population. Every pup is with its mother. Even on the weekends! Every mother is a single mother. Not only that, they seem to be itinerant. They never have a nice place where they can settle down. In effect, seals couch surf. Family values wise, they are just not that impressive.

River otters have a whole other thing going on. They have major scatological issues. It must be psychological. Poop seems to play a large role in their lives as they scatter it willy-nilly along the shore on rocks, docks, decks, boats, prawn traps, life jackets…but I digress.

I made a small square wood platform for the ravens at the corner of our deck railing on which we place food. I call them when it's time for them to dine. Yes, I talk Ravenish or, perhaps, Ravenese. I'm not sure which it is. And I am not fluent. I only know, "Come and get it!" I yell my last name a few times—"Cawx, cawx, cawx"—and it works. They almost always come and, when they do, they always get something. Pre-dinner offcuts, post dinner leftovers and, of course, the odd treat keep them checking in. They are good, albeit somewhat quick, dinner guests and we enjoy their company a great deal.

However, despite being perfectly dressed for an evening out, they are not very nocturnal. In fact, they seem to shut down for the day around dinnertime and, despite my best raven calls, will not show up again until early the next morning.

Typically, when they come by, Jack sits on the platform and Liz sits in a nearby tree. We dole out a lump or two of something for Jack and after he scoops it up and flies off we put a bit more out for Liz who comes in to see what's left.

They like cheese. They prefer meat. They don't seem to like prawns and we never feed them bread or anything they couldn't theoretically get in the wild. More than once they have had salmon, steak and even whole raw eggs in the shell. They don't break the eggs; they just pick them up and fly away with them held gently in their beaks.

They are grateful for our handouts, especially when they have chicks in the nest. And we know this because, every now and then, even though we're not getting any dinner invitations, Jack leaves us a present of something wretched.

One time it was a couple of clean white vertebrae from some poor mammal no longer needing them. Last year we received a regurgitated parcel of semi digested organic matter, not unlike a cat's hairball or an owl's dinner rejects. We were moved both times. It's the thought that counts. Sally likes the bones (I have no idea why) but we were somewhat perplexed by the avian cud. I couldn't help but think of that old expression that "something was stuck in his craw" and that, perhaps, this was his way of saying that it was me. I chose to turn the other cheek and, as with so many other surprise gifts, discreetly disposed of it.

And I am glad that I assumed the best. Today, the raven declared his love, if not for both of us, then certainly for my wife. She tends to serve food up more regularly than do I. On the raven's platform, there suddenly appeared a sprig of elderberry. It was a beautiful spray, complete with a couple of dozen delicious looking red berries. The only thing missing was a small white cardboard box and a card. Clearly we have a friend and neighbour, if not a trans-species suitor. We really don't know which, but we wouldn't judge either way.

So now I do believe Jack likes us. Mind you, I am already smitten with him. He can call my name. But, to be fair, with the last name of Cox one could argue that the raven may like a local Smith, Dempsey or Matheson better, but has a limited verbal command of the local address book. I may win the popular vote simply because I am pronounceable by beak.

These interspecies relationships can sometimes be a little tricky, though. We so easily anthropomorphize the actions of animals and, I am sure, we are one hundred percent wrong virtually one hundred percent of the time. But how else to explain a dollop of processed mouse or a gift of berries? It's affection. It has to be.

Who can blame them? We look really cute, especially when we twitch our little faces. We have such funny little habits. We scurry around and look so busy all the time. C'mon, what's not to like?

Given how well things were going, I tried getting up close and personal by feeding the ravens from my hand. Direct. I stretched myself out, splayed over the deck railing as if I had been stepped on by a giant and reached out as far as I could. Jack eventually snatched the rather elongated piece of cheese I held out. This tactic went on for a few days and then Liz got in on the act. Then, so did Sal. Finally, Sally could feed Jack while standing normally. This may not be ecologically correct or whatever. Naturalist club members may be collectively grinding their teeth but, for us, it was special.

Jack rarely speaks. On occasion, if the eagle is in his favorite tree, he'll rebuke him a few times. But the eagle is either deaf or doesn't care. The disagreement always ends the same way. Jack sits sullenly in another tree close by until his point seems to be made and then he flies away darkly.

The Ravens have trained us well. Normally we feed them as we see fit. On our own time. At our discretion. Not so at hatching time. When the new family members arrive Liz and Jack fly over and just bloody squawk until they are given something for the babies. Then, when the chicks fledge, they bring them over to our house to show the young 'uns how it is done. The instructions delivered to the young are unbelievably ear shattering. Some teenaged doofus sits in a tree and his mom and dad sit nearby just hollering and squawking as loud as they can until the youngster does as he is told.

"Just stand on that little platform and yell at them. Do it loud now! Louder! That's it. They'll come. Pretty slow sometimes, but just keep it up. You'll see. After them, we hit up the neighbours. Come on now!"

You can call that anthropomorphizing if you like, but the sounds, the delivery and the resultant actions pretty much prove it is raven parenting.

One morning Fletch, one of the fledglings, came by. Sitting at my computer desk I could see him land on the deck railing near the window. He pecked at the glass a bit. Then he pecked the window frame. Then he looked up and down and all around, practically turning himself upside down on his feet. Finally, he pressed his head with one beady, black eye tight against the glass and peered in. And there I was—peering out at him. We were inches apart.

I tried to move slowly in an attempt to get the camera. I was thinking I just might be able to get a close up through the window. But, no luck. Every time I moved, he flew off. So I just went back to work.

Twice he came back, though. Each time that he peered in he was quite obviously studying me. I was fascinated by his behaviour. He was in learning mode and what better thing to study than the big guy who feeds him now and then?

Of course, when a raven is curious, things can get messed up around here. The young 'un flipped up the front door mat, pecked a few holes in the deck furniture cushions and generally invaded, investigated and violated all he could find worth engaging with.

He is one of four offspring. Usually ravens have only two, although if they are doing well in their world, they might have three. Our spoiled rotten buddies had four this year!

One of them is a bit of a runt, though. His feathers are coming in a bit late, he is a bit smaller and he just looks a bit goofy—a geek in a ravenesque kind of way, if you will. But hopefully he'll be fine.

Jack still puts food directly into this youngster's mouth sometimes, but he is flying pretty well, although a severe bank is not yet part of his aviation skills repertoire. When he attempts a quick turn, he falls from his loftier elevation and has to catch himself half way down to the ground. It is hard to watch—especially the first few times. But he is still in the air and seems to be getting the hang of it.

The other three are good to go and I suspect that they will be shown the door as soon as the little geek is ready. The parents are quite egalitarian about that sort of thing. The rule seems to be that when the fledglings go, they go together. So, right now we have six ravens and soon there will be two. Sometime in the near future the elder raven will deliver the hard news.

"Okay, now about that little platform—that square is mine, not yours. You have to get your own little square. So, get off the square. Now! And stay off all the little squares in this immediate neighborhood. I am not telling you twice!"

And that will be the beginning of the end for this year's family. By late June, it is back to Liz and Jack only. The kids have flown the nest.

With the kids out of the way, Jack swooped in and settled on the deck railing beside Sal who was sitting in a chair. He strutted his way closer and gave her a "look at me" stare. Sal stopped drinking her tea and watched. Jack sucked his craw down and splayed his neck feathers out. He scrunched down—presumably for effect. At the same time, he made a huffing and puffing sound, like wheezing in and out. Did that for a few seconds. He finished with a loud sigh.

After that little display, he resumed his proper raven posture and gave Sal "the look" again. Sal stared back stunned. Jack looked at her and repeated the display and performance. Sal remained stunned.

Jack did it again. After awhile Jack concluded that Sal just didn't get it. He gave her a disdainful look, shook his head in seeming frustration and flew off. She could almost hear him say, "What a ditz!"

Sal was beside herself.

"David! Jack was talking to me! Honest! He was trying to say something. I think it was kinda intimate stuff, maybe. Who knows? It was sort of whispery and he was all fluffed up and made these weird sighs and wheezes. Jack was talking to me!"

"I dunno, Sal, hard to tell with Jack. He *is* a raven. They have a sense of humour. I think he was just messing with your head. Probably went back to Liz and they're just cackling over how he got you going. I think he knows a patsy when he sees one."

"Really?"

"No, sweetie, I have no idea. But *I* know a patsy when *I* see one!"

So we have no idea what Jack is up to but I have to hand it to him. He comes up with something new all the time. Boring, he is not. Liz? Well, Liz has her issues. A little harder to get to know our Liz.

But seriously (*yes*), when a wild animal acknowledges your presence in an unmistakable way, it's profoundly humbling. But when one of earth's more intelligent creatures makes a gesture that seemingly accepts you as a neighbour at least and, perhaps, even as a friend, it is absolutely magical.

Jack watching *us*

Goats on the go

-19-

Natural Forces

Living the remote life can be somewhat limiting in winter, even if we pretend otherwise. And some of us living out in the wilderness do tend to kid ourselves. We have to. Sometimes there is nowhere else to go.

The Pollyanna-esque attitude adopted by some requires the winter restricted forest denizen to happily roll suet and seeds into foodstuffs for birds as some kind of salve to the dreary, short day blahs. Staving off depression by feeding the birds doesn't work for me. Shooting them might. I tend to get a bit grumpy, it seems.

These overly merry folk also joyfully stoke the woodstove with armloads of cheerily chopped wood and whistle a happy tune while doing it. Or so myth has it. I can't do that either. But some can. I do like watching Sally fetch wood. However, sometimes even she, a Tinker Bell wannabe, gets down in the winter dumps.

I usually like a *little* winter. I like the cold, the snow and the hot toddies. I like a roaring fire in a hot woodstove. I even like the vision of myself as the intrepid coastal guy out in a storm in a small boat or carrying armloads of wood in my burly, plaid covered arms. But it's the vision I like, not the reality. The reality sucks. The key word for me is "little". I like a *little* winter.

The end of October represents the onset of winter for us. Didn't use to. When I was living in the city winter always happened without me noticing. One day I was driving in the rain and the next, I was driving in the snow. "Wow, winter!" I exaggerate a bit, of course, but I was definitely not in tune with the seasons back then. There is such a thing as an urban cocoon of sorts. Cars, underground parking, heated garages, malls and large urban buildings isolate you from the elements and, as necessary and civilized as that is, it is also a subtle form of denial.

Out here, it seems, you can tell the very day the season shifts from fall to winter. There is suddenly a nip in the air. One day we are in shirt sleeves and the next we are setting the fire. It is easier to stay in touch with the health and well being of our planet when you are in direct contact with it. Of course I am trying my best to stay insulated, if not isolated, myself. We will soon start to diminish the wood pile at a prodigious rate.

Yesterday I began to fill the indoor wood bin from the outdoor shed. We usually stack a week's burning inside to have it handy. It is a tiny chore but marked because it signifies the seasonal shift. Officially, it is now the "cold" season.

Sal went through our clothes and put away the summer stuff and pulled out the long sleeved stuff. Again a minor chore, but symbolic. And so the next week or two will go. Things put away. Other's pulled out. We now seem to mark the seasons quite consciously and even, to a significant extent, live by them.

The dogs, as always, alerted us to someone pulling up to our beach. This time it was Rieko and Brenda waving from their kayaks. We grabbed our jackets and went down to the shore to pass some time.

"We just dropped by to say goodbye. We're heading off to Mexico tomorrow!"

They will join a portion of our neighbours who will be spending time in Mexico drinking too many Margaritas and suffering Montezuma's revenge along with sunburns. They are the sane ones.

Socializing is making a shift for those of us left behind. Dinner parties are now mostly out of the question. No one wants to return home by boat through treacherous waters in the dark. It can be dangerous, especially if the weather is bad. So we will have guests for lunch instead. We'll adjust for the weather, accommodate the diminished daylight and still have a good chin wag now and then.

We will use this time to begin hunkering, however that shows up. It usually means making sure the woodshed is full, planning some indoor hobbies and trying to finish a few outdoor projects before the weather deteriorates. It is a time marked by making sure the door is kept shut and the larder is full and the fuel tanks topped up. Hunkering down for the winter is not what it used to be in the old days, but it is still a phenomenon out here. We still tend to hibernate a bit.

Where it has been bright and vibrant with fall's colors a few short days ago it is now foggy grey in the morning with a washed out respite of weak sunshine in the afternoon that soon darkens with fog towards the end of the day. It *feels* like the End of Days.

The wind's howling. The seas are up. Bits and pieces of trees are whizzing by. Winter is here. Neighbours aren't, though. The last of our close neighbours have left. Miles and miles without a soul around but us. Even boat traffic has dropped way, way off. Fantastic!

This kind of isolation grows old if it extends for too long but, for us, it is usually brief. There are still some year round neighbours who are just a bit further away. They'll come. We'll go to them. Eventually. There will be companionship. But there is always a feeling of separation around this time as the summer people and the snowbirds leave.

Occasionally a winter crisis is created as a result of the inclement weather. It *can* get a bit challenging. Once, when the logging road on the adjacent island was covered with snow and fallen trees, we called the road crew to find out when they were bringing in a snow plough so that we could follow it out to get food. It took a while before they made it and by the time we got out we had racked up $138 in overdue DVD fines at the Petro-Canada gas station/video store. Mercifully we were forgiven due to the circumstances.

Another time we arrived at our car, parked on the adjacent island, to find it battered by a tree blown over by high winds. A neighbor's car was impaled through the hood by a ten foot section of tree trunk and another had its roof crushed by the same tree. Thankfully our vehicle was drivable, albeit missing a passenger side window and having incurred enough damage to eventually be written off.

I have eschewed the locally recommended remedies for the winter blues because, well, just considering those remedies depressed me further. Lots of people gather at the community centre and sing on Mondays, do yoga on Wednesdays and swap lunch dates in between. I can't sing, look ridiculous in lululemon and sometimes wonder at the wisdom of small boat travel in a winter gale for lunch. So I decline as a rule. Mind you, I don't get invited much either so there is no real conflict there.

The resident locals do remain pretty busy, though. Building still goes on, albeit slowly. What little commerce there is continues at a reduced rate. The kids attend school and the parents and the rest of the community attend to the kids. And local events from guest speakers to protests, from weddings to funerals, from work parties to traveling minstrels and from community meetings to all hands on deck emergencies keep the juices flowing.

So don't get me wrong. I love *some* of the winter. It is beautiful in a harsh, deprived kind of way. Like a kid, I still marvel at the first snowfall. But, unlike kids, I dislike it intensely by the second day. I enjoy reading until I am bleary eyed and I especially value that most rare of people, the winter guest. Mind you their appeal lies in their rarity. Wouldn't want too many of the blighters, now, would we?

There was a hole in the huge stone breakwater at the Campbell River ferry terminal large enough to drive a car through. Seems the rough seas made it during a big storm. We get several big weather systems going through in the winter. The prevailing winds are from the southeast and bring rain, slightly warmer temperatures and are of little threat to us, although the seas can get pretty bad in some places.

The second direction we get wind from is the west and it can blow pretty hard and the temperature usually drops some. But, because of the configuration of the islands and our place in them, we usually remain mostly unscathed. I like the westerlies.

It's the Bute wind that kicks butt. Coming from the northeast, it roars over the glaciers and out of the fiord-like coastal inlets. It is a bitterly cold, hard wind that brings freezing temperatures in winter and can occasionally reach hurricane force. It packs a real punch and more than one family has had to move out of their home for a few days or, more often, not been able to get out, due to the almost instant freeze up and high seas. Turn on a garden hose and pump out a strong, steady stream and it will freeze in mid flow when a Bute hits. Go out in a small boat and the salt spray will freeze as it hits you.

It's pretty nice inside our house, though. Cozy. Warm. Sal is planning lunch for six tomorrow. I am not as keen to entertain when it's freezing out and the guests have to come by boat but Sal has a social accounting system to reckon with and so we all convene now and then, whether we want to or not. Whoopee! I ask her about the logic of this and she says, "It's almost year end. We still have some payables!" She may be missing the hospitality concept a smidge.

The problem for me is that the plumbing gets close to freezing up. I have heat tape around it but I have to run the genset to keep that functioning all the time, which seems a bit silly. I usually just drain the system so I don't have to worry about freezing *or* running the generator. I'll recharge the system before everyone arrives for lunch and once they've gone home I'll drain it again. Heat tape and genset on while guests are here. Party preparations are a little different out here.

I sometimes plan on going to do some work at the community workshop in winter but occasionally it is just too cold to go out. Sal, of course, does not let that stop her and she heads out to get the mail at least weekly. But if the wind is gusting up, the mail plane doesn't come anyway. So sometimes we just stay put. That's what winter's all about.

Describing this winter hibernation as slow paced, relaxed and comfortable still makes it sound more stressed than it is. I'm even more laid back than that. Think big giant gummy bear. In a robe.

However, all good things come to an end. We eventually have to go to town. We get a bit low on things such as milk and chocolate. We can do without milk, but other things are just way too important. Sal decides when to go to town, regardless of the weather. As she says, "There will be chocolate!"

So we spend the next day in town getting supplies. It was late in the day by the time we got off the ferry on the adjacent island and we still had to load the boat and head up channel to get home. I could see the fog bank rolling into the bay where our boat was docked. Scheduling was giving way to trepidation.

When we finished loading it was near dark, cold and the fog had filled the bay like a flood. We couldn't even see the fuel barge at the end of the dock. Visibility was about fifty feet and seemingly getting worse. We made our way to where the boat was tied up and, like all self absorbed guys with an agenda, I was trying to figure out a way to traverse the ten or so miles and the narrow passages of our route home despite the obvious problem. I stood at the end of the float and looked into nothingness.

One of our neighbours was at the gas barge filling up. Bruce had lived on the coast for much of his sixty years and has navigated the channel every day or so. He seemed to be preparing to leave.

"Hey Bruce! You're not planning on going out in this are you?"

"Yup."

"But you can't see! I mean, I know you have a compass but that's not good enough. Is it?"

"Yup."

"You sure?"

"Yup."

"Hmm…well, if you're going and you are confident, I'll follow you to your place and we're only another mile further north. I'll crawl along the coast for that last bit. Hang on. Give us a minute. We're going to follow you across the bay and through the passes. We'll tuck in behind you until we get to your place."

"Uh, well, I dunno...that seems to put a lot of responsibility on me, Dave."

"Actually, it doesn't. If you really think about it, all the responsibility is on my shoulders. You are free of any burden."

"How do you figure that?"

"Well, see, it's like this. You're going anyway. We're following you. Should you falter or hit a rock, I'm right there and I have to rescue you. Huge responsibility. But, if you succeed, there is no incident. You get nothing but credit. You're the hero. So all I see is upside for you."

"Yeah. Okay, I guess you're right. We'll leave when you're ready."

Bruce's boat is a slim, thirty footer, only five feet at the beam. It sits low in the water like a canoe and, even going full tilt, produces about as much wake as one. Our boat is a new (to us) beamy twenty-six footer and, despite the shorter length, it is at least twice as large in volume. It pushes a lot of water until it gets up on a plane and it is only then that it is easily steered. At slow speeds it tends to lurch to and fro and plow through the water.

Bruce's boat left the dock and Sal and I tucked in behind him. Many of us don't use modern navigational aids or equipment and, in Bruce's case, that Spartan outlook carried to lights as well. He had one very small white running light on his stern. When he was forty feet ahead of me, he disappeared into the fog. At thirty feet, it felt like I was going to drive right over him. Following the leader was extremely difficult and, worse, if I failed to keep close, Bruce might just blend into the fog and there was no way to find him. Go a bit too quick and I'd end up in his lap.

By the time we had traveled across the mile wide bay, I was pretty much convinced that this was not such a great idea. Unfortunately, turning around was not an option. I left the dock with the conviction that I could easily keep Bruce in sight but it became evident that doing so was going to be more a matter of luck than seamanship. The fog was getting thicker and one moment Bruce was virtually underneath my bow and the next he was gone with only faint traces of a wake to prove his existence.

At the far end of the bay is a tricky and narrow pass between a few small islets. It is a dog's leg and narrowly defined; a fifty foot wide space surrounded by reefs, rocks, shallow water and requiring a few tight turns at just the right time.

Bruce drove at about three knots for half an hour on a compass bearing approximately due north. He didn't deviate much. He seemed unerring. I'm not sure he could see the bow of his boat.

About forty minutes out, he turned right. So did we. Three minutes later, he turned left. I followed. Then it was an hour or so more of simply running blind.

I lost him on a few occasions and looked for his boat's wake for a clue as to where he was. But the sea was a bit choppy by then and what little wake that existed was as much imagined as seen. At one point I was convinced that he was gone and I was looking left and right to make sure that I didn't pass him. Whoa! Almost landed on top of him! He had been straight ahead.

To Bruce's credit, or dysfunction, I never once saw him turn around to look for me. I came up too quickly, and I fell back into the nothing. I almost passed him and I almost lost him. Several times I almost ran over him and I honestly don't think he ever noticed any of it. Sally and I were sweating.

After over an hour of this I confess to being exhausted and not a little frightened. Then Bruce stopped. I almost rammed him again.

"I'm home." he said. "Would you like me to accompany you to your dock?"

I looked around. It was all grayness. I peered into the wet bleakness and saw nothing. Then, just as I was about to question him, I glimpsed a shape that I made out to be another boat at his dock. He had not missed his destination by even a foot.

"Yes, please. Sir! I have no hesitation in following you anywhere. You have radar in your head! Lead on!"

Twenty minutes later Bruce stopped again.

"You're home. See you later!" And he turned around and disappeared.

Sure enough, just a few faint lines of our dock appeared through the mist. We *were* home. There is no getting away from the fact that Bruce did well. But he topped himself later.

I was at the local store a week later and sang Bruce's praises for his piloting skills to a neighbour. She laughed.

"Bruce told us the story, too. Seems he was planning on taking the long way around the islets instead of the shortcut because he wasn't sure if he could find it. He was actually aiming to be half a mile further east when he saw the entrance to the pass. He was just as surprised as you were!"

I don't know the truth. I prefer to believe that Bruce is special.

-20-

No One Gets Us

There are so many positive aspects to living remote, although I won't go through them again. You already know about the ravens, the seals, the orcas, clean air, blah, blah, blah, gorgeous scenery, blah, blah, blah…but of course some things can be inconvenient.

The municipal elections were coming up and we wanted to vote. It's not easy. First off, the voting booth is on another island. So we have to travel in winter in a small boat and then drive through the forest on a logging road (if we are not snowed in) to get there. Say, two or three hours minimum, given good passage. Longer for those who live further out.

Mind you, we chose to live out here but, on the other hand, this is our regional district election. You'd think that, if anyone understands our situation and the logistical challenges their constituents face, it would be the local government, wouldn't you? You'd be wrong. Our local representative, Jim Abram, is well aware of us islanders and our issues and represents us extremely well, but unfortunately the office staff isn't always as knowledgeable.

The Feds understand. They set up a voting station here on our island. So does the Province. But the government most locally oriented doesn't seem to know from rural. They just don't get it.

Well, in theory they do. Seems we can vote by mail. But, of course, because the nominations just closed the mail-in ballots won't be ready for a while. Tick tock, tick tock. Voting day is less than a month away.

"Hello? Uh, Mr. Elections fella? If we're going to vote by mail, shouldn't we get those ballots pretty damn quick?"

"Can't. We've got to wait for the forms to be printed."

"You mean the ballots?"

"No, the forms. You ask us to mail out a form. When you get it you fill it in and send it back. When we receive it, we send out a ballot for you to mark and then you mail that in."

"Well then, you may as well not bother. The mail plane schedule is often disrupted in winter when the weather is bad. Even when it gets here, people have to come from miles around in small boats to get their mail. If they take their mail home before looking at it, they may not get back to the post office for a week, or maybe even a month, to return the form."

"Well, look on our website in a few days. We'll have a downloadable form that can maybe save time on that first step."

"Yeah, great. Trouble is a lot of folks don't have internet or a printer. And if they do, internet service here isn't always reliable."

"Hmm…well, maybe I can send out a bunch of forms to the post office without waiting to be asked. People can pick them up there, fill them out and get them back to us right away. Can you give me the post office phone number? I'll have my assistant arrange it."

"Well, that's a good idea. But the post office doesn't have a phone. Or electricity. Not even lights. Or even a bathroom. Can we just come in to the district office any old time and vote? Most everyone will get into town at least once within the month. That should cover off the bulk of us."

"Well, I guess…but you'll have to prove your identity. Real proof. And an actual address. Not just a post office box."

"Well now, that seems fair. Except no one has a real street address. We don't have any streets. No street lights. No stores. No district water supply. No provincial hydro. No police. No fire protection. No amenities. Only thing we got is @!#&^^$ taxes. No offense."

"Well, can't you just write in a description? Like old rotting houseboat on the beach or something?"

"That might work fine for Old Ted. He's the one living in a hollow tree trunk on the north side. And Tiny and his wife inhabit the top deck of a sunken boat in East Bay. But it might not work for the big cheese CEO with his five thousand square feet of upscale country home or that real pretty estate belonging to a movie star. So, I dunno. Can we just address our ballot to that big old government building with all the bloodsucking sloths in it? Would they zero in on you pretty quick?"

Sally and I sent our applications in at the same time. I received my ballot. She didn't. Some bureaucratic glitch had her living on the wrong island. She straightened that out and a ballot was put in the mail for her but when a big storm rolled in and the plane didn't fly we realized it wouldn't reach her in time to mail it back. So we went to the district office on our next day in town.

"Sorry, your ballot's now in the mail. Can't let you vote if there is a ballot flying around out there with your name on it."

Sally wasn't able to get the ballot back in time to vote.

I confess to being surprised by the misconceptions of city people. Don't misunderstand me; I was just as guilty before moving here. Probably more so than most. I had no clue what it meant to live rural, let alone remote. The average urbanite just doesn't understand that it is quicker to fly from Vancouver to Toronto than it is to get from Vancouver to our island. They don't get that cell phones don't always have reception out here, even though we rely on them.

For our cell phone to work well at our house it has to be physically attached to our large Yagi antenna, with another piece of equipment called a booster also installed. That renders the phone no longer portable. We can't carry it around like we could in the city where there is service everywhere. So if we are away from the house, even working outside, we pick up our messages only when we get home. Like the old days when everybody had land lines. It's freeing not to be on call twenty-four hours a day but a difficult concept for some to understand in this era of instant communications.

"They" don't seem to understand that there is no address for us other than a post office box. When I changed the address on my drivers' license I was asked for a street address. I tried to explain there was no street and I had to get to my home by boat. Once this was understood there was still a dilemma for the person on the other end of the line.

"There's a box on the computer screen for your street address. If I don't fill it in, the computer won't accept the change."

In a rare flash of brilliance I recalled that it didn't matter what address I provided.

"Try 1-2-3 Doofus Drive."
"Oh good, that works! Can I confirm the spelling of Doofus?"

Our community is reliant on a government dock. All coastal communities are. Maybe five or six people leave their small boats tied up permanently. But, over time, everyone in the area ties up at the dock at one point or another. The dock is the hub of the community. It is our parking lot, the town square and the sea port for outsiders. It is essential. It is where evacuation takes place when there is a medical emergency, as I have experienced. It is part of our life line to the outside world.

Our dock accommodates the post office operated by Canada Post as well as providing moorage for a rotating flotilla of boats which, on a busy day, might number twenty. One of the boats belongs to the teacher at the school, another to the school custodian. A few belong to community members volunteering at the school. Another space, now and then, goes to the postmistress. One end of the dock is reserved for the mail plane that comes three times a week. Percentage wise, the government itself uses the dock the most.

Government docks used to be operated by a federal government agency, Transport Canada. Transport Canada is nearing the end of a decade long program of divestiture. They don't want to be in the business of operating docks anymore. They want to privatize them or, as is the case in our community, offload the responsibility to local government.

Many small communities on the coast don't have enough people, and consequently boats, to warrant paying a wharfinger or a manager, or even a dock boy to collect fees. The facilities do not have enough moorage space to generate operating capital. Therefore it's not feasible to privatize them. But people out here need docks more than people in the city need mass transit. In fact, this government plan is not divestiture as much as a dereliction of duty.

Some bureaucrats from another government department came out to pay us all a visit. Nice folks. They came to see the final portion of the road on the adjacent island that leads down a steep hill to the water and our community dock. This dock is where we park our boats when we head in to so-called civilization. But we also bring our small boats onto the beach next to the dock to load heavy supplies and equipment directly from our vehicles. Getting down the final hill to the water is critical to bringing out building supplies or taking an outboard in for repair and we were hoping to have it maintained.

But it seems there is a question about whether that final steep portion of the road is actually a road. Apparently it is not officially called a road and is thus not recognized as one. It may not exist. Even if it *is* there and cars drive on it as a natural continuance of the real road.

"Well, this isn't a road. And, if it was a road, it wouldn't be a road we recognized. And, if you disagree, the best way for us to determine if it is a road is for you to take us to court. If the judge says it is a road, then it is a road. Until then, we are pretty sure it isn't a road."

This helpful bureaucrat is talking about the road he just drove down to meet me. The phantom road.

"Well, we're happy to take you to court. But I don't really want to fight the government. Too exhausting. If we take you to court, will you argue with us or just roll over?"

"My job is just to present the facts. I don't argue one way or the other."

"All right then. Thanks. I just may see you in court. In the meantime, do you want to walk down the road, and head across the channel to our island and come for lunch?"

"I'll take this trail here to your boat because I don't see a road. But this trail will do."

So, off we go in a real boat on the real ocean though I may have been delusional at the time. As we traveled, I was thinking of serving an empty bowl and calling it lunch. If the fellow looked surprised, I'd say, "Well, take me to court. Maybe the judge will see this as lunch. And if he or she calls it lunch, then it is lunch. If it is not officially a real lunch, then I'll serve a real lunch."

But I am not a petty man.

I like this bureaucrat. He laughs at my jokes. And he seems harmless enough. He is retiring soon. He's fairly benign. And that's how I like 'em, benign and retiring. Invisible is good, too. A not real bureaucrat is a good thing. I kinda hope they downsize the Ministry and there is no replacement. That would make him really not real. And then there would be no road and nobody to tell me there was no road. 'Course, I'd still drive down it now and then.

In contrast to various government departments, the Campbell River urbanites are often pretty good at "getting" us. One of the ways it shows up, though, is quirky. When we go to Save-On to shop, sometimes the store is out of something we want, or the produce is withered or past its prime. Such is life in the grocery business. But, of course, we have no choice and so we take it anyway. Often the cashier, suspecting that we are from the outer islands (wearing gumboots is a hint) will say, "Geez, that lettuce is pretty droopy." or, "Hey, those avocadoes aren't very good."

"We know. Have no choice. We won't be back for two or three weeks. Weather permitting."

"Right, outer islands, huh? I'm not going to charge you for this. Not worth it. Sorry we don't have better."

That does not make the lettuce crisper but it is an exceptionally nice gesture and recognition of who we are. And, I suppose, that is what this is all about—it really *is* great when someone gets us.

-21-

Doing Their Thing

Once a month a group of women down implements and tools for a day to join the latest gathering of rural booklovers. Lots of comings and goings, to-ing and fro-ing, by sea between the local islands. Small, mostly open boats, carrying women clutching various potluck dishes and a few bottles of wine, will form an irregular ragtag flotilla coming together from throughout Discovery Sound. British Columbia's best book club meets at the home of its members, a different one each time. The hostess will serve coffee and tea and the rest of the contingent brings food for lunch.

The book club is not British Columbia's best because of the food, the books or the loyal following. Nor is it the best because the club, Sally or I think it is. It is the best because it is deemed so by the Canadian Broadcasting Corporation.

The CBC ran a contest to see who had the best book club in the province. It seems that having twenty or so members for twenty-five years is a good start. The clincher was that the meetings move every month and that each chatelaine's home is on a small, remote island with most having water access only. Usually about twelve or so women head out in boats in all kinds of weather to attend the meeting. They come from five different islands and they come singly, in pairs and bunched up in their small boats. Kayak travel is not uncommon.

Sometimes the tide tables have to be consulted to determine if rapids can be safely negotiated on the proposed date. These women are dedicated.

While still in our building stage, Sally had volunteered to host the December meeting. I am not so sure that her motive was pure hospitality, however. She volunteered in August when we had not yet finished the house. No plumbing, electricity or furniture. Walls not painted. Kitchen unassembled. I assumed the offer was a prompt for us to work to a deadline. I was right. When she told me, I laughed, "Well, these women are good sports. I'm sure that bare plywood floors and a bucket toilet will be okay."

"Not on your life, big boy. We just have to pick up the pace. This place is going to be finished by the eleventh of December. Now, let's get to work!"

Book Club was held on time. The women sat on sofas and chairs, walked on Persian carpets over finished hardwood floors. The water was running, walls were painted. The wood stove was ablaze with heat and the kitchen stove was warming the potluck dishes. The toilet worked. Sal was pleased. I was dead on my feet.

Book Club hosted by Sal in December became a yearly tradition—weather permitting. But who are we kidding? It would take a hurricane, sleet and minus zero temperatures for cancellation to be considered and, even then, some of the women would still make it. A few years back the December meeting was officially cancelled due to a big storm making travel by sea and road (falling trees) treacherous. A small group of intrepid women showed up anyway. The main reason for that, of course, is that they all really like to gather, eat, drink and hobnob. It's their thing.

The second reason is that Book Club is deemed all the more necessary in the depths of darkest winter. The members feel they need socializing even more at that time. And they are right. Winter marks the onset of potential "Bush Disorder" (not to be confused with a similarly named, but different problem, experienced south of the border) and, if it is a short winter, there are usually only a few sufferers. But if it is long, dreary and harsh then getting out and about is one small way of dealing with it. Every year someone is noticed as acting a little "bushed" and the old, isolated bachelors suffer the most. The women of Book Club seem to fare the best. It is not a coincidence.

The third reason for good December turnouts is that Sally serves a rich and plentiful homemade rummy eggnog that is to travel through Pauline's perils for. Naturally, no one would travel tens of miles by sea in an open boat in winter merely to get a cup of eggnog. Unless, of course, they had tasted it the previous year in which case the seed of temptation would have been well and truly planted. The smiles are broad when the women leave. And the bowl is always emptied. Trust me. It's the first thing I check when I am allowed back in.

Which brings me to the Book Club's sole rule—men are not allowed. I have to sit in my shed or go to visit John. Picture John and me and Roger, another dour spouse, killing time in each other's company while the bookish festivities are underway up at chez Cox-Davies. We sit in John's shop until we get hungry and then drink tea and eat peasant sandwiches consisting of a slab of crusty bread folded over a smaller slab of cheese and a chunk of salami. Repeat as required. Roger got so sleepy, or bored, that he lay on the couch and had a nap. John and I went out and cut up a few logs. The hours crawled by. Finally I got a call on the walkie-talkie, "Sweetie, you can come home now, if you like. Book Club is over."

Last year I stood in the shed for three hours until Sal came out and said I could join our dogs in our bedroom if I kept as quiet as they did. So, I got to spend the last two hours of Book Club shut in my own room with two dogs and happy for the concession. It was bloody cold in the shed.

One year I just puttered about in the rain. It was pathetic. Never mind. In a few years I'll be eligible to phone the elder abuse hotline and don't think I won't! That is, if I'm allowed in the house to make the phone call.

But just because I don't attend doesn't mean I can't write about the meetings. It might mean I don't have a clue what I'm talking about, but I doubt that very much. I mean, when has that ever been true?

I don't think that fashion comes up much in conversation. These women are too practical to bother with such nonsense. The Canucks don't rate highly, either. Neither would the Oscars or any of the other more typical water cooler topics of urban folks.

They might discuss their gardens, home repairs, boat repairs, a dead sea lion, and other local flora and fauna, though. Wolves, certainly. Recipes, maybe. An environmental issue, probably. But actually I am not sure. I really have no idea what they talk about, but the meetings last about four hours and only an hour is spent discussing the chosen book.

"So, do you guys ever talk about me?" I once asked Sal, somewhat beseechingly.

"No, sweetie. We never talk about you or any of the husbands. Sometimes a kid or grandchild."

"But what about some guy who sets himself on fire, falls out of his boat or runs off with a bar maid from the Heriot Bay Inn?"

"Nah…men do that all the time. These women have all had those experiences with the men in their lives already. It's old news, like dog bites man."

"So, we never come up?"

"Well, generically, sometimes. We might talk about men but generally just to condemn them all to hell and then we move on to lunch or gardens or something nice."

In theory, anyway, we men should be doing something like the women do. A regular poker night, a pub night maybe, a sport that we play together. Or something. But we don't. And none of us are organized enough to get the food thing handled, so we'd just sit around and get hungrier and hungrier until it was time to leave. And we'd all be ticked as hell by then, too! Doesn't sound so great to me.

We have a pretty high proportion of males out here who prefer to be alone, anyway. Independent whacked-out old loners whose only real connection to one another is an inclination to conspiracy theories and perhaps a little substance abuse. Any male bonding is usually done in the summer when it is warm and sunny and we can hammer or saw to drown out the other guy's inane chatter. We old codgers just aren't as sociable as the women. Nor do we like each other as much as they do.

And, even if we did like each other more, most of the old guys around here are deaf. So conversation is limited at best, nonexistent most of the time and we don't even get near one another much in the winter. Old guys just don't congregate. It ain't our thing.

Of course the books read at Book Club aren't our thing either. It's a given that the book will be some kind of bleak misery depicting the slow death of a crippled child born in Calcutta during the first World War and having to live in a culvert all her life.

Or, perhaps, a four hundred page exposé on the death of the Whistler sled dogs as experienced by Elsi, the only dog to survive. She just knew something was amiss and hid under the porch. Author? Should be Margaret Atwood, of course. These gals thrive on that stuff.

"I read this wonderful book about a woman who lived thirty years disguised as a man working in a steel mill in Philadelphia as a union leader. She had two children she raised in secret while practicing Tibetan Buddhism and teaching yoga."

Women, of course, are the victims of outrageous misfortune and evil men. But they are essentially invulnerable, outliving the pedophiles, rapists, slumlords and boyfriends who have made their lives miserable. Then they write a book. I am pretty sure we spell them W-O-M-A-N.

Another Sunday. Book Club day again. Women in boats carrying pies and casseroles. Freezing weather. A few hours of chitchat about Chick Lit and this and that and then it is again with the seas and piercing wind trying to make it safely home before dark and even colder temperatures. Gawd! They sure know how to have a good time, eh?

A year ago, while the good times rolled on, a fogbank rolled in. Sal didn't have her compass with her. When the members dispersed another woman, also lacking a compass, claimed to have extraordinary fog penetrating abilities. So the two of them headed out in their separate boats guided only by misplaced confidence and a general idea of where each other was. But my wife had her walkie-talkie.

"We are heading out now, sweetie. See you shortly."

Half an hour later, "Well, heh heh, we missed our island and ended up going the wrong way, but not to worry, we found each other and are heading out again. See you soon."

Half an hour after that. "Well, it's just amazing how this fog can trick you. We ended up—well, never mind. We're leaving again. Don't worry!"

She did a few more turns in the fog, and eventually was able to follow a neighbour across the channel who *did* have a compass on *his* boat. When she caught a glimpse of a familiar headland she followed the shoreline and finally arrived home safely. I was a basket case.

Book Club Photo: Jeanne Stoppard

Towing water tank to site

-22-

Dear Prudence

Ease of access, or in our case difficulty of access, and materials handling go hand in hand. There is not a single piece of wood, a screw, nail or any other building product that I have not handled several, if not a dozen times, before actually putting it in its final resting place.

Think about it. I pick up a bag of Redi-Mix concrete at the building supply store and put it in my vehicle. That is lift number one. I pull it out of the back of the truck at the dock or the beach (number two). Then I lift it into the boat (number three).

After the boat trip I lift it out of the boat (number four) and pass it to someone (Sally) and she puts it down ready for me to carry up the beach to the funicular, once the boat is tied up (number five). Then I take it off the funicular and carry it to wherever I'm going to store it (number six). Some days later, I'll pick it up and carry it to where I'm going to mix concrete (number seven) and there it sits awaiting its turn to become useful. I pick it up to pour it into the mix (number eight) and then carry the slurry to the forms and dump it in (number nine). Nine lifts of fifty-five pounds each time works out to just about five hundred pounds of lifting. For each bag.

One of the consistent mysteries of coastal life is that the heavier the load, the lower the tide. A cruel corollary to that is the government's requirement that a cabin be situated at least fifty feet back from the high water mark so, as is often the case on our wild and rocky coastline, this means a hundred or so feet up a steep incline. It seems that whenever you have to carry things to or from the boat it is low tide. It is the real life equivalent of the old joke, "We walked five miles to school every day, uphill—both ways."

You can't change the nature of the tide but, if you are willing to wait it out, it will, of course, eventually reverse and work for you. When I have the patience to wait for the tide to rise it saves me traversing a kelp covered, barnacle studded irregular rocky beach. The heavier the load, the more it is worth the wait. But, as I have little patience and don't expect a personality change anytime soon, I decided to employ a few mechanical aids in the meantime.

I built sea stairs to traverse the intertidal zone. They are common in Europe and many old harbors on the Eastern seaboard. We don't see them much on the west coast because our generally better protected waters make the more convenient ramps and floating docks practical. But they still have a place. Big city sea walls often sport a set or two of sea stairs. Some sea stairs are mortared stone. More typically they are simple concrete steps descending towards the low tide mark from a few feet above the high water mark.

Mine are a bit different because I chanced upon some exceptionally heavy galvanized steel grates at a scrap yard. I admit that when I first bought the grates I had no idea what I was going to do with them. They were just such a good deal and so incredibly cool I couldn't resist. I even stored them at a friend's place because I couldn't in any way justify their purchase to Sal. But finally inspiration struck.

I cut each grate in half to make two stair treads. I managed to get twelve treads that would cover the better part of the sixteen foot range from low to high tide. The top of the set of sea stairs ends at the bottom of a steel ramp which accesses the lower deck. I made the steps small, unobtrusive and removable and they do no harm to sea life. Quite the reverse. The barnacles and seaweed seem to find them more enticing than the natural rock.

My friend Brian, who was instrumental in building the funicular, built a crane which we placed on the lower deck. He took my basic design and improved on it. The crane lifted heavy loads right from the boat onto the funicular. It was sturdily built and worked like a charm. However, you may notice the use of the past tense here.

That's because my beautiful crane collapsed. It was lifting seven hundred pounds of lumber off my boat. The whole bundle was coming up nicely and then the crane slowly slumped over, tumbling the load onto the beach. That was a slow-mo surprise! I stood there trying to figure out what had happened and I was finally able to process it. One of the solid steel support legs had been bolted into rock. A huge slab of it had sloughed off from an even larger rock—the planet. The crane was intact, albeit horizontal instead of vertical. Fortunately my neighbour Robert, who was helping me, and I were unscathed. But the planet had failed me!

The crane is gone but the sea stairs remain and have served us well. One day we were taking our son Ben and his partner, Katie, to the next island to catch the ferry. The timing was such that we couldn't wait for high tide. The current going by was running at a couple of knots, which makes a landing on our shore even more of a challenge. Picture me approaching a rocky, slimy shore in a small boat. As soon as I slow down, so as not to ram into the rocks, the current takes effect to render me virtually out of control. I am somewhat used to this exercise, but still, it is no walk in the park. More like a crab walk in a river.

Usually when the tide and currents are this bad we go around to our dock and depart from there, like civilized people. But getting there is a long schlep, especially when you have luggage and a puppy crate to carry, not to mention the puppy. The battery in my car had died a couple of days prior so we also had a recharged car battery, a truly leaden weight, to get down to the boat.

Because of all the baggage, we opted to load from our shore, despite the less than ideal conditions. I went to get the boat from the dock with Ben and Katie and the puppy. Sally went down to the shore and awaited our arrival. She stood on the lowest step of the sea stairs in order to pass us the luggage, battery and dog crate. That was the plan.

I came around the point and nudged the little runabout close to the bottom of the stairs. Sal hung out as far as she could while extending the car battery at the end of one arm. Ben, on the bow, stretched over as far as he could to take it from her. As the boat swished by sideways at two knots the transfer was accomplished on the first pass. I circled back and made another pass for a piece of luggage.

And so it went until, after five or so passes, everything was transferred and it was only Sally who needed to get on the boat. At this point it was pretty full with the dog crate taking up most of the room on the bow. As I brought the boat around Sal took a flying leap and landed like a cat on the small patch of deck left for her. She settled into the boat as if it was the most normal thing in the world.

Some years ago, when I was playing at being a businessman, I bought an expensive pair of Florsheim shoes. This may seem irrelevant to living off the grid, but bear with me. Fancy shoes were part of the uniform of the team I was working with at that time. I had worn the shoes for a day when the heel fell off. It was irritating and I took them back to the store with a glower. I was polite and restrained but this second trip was cutting into a busy day and my annoyance must have shown through.

The storeowner replaced the shoes immediately and gave me a couple of pairs of "lifetime" socks. At first I refused the gesture saying that it was not necessary.

"Please, sir. We wanted to make a good first impression and we failed. So, I really want to make a much better second impression. I want you to leave a satisfied customer and not an angry one. If I can accomplish that, you'll come back."

I accepted and, of course, I went back for as long as I was in the game. But I never forgot the lesson, or did I?

A few years ago I had a disappointing encounter with Superior Propane. I had signed up for delivery because of their telephone marketer's generous promises. However, the service promised turned out to be only available to customers back East. Because I live where I do the company withdrew the offer their employee had made. They made a half-hearted attempt at consolation and I use them to this day but, for me, the relationship had always been a bit strained. They, of course, have many, many customers and, to them, I am just one of all the account numbers in their computer.

However, a recent bill I received from them was in error. They had overcharged me in the amount of twenty-five thousand dollars. Mind you, in retrospect, that is the best kind of error. Overbilling me only a few dollars might have gone unnoticed.

I had no choice. I emailed them and told them of their error and, further, I mentioned my original disappointment. I was polite but pointed. I must have managed to glower by way of email. It is an art.

They replied quickly, apologized profusely and told me the billing problem had been rectified. But then they went the additional step of addressing my other complaint. I hadn't expected that.

"That you would ask me about my original complaint is good enough. Fuggedaboudit. It was years ago. The employees involved have likely gone. The world moves on. And so do I. We'll let it go."

"No sir. We want to make it better. We messed up and we want a good relationship, not a poor one. We'll do the right thing by you this time!"

And they credited me with a free fill up.

Sometimes a faux pas can be an opportunity. Sometimes it is just another screw up in a world of screw ups. But the good part is that an error fixed with grace and sincerity is long remembered. I still remember the shoe store manager thirty-five years later. But now his file in my memory drawer just got a little bigger. I had to shuffle him over to make room for Superior Propane.

Propane is delivered to us by barge. As is diesel and gas and anything else that we can't or don't want to schlep ourselves in our own boat. The barge is quite a sight—an impressive one hundred and fifty feet of vessel with a substantial wheelhouse and crew quarters at the stern.

We never know what time of day the barge will arrive or even exactly which day. But it is almost always within the first three days of the month. Bad weather or an important client with an emergency delivery takes precedence over our relatively miniscule deliveries.

As dusk enveloped the channel one evening, and we were about to sit down for dinner with Jan and Pat, we saw the barge heading for our beachfront with a bone in its teeth. That means a frothy bow wave for all you landlubbers. Dinner was on hold as we rushed down to the shore.

Captain Tom and his crew were coming and they were ready to pump! It was time for our semiannual fill up. With his usual deft touch, Tom dropped the thirty foot wide steel ramp and ran it up the inclined rocks to within a foot of the stairs to our generator shed and then left the helm under the watchful eye of the GPS system which keeps the barge perfectly positioned. He stepped out to greet us while Lorne and Bob dragged the heavy hoses to our waiting propane and gas tanks.

It's a funny relationship. We are very fond of the crew members who are always incredibly cheerful and competent no matter what the weather is doing. Yet we encounter one another for fifteen minutes twice a year. In theory, it is all business but, in reality, it is a warm, friendly encounter with people we like and trust and, admittedly, on whom we are somewhat reliant. They don't need us to be there when they arrive as they know what to do better than we do, but we always like to be around simply because we like to see them. If it is mostly business, it's the kind I like.

Jan and Pat enjoyed the impromptu visit. We certainly know how to entertain dinner guests.

I finally had to admit that I was coming to the end of an era in my materials handling and storage. Dave's hardware store's inventory was beginning to touch bottom. The well was pumping brown. I was running out of things. I could hardly believe it.

When we began building I bought all the required supplies I thought I could possibly need for each stage and I never skimped. Why buy one pound of screws for ten bucks when I could buy ten pounds for thirty-five, or whatever? It was basically just good math. But at first Sal didn't get it.

"Sweetie, why are we buying fifty pounds of three inch galvanized casing nails. You said we just needed a few."

"Yeah, well, we do. Just a couple of pounds, actually. But the price is good and one always needs three inch galvanized casing nails, eh?"

"We've never needed even one before. You sure?"

We'd get the nails and, for good measure a box of four inch and two inch plus a bucket o' screws. Sal just shook her head.

She had good reason. I didn't really know what I was talking about. I didn't really know anything except that going shopping was such an incredible drag. I decided that if I had to buy one small item, I'd buy a dozen and, with that simple extravagance, I'd have a replacement for the one I dropped and lost, the one I ruined by cutting it too short and the two I lent my neighbour. Simple logic: I'd still have seven left that would likely suffice to save me from having to ever shop for them again. Just think of the fuel savings alone.

And Dave's local hardware store was born.

This mad way of stocking inventory has stood me in good stead. Whenever we needed something, we had it. Always. One hundred percent. And, over the years, my reputation grew. As we were building Sal beamed at me frequently in ever growing appreciation of my foresightedness. I was golden.

But all good things come to an end. Even Mike Tyson eventually lost. And it was a shock when it happened. I simply wasn't prepared. I didn't see it coming. I was caught flat footed and empty handed. And that feels bad when you are standing amongst three buckets of extra nails. Yes, we still have forty plus pounds of three inch galvanized casing nails.

I thought I was covered. It is hard to describe the feeling of not being covered. Naked, perhaps? There was a hint a few days before this grim realization.

"Dave? Robert here. I need a dozen or so one inch, fine threaded bolts with a flat head. For drawer pulls. You got any?"

"Probably. I'll check. Get back to you in a few minutes."

And I searched high and low. Searching is always done in a mild panic. There is no system, really. Well, in a way there are actually two systems. The vague, imprecise, running tally I have in my head that starts with hmm, I am thinking that they would be somewhere near the end of the lower level bench...maybe near the carriage bolts...possibly...if I have any...

And then there is the more reliable system.

"Hey, Sal! Do you know where the little bolts are? The ones you might use for drawer handles?"

"Have you tried the tote labeled drawer handles?"

And that system has sufficed for years. It's a great system if Sal is home. Or if she is nearby and has turned on her walkie-talkie which is highly unlikely. Our gal Sal likes to leave it turned off at the bottom of her pack. It is quieter that way, she says. Still, all in all, it has been a good system. We usually have the goods.

Until that fateful day. I had to put my ego aside and tell Robert that Dave's hardware store is out of stock. Should I put it on back order?

Not only had I discovered that we were out of small bolts for drawer pulls but we were out of two inch galvanized nails as well! I managed by using silicone bronze—a material both rare and expensive.

My inventory had let me down. I felt inadequate, a feeling I am familiar enough with to know when it is upon me. Yup, it was inadequacy alright—inventory dysfunction. Came up short, if you know what I mean.

This gave me a weird dilemma. Do I replenish the inventory? Would doing so just be for reasons of ego or am I going to maybe build something else? And, if I am not going to build again, what about the smaller projects? Don't they need inventory, too? And what about my standing with my neighbours? Is my basic personality attractive enough to keep my friends without my stock of supplies? Do I dare risk finding out?

And worse, where to start? There are quite a few depleted items. Many half-filled jars, tins and boxes, tubes of goo and various things I have forgotten about. What do I have? What should I get?

I dunno…maybe I'll just get out of the lending business altogether. Retire from hardware supplies and get into something where the basic goods are guaranteed to be there. Maybe carving wooden ducks or something. I've got wood up the yin yang. Perhaps that would be the prudent thing to do.

-23-

She's a Woofer

It was a few years after our arrival on the island and Sally and I were at a party at a neighbor's home. I thought I knew everyone, but it seemed I was mistaken. My host and I were talking when a young woman walked by with appetizers.

"Who's that?" I asked.

"Woofer," he said.

Now I don't feel the need to defend the planet from sexism or rudeness in all its manifest forms but "woofer" seemed a bit harsh, even to me. I gallantly rose to the occasion.

"Oh yeah? I'll admit that she's no Angelina Jolie but, really man, calling her a "woofer" is just plain rude!"

"Dave, Dave. Calm down. "Woof" is spelled W-W-O-O-F. It stands for World Wide Opportunities on Organic Farms. It's a volunteer program. Hosts feed and house young people, often from other countries, in exchange for farm, ranch or homestead work. Typically, hosts have rural homes on acreages, like us. Jen is wwoofing here. She's from Australia. She'll help out in the garden and maybe chop some wood and then, in a week or so, move on to another host."

And here I was thinking that maybe just a new hairdo and bit of makeup might help the situation.

But I was hooked on the concept. I contacted WWOOF, sent in my name with a brief write-up, paid my dues, and waited for the wwoofers to bark at my door. Sure enough, Sarah and Constance soon contacted us from England. The game was afoot.

These two young school teachers arrived all pasty white and very British. I didn't think they'd make it up the trail, let alone work like the Sherpas I'd hoped for. But they were delightful company those first few hours and we had a great introductory meal. They did the dishes without prompting before they took to the guest quarters, so Sally was already fully on side.

Log hauling, bucking and splitting were scheduled for the next day. Then carrying and stacking. I intended to start slowly and quit early as is my usual practice with just about everything except reading and drinking Scotch. They'd have none of it. These two young women were farm girls and knew how to work. It was hell. I couldn't get them to stop so I kept bringing up logs. We put in a lot of wood that day. Finally we quit, had dinner and they did the dishes again.

I was starting to enjoy this wwoofing thing. It's nice having young people do as I tell them, an experience foreign to me since my own kids were about six years old. These two were even polite enough to suffer through a few of my stories. No choice, really, as we don't have television. Naturally, they went to bed early.

But the next day, of course, was different. They were off the job. No work. They went kayaking and, while they were out on the water, found and towed in a log that was drifting by. Brought it in by kayak. Not an easy thing to do. They added it to the pile awaiting the next day's work. They had good attitude in spades.

And so it went for a week. When Sarah and Constance left for another wwoofing gig they left as friends, with their legacy our winter's firewood. It was a good experience for all of us.

Since then we've hosted many wwoofers and enjoyed almost every single one of them. I am still in frequent touch with Christian from Eastern Europe who came with his friend Leanne from the Maritimes. Before arriving at our door he and Leanne had worked at a dog sled outfit up north where they looked after the dogs and worked their way up to driving clients on dogsleds.

Christian worked like Paul Bunyan and ate like his ox, Babe. Financially it was not quite the same great deal as it had been with the two school teachers, but we were only out a few pounds of potatoes and a steak or two. Christian and Leanne were both hard workers, bright and interesting. Good company too. Christian regaled us with tales of growing up in East Germany. When he was a small child his father had driven him for many hours to witness the fall of the Berlin Wall.

Each wwoofer is different. Some speak English poorly, some not much at all. Some are small and unskilled; others are Amazons and work like machines. Generally speaking, they are all willing workers, often from out of the province, and more often from out of the country, looking for a natural experience in a family setting. They need a place to sleep and put their belongings, some inclusive family time, usually around meals or chores, and some free time. And they need good food. In exchange for room and board they work half a day or one day out of two, although many wwoofers help out a little all the time.

We learned how to evaluate our wwoofer applicants in our email exchanges. Shakespeare wrote from Gambia. "I want to come help and…I have five lovely children." Sheesh. I don't think we can accommodate six people, even if five of them are lovely. Truth is, this is not a good place for little kids. If they tip over on our slope they'll keep on rolling right into the sea. Not good. Sadly, we had to disappoint Shakespeare.

Our next wwoofer, Phoebe, came from Australia by way of a seven year work stint in Jolly Olde England. Her accent was just wild. A thirty year old worker with youth offenders, Phoebe is smart, capable, strong and pleasant. We did a little logging of dead and windfall trees and managed a good day's work in less than four hours. Which is good, since four hours is about my limit. I always vow to work wwoofers like dogs (seems fitting) but we never do.

"You have to do the dishes!" I say, sternly.

Sally adds, "If that's okay with you?"

Our supine wwoofer looks up from the couch, "Okay, but since you are up, I'll have a bit more wine."

There has to be a happy medium.

Actually, I am only kidding. All the wwoofers have been good, save one French couple who were very pleasant in a social setting but felt obliged to stand back whenever work was being undertaken.

When Lilou and Jules showed up, the chores I had scheduled at the time were simple. I was going to put in a new window in the boathouse with which I required some assistance and as well we were going to clear an area of beach by carrying small boulders from one part of our shoreline to another. Each boulder was between the size of a cabbage and a bowling ball—heavy, but still manageable by one person.

They couldn't seem to walk and carry a rock at the same time and demonstrated no inclination to master the skill, either. The window installation was rocket science to them—beyond their intellectual grasp. They looked at the tools I gave them as if they were ray guns from the Planet Zorg. They stood dumbstruck the whole time. They were very nice to be with but labour was not only beneath them, it also seemed too challenging. They just didn't seem to get it, even as we were doing it.

I'm not kidding. I'd say only the wheelbarrow was a concept readily grasped. How the hell these people got from their home country all the way to our island is a question I often pondered after seeing them trying to work the garden hose or use a screwdriver.

"So, Lilou…? What did you do in France? Before coming here?"

"Ooo...ah teaze de Onglais, eh? Ah am a Onglaiz teazer fo den 'ears, eh?"

"Wow! Interesting. What is the name of that tool in French?"

"Ah 'ave neder zeen zat tsing beefore. Whad iz zat?"

"We call it a shovel."

We share our wwoofers with other hosts now and then, especially if the wwoofers want to stay on in the area. This couple did. We shared those school teachers pretty quick, hoping they would find a better fit with someone else. They made a favorable impression at one of the local lodges because they liked working in the kitchen. As it turned out, they stayed around the islands for a month or so before returning home to France.

The other night at a dinner party, Judith asked, "Have you heard about Lilou and Jules? Seems they went back to France but once there, felt they needed to become more independent. They wanted to be more competent and skilled. They quit their jobs and immigrated to Canada last summer. They are working on a cattle ranch in the Chilcotin."

"*What*? They are the last people I ever thought would do something like that. *Oh my gawd*. How are they doing?"

"Well, they are riding horses, herding cattle, mending fences and building things. Really into alternative energy, too, I gather. I saw a picture of the cabin they built for themselves. It was pretty good!"

"*What the hell happened to them?*"

"Well, Lilou wrote to tell me that their time on our island taught them that they were lacking in real life skills and they were very impressed with all of us and how independent we were. After a time in France, they decided that they preferred to live our way and made application to come to Canada. They got a wwoofing gig at a ranch and are now employees. They are really into off the grid learning and are picking up skills wherever they can. They've both signed up for a course in heavy duty mechanics. They seem pretty pleased with themselves."

I picked my jaw up from the floor. I stammered. I was stunned, to say the least.

"Those guys were the least capable people we have ever encountered and bear in mind that we, ourselves, are barely functional out here. I would never have guessed that happening in a million years. That's *astonishing*."

"Yeah, that's what I thought. Pretty cool, huh?"

But back to Phoebe. We finally managed to work our wwoofer like a dog. Unfortunately our primary experience is with Portuguese water dogs so Phoebe went paddling. Sally, Jorge, John and Phoebe took the kayaks and paddled through the narrows. The tides and currents at this time of year are moderate so they could explore the nooks and crannies of the islets that form the constriction that is the pass. They could see what can't always be easily seen. Mostly just more rocks and Christmas trees, of course, but at one point they came upon a small, dry rock with a couple of dozen seals lolling about. Seeing seals a few feet away from a kayak is a neat experience, especially for a young woman from Melbourne via London.

They also caught a glimpse of a sea lion and, naturally, there were eagles and other winged denizens of the area to view. The paddle was quite a few miles long and took a few hours. All good.

While they were away, I worked on a small deck extension to make hanging the clothes on the clothesline easier. Yes, that's right–we hang clothes on a line. The clothesline extends through the trees so finding bark and twigs in my sock drawer is the norm. Paw prints on the sheets tend to mystify me, though. Just how does a dog get a muddy print on a sheet hanging six feet off the ground? More mystifying is the fact that the first time I noticed it there were a series of prints as if a dog had walked across the sheet.

"Sally, how did the paw print pattern come to decorate our sheets?"

"Never mind, a little dirt won't do you any harm!"

"But, really, a little dirt kind of defeats the purpose of washing them in the first place, doesn't it?"

"No. This is just a little clean dirt. We wash the sheets to get rid of the dirty dirt."

Seems the dogs generate clean dirt and we, in our sleep, make dirty dirt. If only it were so. Maybe Phoebe should be doing the washing? But she's heading off to trek in Nepal.

Because she is going on a trek, we invited Judith, Rob and Laurie for a send-off dinner. Rob and Laurie are world class mountaineers and they gave Phoebe tips on hiking gear, hostels and other things Katmandu.

Normally, I would listen attentively to that kind of discussion so that I would have the information for future use. But I didn't listen so closely this time. I am unlikely to go hiking in Nepal anytime in the foreseeable future. At least I hope not. A sure sign of getting older is striking things off the lifetime bucket list without having done them.

We host wwoofers for a number of reasons, one of which is for the fun of meeting nice young people and sharing our piece of the world with them. But we do always need to get in a few cords of wood for each winter and that chore is one that we have found wwoofers enjoy and is easy to get their help with.

Rod and Julie arrived in the spring specifically to help us with firewood. They are wwoofers from England in their late twenties. Traveling around the world on a budget, their goal is to do so without taking a plane. Nice couple. We took them up to the Arts and Culture Day at the school and they mingled with the fifty or so local people in attendance. We returned home in the rain and, since already wet, we decided to start on the chore of building the woodpile.

Hurting my back riding my son's motorcycle through a backstop the previous summer hadn't helped my woodcutting abilities. I could still feel the injury. I didn't yet have the log splitter so I was going to leave the splitting to the young people.

Well, first I had to teach them how to do it. And at least I *look* like I know what I am talking about. I wear one of my plaid lumberjack shirts and my heavy boots. I'm not light and, put as nicely as I can, I am somewhat compact. Some might say dense. Like a boulder packed in bubble wrap. But not just a little of that is muscle. Plus I have been doing this chopping thing for a while. I have the rhythm. So, I pick up the splitting maul and, with indicating barely an effort, I split a piece neatly and efficiently with one blow. Impressive, if I do say so myself.

Then I stop and hand the implement of destruction to the smaller of the two—in this case, Julie.

What they don't know is that the piece I chose to demonstrate on was pre-selected for being knot free and dry. A real logger could have split it with a large spoon. Still, it looks impressive and it is to them. So, then I give them a knotty, green piece of spirit breaking wood and say, "Here, Julie. You try!"

The results are predictable but Julie doesn't care. She wasn't looking forward to swinging an eight pound maul around anyway. But the contrast of my proficiency with Julie's lack of it is what we are going for. Rod can see that this is his chance to impress me and, more importantly, Julie. His hormones are rising to the challenge. Like sap!

I discretely remove the gnarly piece and give him a nice dry, easily split round. He whacks. It usually still takes a few good swings but he gets through and we all "oooh" and "aaah" at his burly man-ness. Julie looks on approvingly. And the guy is hooked.

Young men, eh? I go in and get a few ibuprofens for my sore back and go out to encourage the macho display a few more times before getting the chainsaw to cut more rounds for the now sweating, macho man splitting machine.

But all is not quite right. Not yet.

I whisper to Julie "I gave him an easy round to split. I gave you a hard one. Doing it this way means he is proud of his work, you see. It encourages him. I hope you don't mind? If you want to give it a few whacks some time, I'll get a regular piece for you."

"No. I don't mind. I do the same with him, myself. Give him something easy and then oooh and aaah. He falls for it every time. But I had no idea guys were on to this."

"Just getting in touch with my feminine side. Have to. My masculine side is sore and hurting. Gotta get smart like you women."

I split a few more rounds for them to set some sort of standard and then, before my back packs it in, I stride off with a bit of a macho challenge.

"It's not muscle work, it's just rhythm. You should get good enough so that you can just whack and whack all day.

Rod split all afternoon. And before I had a chance to get a round for Julie she had decided that she could split wood too and when I eventually went back out, she was hard at it. She returned to stacking for a while but later she took the job of splitting from her partner. She was going to master the maul and chop like a logger.

And she did! It always takes a while to see who has it and who doesn't. Splitting really *is* a rhythm thing. Strength *is* a factor (even though I lied and said it wasn't) but the real role of strength is in keeping the maul and the chopping head straight and true at the moment of impact. A strong person hitting slightly off target wastes their energy and gets nowhere. A weaker person who hits dead on will split wood. Julie got it. She then found a good rhythm. And the wood started to *fly*.

It was only for half a day because these two, being English and not living near a beach, were amazed at ours. (But really, how far away from a beach can you get when you live in England?) They couldn't get over the plentiful and free seafood. They gathered and shucked oysters for dinner and dug a bunch of clams for Sal's famous chowder. I took the opportunity to have a brief nap. Old guys, eh?

At five o'clock it was time for a glass of wine. So, we had one. Rod and Julie joined us when they returned from kayaking. For us, it was a normal day—a productive one, a physical one and a nice one. For them? It was marvelous.

And that is the main reason for hosting wwoofers.

-24-

Cultivating the Rock

We finally planted a vegetable garden for the very first time. Well, we tried to, but we didn't really know what we were doing. Of course, no one expects you to know much about gardening out here until you have been around for a few years but we were coming up to the end of our probation period and we knew that we would be judged somewhat if we didn't come up with a crop. The pressure was on to produce produce.

The thing is, having a garden is difficult when you build on granite. We don't have much dirt. Well, none, really. So I built raised garden beds totaling about eighty square feet and then we proceeded to dig and scrape dirt from wherever we could find it. Sally and our wwoofer, Alice, did most of that. I built the boxes three feet high so that I wouldn't have to bend over too far to pick the avocados and strawberries I envisioned…maybe a few cherry tomatoes as well.

But, when you think about it, eighty square feet of garden that is three feet deep has a hell of a volume. We scrabbled for dirt until we got bored and then added some purchased steer manure and peat moss. That still wasn't enough so we added seaweed, compost and a few log ends. We really had no idea what we were doing, other than guessing that log ends possibly weren't the best ingredient for good soil. But we were desperate to fill the seemingly bottomless boxes.

Then Sal went to our local market day and bought some local plants from some of the local gardeners. Our neighbour, Bruce, not only navigates through the fog, but he grows wonderful plants, including Godzilla tomatoes, so he was our biggest source. Sally planted a salad garden that included lettuce and onions, beans and peas, squash and tomatoes and, for reasons unfathomable to me, marigolds. We got marigolds up the wazoo.

Actually, we got it all up the wazoo! Lettuce plants are trying to elbow each other aside. We have the squash plant from hell trying to take over the whole box and then some. We have broccoli that rivals old growth trees and we have tomatoes like Rambo has bullets. The cauliflower we grew was too big for the kitchen sink. *Oh my gawd.*

Part of it is because of the record setting sunshine and Sal's religious devotion to watering the farm daily. Hard *not* to thrive under those conditions. But, really, our eighty square feet is producing as much as the Fraser Valley. We could fill a supermarket produce section.

'Course half of it is &#%$!* marigolds but Sal claims they are edible so I shouldn't complain. I just don't see myself with a mouthful of orange flowers, I guess. I don't see myself eating the squash from the Little Shop of Horrors either. I don't want to make enemies of that kind. It's creepy in every sense of the word.

When it comes right down to it, I am a little ticked that I don't have the much anticipated strawberries and avocados but, it seems that avocados, at least, require a special touch of some kind. Like Costa Rica. We keep saying, "Well, this was just a learning experience and we now know not to plant so many marigolds and beans." Of course, I am thinking, I already *knew* that! It was *you* who planted an acre of marigolds and you who must have bought the squash plant from Monsanto's lab!

But I don't dare say it because Sal would simply arch an eyebrow and say, "Fine. You do it then."

Then we'd be back to a compost bin, a bunch of flies and a box full of dirt. It is counter intuitive, I realize, but I know enough that in order to keep my mouth full, I have to keep it shut!

I am pleased to report that our garden passed muster from our local visitors. A few comments here and there from our island neighbours, but the basic evaluation, "we've done well". Everyone is in agreement that the squash has to go (it is either it or us) but, otherwise, it has been encouraging. And we learned some things. Seems planting peas is good for the garden. Who knew? And we can cut back the tomato foliage earlier to accelerate the ripening process somewhat. Wahoo! Does it get any better than that?

Worms. Are they worth it? Our garden seemed to be doing pretty well but I read somewhere that worms were a good addition. And so we got some.

I got the first batch of worms the hard way—digging. Sally and I boated over to an abandoned homestead and dug in the area that had been the garden in years gone by. We assumed correctly that there were worms there and we ferreted about until we had a handful. It is much harder than it sounds to find a good handful of worms but we thought we had enough. We went home and put them in the compost.

About a week later I poked around the compost looking for worms. They were gone! The little blighters had made a break for it and were on the lam, so to speak. It was discouraging. But I adjusted emotionally and we carried on.

This year, I was once again struck with the desire for worms but I just didn't feel like digging so I went online instead. Enter Garry the Worm Guy at www.redwormsbc.com. Garry sent me two pounds of red wrigglers by courier to a friend in town. I picked up the worms at the same time I was picking up a guest and they rode on his lap all the way home.

And today, while Sal and our guest were out gallivanting I built a worm house. Wet shredded paper on the bottom, a layer of worms and dry shredded paper on top with a bit of compost material.

"I don't think you did it right", said Sal when she came home.

"What's wrong?"

"I dunno. It just doesn't look right."

I didn't know how to respond to that. How can worms in a box look right or wrong? Was Sal a worm in a previous life? Who does she know that I don't, who is connected to the worm crowd?

"Waddya talking about?"

"All I am saying is, if they all die, it's your fault!"

So now I am worried sick. All I wanted was to have a box of happy worms.

As it turned out, she was right. Again. The worms somehow made an escape from the plastic tote that I had modified into their new digs. Pun intended. And we were wormless once again. I gave up on worms. Mostly because they gave up on me. If they come back—no questions asked—I will take them in again. But I am not holding my breath. I think we are going to have to farm sans worms.

"Oooh, what are those?" asked Sal.

Bending close to examine the garden plant in question, Laurie said, "Spit bugs!" She then picked one off and they both examined it closely.

Not noticing what Laurie did immediately thereafter, Sal asked, "Are they okay? Or do I have to get rid of them?"

"You have to get rid of them."

"Okay, fine. What do I do with them?"

Laurie looking at Sal like she was an idiot child (Sally's own words, I swear!) said, "Squish them of course!"

"Oooh, yuck!"

You can take the lady out of the city but it is hard to take the lady out of the lady. Sal has always been a bit squeamish about such things as squishing bugs, bonking fish on the head or killing mice, anything like that. And that is even when *I* am doing it. She won't even yell at the dogs. I am not one hundred percent sure that butter will melt in her mouth, to be honest. So, if we need a little ugly, she looks to me. Well, so do a lot of people, actually.

Mind you Sal has grown somewhat over the years and can now yell at me without any qualms whatsoever. I take credit for that growth. Hmm…she took to that pretty early on as I recollect. Made it look easy, too. I must be a good teacher.

This is a woman more than willing to brave the winter elements in a small boat to get to Book Club with her casserole intact. This is a woman capable of carrying and fixing small outboards, within reason, and this is a woman completely unafraid of chicken busing through El Salvador. Well, until she was actually there and doing it, that is. Then her courage waned a smidge. Along with mine, by the way. This is a woman unhindered by fear. Or common sense, sometimes, if you ask me. She's got guts.

But step on a bug? Kill a mouse? Not a chance! The point? Some things out here in rural land are a bit closer to the bone, a bit less civilized. Harsh. It can get mean out here. You just have to get your hands dirty. And sometimes they get bloody, too.

Sal will get her hands dirty. She's a trooper that way. But she is Gandhi-esque when it comes to life. Any life. She just won't take one. She just says *no*. So, I have to kill stuff.

Don't get me wrong. I am no wanton killer. I have a heart. Honest. But, I am sorry, our house is for us, the mice and ants have to live elsewhere. If they persist, they will cease to exist. You can quote me on that. Remember I once had to dispatch a mouse with the sharp end of a shovel? It wasn't pretty. But he got a decent burial. I'll go that far. It helped with my pain, if not his.

I even have no real problem bonking fish. It seems logical in a want to eat dinner kind of way. But I hate it when it takes more than two bonks. I feel like a clumsy murderer when I am bashing about the bottom of the boat and it is screaming at me in anguish. Or so I imagine. Gruesome, but I cope.

If this keeps up, I may even end up hunting a deer some day. However at the rate I'm going I'll be in my nineties. Maybe. Oooh, yuck!

Before we know it, it's time to start planning the crops again. The last of our seed catalogues has arrived and we have to order in the seed to till and plant the back forty. Feet, that is.

Talk about transplanting the yuppie view of the world, eh? We have a garden all sitting pretty in raised beds and, counting all the seed and garden catalogues that have arrived so far, we have approximately two hundred and fifty square feet of extravagantly colored printed page! That's right—three square feet of glossy catalogue for every square foot of garden. I call that the yuppie ratio—magazine coverage versus the real thing.

Given our gardening track record there is no way we can justify killing a tree to make the paper to publish the catalogue to entice us to buy the seeds that grow marigolds and the squash from hell. But the catalogues keep coming.

The yuppie ratio shows up in Lee Valley catalogues, too. I have almost enough Lee Valley catalogues to construct an Adirondack deck chair from them.

It isn't easy being a green and hip consumer, but West Coast and Vesey Seeds are trying to bridge the gap for us all. And I am going to have to build another garden box this year in an effort to justify their work. To me, this is just an exercise in exercise.

Sally is hooked, however. She pored over the latest seed catalogues, reading the write-ups on turnips, vintage grape strains, multi-hued tomatoes and heritage apples and pears, conveniently ignoring the fact that we are located on solid granite and any apple trees grown in raised beds will produce very little in the way of pie filling.

"Oooh, I think we should plant spinach and kale this year. What do you think?"

"Well, we grew kale last year and had so much we fed it to the dogs. We also grew marigolds that grew like billy-o and we didn't eat any—but at least they were pretty. And let us not forget the squash that we not only didn't eat, we were afraid to make angry! And then there were the bushels of green tomatoes that covered the living room for a week waiting to ripen that, come to think of it, I have not seen hide nor hair of since."

"They got turned into green tomato relish. But, yeah, we have to choose more carefully this time, I guess. I was just surprised that anything grew at all. It was so much fun!"

I love her attitude. But it is not a reality based one. She sees the Garden of Eden. I see a box not much larger than a coffin…beckoning. Our visions conflict.

I suspect that we'll have a mixed salad of things that we'll toil over and yet our diet will change very little. It is Save-On based, as you have probably gathered. We'll buy organic, of course, and be sure to get our produce from within one hundred miles but only a portion will come from within the nearest hundred feet. Of that, I am pretty sure. Maybe some squash. The marigolds, however, will grace the table almost all year and for that alone, it is all worth it.

-25-

Living off the Land

We are not pretenders. We are genuine off-the-gridders, real tough guys. We got our solar panels, our gumboots, our big batteries. We even got chainsaws and winches. We have our rural cred, our bona fides. Look out, you city wimps!

Well, you don't have to look out too much. Even though we are definitely in the feral zone, it is only just. We aren't newbies so much anymore, but we are still definitely sophomores—which means "more than soft" in Latin. Plenty to learn.

But good ol' Sal is keeping up the quest. Yesterday, between helping me frame a new deck extension, she started making her own bread from scratch. No bread maker for her. This was the yeast and the kneading, the rising and baking type of bread. It took a while. So did the deck. Man, it was good! (The bread, I mean. The deck still has some way to go.)

What a treat it was to come in at the end of the day. The whole house smelled of bread baking. It was like stepping back in time. Don't get me wrong, Sal *has* baked bread before. There was the five-minute instant bread that came in a Betty Crocker-type box and tasted exactly like the packaging. Once we had a bunch of loaves from some biscuit recipe that tasted like a giant biscuit—go figure. And there were the semi-baked warm and serve types that, all in all were okay, but are not quite right for the true forest dweller.

She actually did make a loaf from scratch once before. Sadly, the flour to bread ratio was not good. We had much more flour all over the house than we had in any one loaf and, with the Molly Maid cleaning service cost, all the extra laundry and the massive flour waste, her cost benefit analysis suggested continued shopping at the supermarket. We probably could have flown to Paris for baguettes, given the expense.

But not this time. This time was good. Very good. One small step up the learning curve for Sal and one giant leap for Dave's breakfast.

Living off the grid is more than actually leaving grids. It is a much larger lifestyle change than simply getting your electricity and water from a different source. The change to our daily activities has been huge and diversified. Many of our neighbours have been here for years and they are constantly surprising me with logical but unusual activities designed to make life better.

Home baked bread is just one of the steps. There are many others. Every year a number of people collect apples from their orchards and press them into juice and such. A lot of folks make jams and jellies. I've mentioned Rieko from down the way. He makes blackberry wine that is to die for. Neighbours come into our bay in the spring to collect the tops of nettle plants which provide fresh spinach-like greens early in the season.

Berries, both wild and cultivated, are picked in season, especially by the winemakers. There are wild mushrooms, of course, but Sal and I are leery of picking the wrong ones so that is left to a few old hands mostly. There are wild onions and other edibles that we might recognize, book in hand, but there are many more that we don't.

We do utilize a bit of seaweed now and then. And, of course, some of our friends and neighbours have fabulous orchards and gardens so, in that sense, we benefit from the bounty of the land.

There's prawning and gathering clams, oysters and mussels, and fishing, of course. I often hear of someone taking a deer in the fall. And chickens are common, though layers are preferred over roasters. And, while there is a cost saving, all this is motivated as much by the health aspect of it. And the taste of things! Many folks have made it a lifestyle choice to fish, hunt and gather, grow and do their own processing. The most productive amongst us could likely survive off the land for a considerable time, if not indefinitely.

Us? Not so much. We still shop. It used to be once a week, then every two weeks, and now we are averaging once every three weeks without any hardship, except a few minor shortages of dairy and some fresh veggies, mostly.

Still, I do not think we will ever rise too high on the off the grid status charts. There simply is not enough time. The good ones just know too much. They can do so much. They are just incredibly amazing at all this stuff—we will never catch up.

One thing we have learned about is prawning. Pulling prawn traps by hand is not so hard. The traps seem to weigh a lot when they are down deep, though, and the rope feels rough on soft, flabby hands like mine but the reward is usually well worth the effort. If there *is* a reward.

And therein is the real obstacle to prawning: coming up empty. It is so discouraging to strain one's poor little hands and back and not get some reward, spoiled brat that I am. Disney taught me that if I try *real* hard, I should get some prawns. Like the Little Fisherman that Could. Sadly, that is not always the case.

But neighbour John got an electric prawn trap puller and I get to use it. All I can say is dem prawns better look out! Now I can drop and lift prawn traps on a whim. Oooh…it is exciting! The worst case scenario is disappointment but *without* sore muscles. Of course, it does get better than that, but saving my back is a close second.

There is no denying the primal satisfaction that one gets from bringing home the bacon unless, of course, one is not allowed to eat bacon anymore. Prawns are the new bacon.

As I get older I get almost as much pleasure thinking about stuff I used to do, or am planning to do someday in the future, as in actually doing it. I figure it's nature's way of keeping older people safe. Don't get me wrong. I don't mind a bit of a walk, a few scrapes and a prick or two from the blackberry thorns. That's okay. That's where my macho kicks in. But when you hike and hike and sweat and fall down and get dirty and then you get bitten by mosquitoes and it's hot and everything…and you forgot your water bottle…and then there are no berries. Well, that's when my macho runs dry. And my tears run wet.

And so it is with most of this foraging, gathering, hunting thing. The fruits of my labour don't have to be as easily gotten as store-bought but they shouldn't be so hard to get that blood, sweat or tears are required in any way whatsoever. One ounce of effort should get two ounces of blackberries or the equivalent in prawns. It's only fair!

Fishing is the ultimate example of a pastime in need of some fair play. If I could get my gear, launch the boat and head off, drop my line and return home with a couple of fish within say, an hour or maybe two, then fishing is okay. Not great, but definitely fair. I could choose to play or not, based on that time versus reward ratio.

For it to be really great, the salmon would have to jump into the boat and clean themselves but they are just not that cooperative. But if you have to go to town to get your license and the motor doesn't start and, after several weeks spent bored out of your gourd with considerable skin loss due to peeling sunburn and you don't have one damn fish to show for it (been there)…well, the whole thing is just stupid, isn't it? And one thing should be clear by now: I ain't stupid. Right?

John dropped prawn traps for us yesterday before he left for his city home. We'll pull them and then reset them as needed. He'll be back to take over again in a few days. It was a nice gesture. But we weren't too excited. The prawning has been poor.

Usually we just set a couple of traps that have provided enough for a few meals and we are content with that. Better the prawns should have fun and stay fresh down there while we have pizza or chicken, or whatever. We'll call on them when the occasion requires it.

Last year, with guests and all, we went through about three hundred prawns. That's individual prawns, not pounds. It was plenty. Sal makes a mean prawn linguini in cream sauce and they are always good with garlic butter or sea food sauce as an appetizer. I sometimes make prawn sushi with avocado slices. I think of prawns like I do bacon—more than a garnish, less than an entrée.

And we needed a few entrées. So, we did a town day lite today. Just over to the next island. We ambled over, did our thing and ambled back. Then we went to pull the traps.

The first trap came up empty but for a single prawn. The next one on the string increased the haul to about a dozen. We were in one of the best areas at the beginning of the season. This was not good.

We went to the next string and started to haul. The traps were not coming up right. It is hard to say what pulling a weight from the depths is supposed to feel like, but I had done it enough to know that there was something wrong. I imagined that there were octopi in there.

We kept pulling and eventually I could see a problem as the traps came up. They were tangled. Each trap was ensnared with the other. It was a jumble of traps. Of course, we kept pulling. We had to clear the tangle at the very least.

But as they came up, we began to see prawns in the traps. Within the next few minutes we had filled a five gallon bucket! Three hundred and fifty prawns! Almost our legal limit. All of them captured in a pile, a jumble, a veritable rat's nest of nets and ropes. Wow! A new prawning technique!

When we were done processing the little sweeties, we had our year's supply! It was a good day.

Big salmon are jumping out in the channel. Guessing from the glimpses I get as they leap, I think fifteen pounders, maybe larger. Every year about this time the chums come and they seem to congregate for a week or so right in front of our house. It's wonderful.

We can't catch them, though. Firstly, one cannot fish our channel. It is closed to fin fishing. The law says. Secondly, you can't catch a salmon, even in an open area, without a special addition to your fishing license issued (for a cost) just for a salmon. Ordinary fishing licenses aren't good enough. The law says. And thirdly, neither Sally nor I are any good at catching fish. Fishing, for us, is boring and unproductive. We just sit there and complain about losing fishing gear. We don't like any part of it. And we're really bad at it. So we don't usually do it.

But it makes no difference, our preferences. The chums don't bite at this point in their life cycle as they get ready to head up the rivers to spawn. They leap, they play and they congregate, but they don't have the munchies. Then they are gone.

The seals don't have to obey the law. So they try and eat salmon even in the closed sections. And they do seem to have a knack for it. The other day, a seal and a large salmon broke the surface of the water fully engaged in a life battle over who gets dinner. The seal had the upper hand but the salmon was so large it was flipping the seal about as the struggle ensued.

Lots of thrashing at the surface but, eventually the seal succeeded and likely took home a doggy bag (another name for chum is dog salmon).

Salmon, it seems, are in danger. But what isn't? Seems the world is on the precipice of an environmental end game according to everything I read and hear. And I believe it. Certainly the climate change people have been proven right. And that has to have implications all over the place. I guess we are doomed. This summer we had close to sixty straight days without rain. It was a record. What a concept, eh—the rain forest without rain.

Our town day lite was a while back so we were a bit overdue for restocking the larder. Supplies were running out.

"What are we going to do for dinner?" Sal asked, "I'm down to reruns and chicken."

"I sure feel like clam chowder. Want to get some clams?"

So, off we went down to the little lagoon right behind our house. It is a steep climb down under the highline and we had strung ropes to use as hand holds to assist us in getting up and down. The lagoon dries when the tide is about halfway out but, at this time of the year, halfway is about as far as it goes. Our window for harvesting was only an hour or so.

The wind was blowing briskly overhead and the wind turbine whined in the near distance. It was the sound of money in the bank and the bank was our batteries.

We clambered down with a couple of plastic buckets and a rake. The two dogs, optimistically carrying a toy each, joined us. Usually the lagoon means play time for them but today they were ignored. Well, as much as two dogs intent on playing can be.

I dug. Sally picked. And we threw the odd toy for the dogs. And within a half hour we had enough clams to make a voluminous batch of clam chowder. It would be enough for three hearty meals.

But the sea had kindly offered up another gift—this time of seaweed. There was a loose carpet of the stuff strewn about so we returned to scoop up a few bucketfuls for the garden. We heaved ourselves up the hill picking our way carefully and using the ropes for assistance while carrying heavy buckets and hand tools. Like Sherpas, only with much more grunting and heavy breathing.

When we returned to the house for tea, the raven was waiting for an afternoon treat and we obliged him. Sal made tea and we sat in the sun watching the clouds shoot by and the odd boat shoot by faster.

As we consciously use more and more local, fresh, wild and free food we are also using less and less processed, packaged and wrapped food. The last time Sal went grocery shopping she remarked, "I never would have imagined that I would be missing not only complete aisles, but I would actually only be shopping around the outside edge of the store! More and more I am simply *not* buying what is on offer. Boy, have our eating habits changed!"

Which is good news. Living off the grid is to prefer the journey over the destination and we are enjoying ourselves no end. The homemade bread and jam? A magnificent bonus!

The author on Wasabi (prawn boat, lumber barge, pleasure craft and everything in between)

-26-

Burping the Fridge

There is a disconnect in the modern world of consumer products. You may know what I am talking about…

We have delegated much of our previously domestic manufacturing to countries overseas. Then the associated customer service for those products has been outsourced to *other* countries. Naturally, that country doesn't speak the same language as the manufacturer's or the customer's. Everyone involved is on separate continents. Apparently it's so much easier this way.

Our fridge is a propane gas unit made in a plant in South Africa. Their head office is in Johannesburg. The Canadian distributor is in New Brunswick. Customer service is in New Delhi. Logic and sanity? That must be on another planet.

It is a ten cubic foot Zero (*not* Sub-Zero) but, being African, it seemed a bit foreign to us at first. For instance, there is no light when you open the door. I was at first disappointed by this lack of convenience until it occurred to me that the light would have to be powered by propane and thus defeat the purpose of the fridge. Anyway, it's dark in there.

It also sports door locks. And, of course, a set of keys came with it. This perplexed Sally and me to no end. Why would we lock our fridge? Why would anyone lock their fridge? Was it in response to the greatly exaggerated tendency of children to play hide and seek in abandoned refrigerators? Had that game caught on big somewhere? Where was UNICEF in all this? The fridge took on ominous vibrations.

Then we thought that maybe the locks were about keeping others from getting at the food? But that made little sense. If you had the money to buy a fridge, presumably you were wealthy enough to fill it now and then. And if it was to keep others from getting at the food, then what were they doing there?

We finally concluded that the fridge was designed for people with eating disorders. That made so much sense to my wife that she is now tempted to lock the fridge and not give me the key.

The fridge worked just fine for two years and, since it is an evaporation-type fridge without moving parts, it seemed almost impossible for something to go wrong. But of course it did. And the evidence was pungent.

When the fridge stopped working it was a gradual process. At first it seemed a bit less cool—but isn't that true for everything after a time? And then we started to lose a bit of food to spoilage and it became obvious that it was evolving into a warming oven.

I called the distributor and was put through to Akbar who skillfully and technically described the fridge's system and the likely problems. He also advised getting in a good gas fitter familiar with such devices. Failing that, he advised taking the fridge in to the nearest repair depot. He politely asked me what country I was calling from and, perhaps not recognizing the name I gave him (Canada), suggested San Diego.

I came to like Akbar but felt the need to point out that items intended for remote cabin applications are likely situated a considerable distance from urban repair centres and San Diego, in particular, threatened even more inconvenience than, in fact, the broken fridge.

This was a surprise for him. But he is not alone. There are seemingly millions of telephone technicians who have never heard of British Columbia. They can program my mobile phone (made in Finland) but don't know that Canada, the second largest country on the planet, even exists.

Sadly, the conversations I have with many suppliers whose products challenge me are consistently illogical. I am expected to understand the programming of the washing machine's software, as explained to me by a techie in Calcutta, but the idea that I could be living remotely on the British Columbia coast is unfathomable to them.

I may have developed a bit of tone with Akbar during our call. In an effort to appease me, and in accordance with policy and procedure, he referred me to his supervisor as if, somehow, the repair job had just become more difficult. I'm sure the truth is he thought that *I* had become more difficult. I bade him goodbye with "Allahu Akbar!" and waited for his supervisor, Abu.

I began to think I might be on a watch list somewhere. You see, for reasons of quality assurance, all of my conversations with corporations these days are recorded. Apparently, it's for my own protection. I must be a verbal danger to someone. Since I do not live in the city and I am quick to adopt *tone*, I am assumed to be a risk. I try to remain calm but I often fail. Hopefully, I am categorized as just a level one threat. After all, I am four thousand miles away and no one understands me anyway. I imagine a yellow bulb flashing somewhere whenever I get on the phone to a big corporation.

Abu, after checking out all my numbers and mother's maiden name (for security reasons, of course) echoed Akbar's suggestion that I bring the unit in to the nearest affiliated and authorized repair depot.

"No can do. I am now verging on being suicidal and I have gas at my disposal. Help me fix it or I'll martyr myself!"

I could feel a shift in the mood. I was talking his language. We bonded. In fact, he showed concern for my condition.

"I wouldn't advise anyone living remote to become a martyr by blowing oneself up, sir. Perhaps you would consider moving to an American city first?"

Sometimes, of course, the technicians are indeed helpful. Abu was there for me. Under his tutelage I took the apparatus apart and cleaned it as instructed and reattached the burner to the gas line and fired the puppy up. A beautiful blue flame enthralled us both, but to no avail. It was warmer inside the fridge now than it was in the house.

Most technicians, it seems, believe that, if at first you don't succeed, you should repeat the process until it dawns on you that you are doing it wrong. And so I did the same thing two more times. Both the fridge and I got warmer. I could feel Abu growing more distant.

Then I remembered an old myth I'd heard about turning one's fridge upside down. I seemed to recall that old gas fridges sometimes suffered from coolant separation anxiety, or something like that, and they needed comforting by being turned topsy-turvy for a while. I have a friend like that, come to think of it.

I asked Abu about it and he said, “Well, it’s true. We call it burping the fridge. It’s a last resort but worth a try. Turn it upside down for five minutes and then right it. Leave it for a bit and repeat the process.”

It worked!

Then there was the composting toilet I, and my friends, had heavily invested in, if you’ll pardon the allusion, that didn’t seem to want to compost. It proved reluctant for several months. This is a disappointing, if not disturbing, situation. You see, it is necessary for the submitted material to compost for it to be removed. If it doesn’t compost, it piles up and turns into a solid mass of significant unpleasantness. If this happens, you have to remove the deposits by reaching your hand into the composter and scooping the unpleasantness out. There is no other way. Trust me.

I called the toilet help line (what a name to answer the phone with, eh?) and spoke with Tandoori. After ensuring that I was the legitimate composting toilet owner that I said I was, for security and recording reasons, she ran me through a toilet checklist. I passed it all, if you’ll pardon the wording. Then she asked if it was more than fifty-five degrees where I lived.

“Sometimes.”

“Well, sir, the composting doesn’t work very well below fifty-five degrees Fahrenheit and not at all below fifty degrees.”

“But, this is a Sun-Mar. It’s made and sold in Canada! There are only a precious few square miles in the whole country that average above freezing, let alone fifty-five degrees!”

“Yes, sir, I know. Have you considered moving to San Diego?”

It was interesting to note at the time of my composting difficulties that the actual toilet didn’t function all that well either. It was of the one-pint flush variety. Basically that means you flush five times. So, I mentioned that to Tandoori, too. I was referred to another country and another 1-800 number.

Sarambah answered. She listened politely to the problem of seepage around the base of the toilet and asked, “Do you or anyone in your family weigh more than three hundred pounds?”

Of course, she was polite (we were being recorded) and put the question as delicately as she could, but my imagination was working overtime. I began laughing. And I asked her if she or any of her family weighed over three hundred pounds and, if so, did their toilet leak?

And so I was referred to her supervisor who, naturally, first took me through the security process. Then she confided, "You see, sir, some people put additional strain on the gaskets. We have a heavy-duty replacement seal kit we can send you but we are trying to confirm that it is a weight related problem."

I've described myself as dense but I'm not that dense. I knew enough to give up.

Maintenance issues are not restricted to appliances. I got a flat tire on my little utility trailer that I park on the adjacent island where we park our vehicle. No big deal. Get in boat, go to neighboring island, remove wheel, replace with spare, take wheel and tire into repair shop. Simple plan. No problem.

Hah!

The first time I go over, I can't remove the bolts that hold the wheel on. The tools don't quite fit right. But, that's okay. I'll just bring more tools next time I come. Wisdom. Patience. Attitude.

I go back another day with enough tools to fix a D-9 Caterpillar Tractor. Remaining calm, I get a wrench and extension and apply my Incredible Hulk bulk to the effort and snap the tool in half. Now I know why they are called Snap-On.

Quick. Get back to meditation, do not pass go…ommmm…ignore blood on knuckles as it is not a positive element to have one's life force leaving the building…ommmm…

Consider options. There is another way, of course. Take chainsaw and heavy sledge. Beat the crap out of the trailer and push remains into the bush. A simple plan. A smidge un-Zen-like.

A mature person would simply go back a third time and try something else and so I will do that as soon as I get mature enough to be able to think of something else.

But, really, it's not about the trailer, is it? No, it is about me. It is always about me. What did I do to deserve this?

Seriously, it is not about me nor is it about the trailer. It is really just another small vignette in the life of one who lives off the grid. Living off the grid also means that my car lives off the grid, too. It lives remote on another island—off another grid. Leave a cell phone in the car? Forget to lock it? Need a thingy from the glove compartment? Well, no quick thing, that. You are a boat ride and a steep hike away from it.

Take the wrong tool? Well, that is another hour or more now, isn't it? The next one doesn't work? Poor baby. Looking at even more hours, hikes and boat rides now, aren't we?

Breathe. Think good thoughts. Ommmm…push chainsaw image from mind…these things are sent to challenge us, butterfly. Be one with the wheel nuts. It will come…so, I look for Butterfly Towing in the yellow pages…

Finally the wheel nuts came off. As did the flat tire. And then, of course, the spare tire went on and so did the wheel nuts. It was easy.

And that was because John did it. He heard me whinging about my challenge and graciously offered to help.

"Ya stupid git! How come you can't take a tire off when you can build a house?"

"Well, it seems a bit foolish but, like, I snapped my ratchet extension in the process and that kinda suggests the nuts have been put on too tight, don't you think?"

"No such thing. Never met a nut I couldn't loosen. Well, there's you, I suppose. Come on, let's go do it."

I grabbed my ratchet and a few sockets, some WD40 and the little car jack. "I'm ready!"

"What the hell are those things? Toys? Is that a three-eighths inch drive? You need half inch and a longer handle, for gawd's sake, man! No wonder you didn't get it. This is a real vehicle, we are talkin'. Not some damn bicycle repair!"

He goes into his shop, gets a ratchet that could double as a baseball bat and one socket, a three-quarter inch.

"Uh, John, I don't think it's a three quarter inch nut. I worked a five-eighth inch socket on the wheel nuts and it gripped up pretty tight. That was the socket that snapped my extension. It was definitely on!"

"Nope, it's three-quarters. I saw it once as you drove by last year over in Campbell River. It's three-quarters. I have no idea how in hell you got a five-eighths on."

So with me shaking my head and him as confident as ever, we went over to the next island.

John popped the three-quarter inch socket onto the first nut, attached the official ratchet of the National Baseball League and, with a deft hand, undid it as if it were bedded in butter. It was embarrassing.

"I have to tell her."

"Tell who?"

"Sal. I gotta tell her. Damn. This will be tough."

"Don't tell her. This can be on a need to know basis. I won't tell her. Well, I probably won't, anyway."

"Never mind, I will. Sheesh. Man can't loosen his own nuts. Sounds bad. Real bad. Still, it's in keeping with my life. Screwing up twice before getting it done right."

"Dave, little girls can change flat tires. You can't make this work in any way except to look like an imbecile. Honest. If I were you, I'd just leave this episode off the record. Your reputation is in enough trouble. You don't need this. Mind you, I will probably have to tell all my friends so it'll get out one way or the other."

"One way or the other? There is only one way and that is you!"

"Well, they say confession is good for the soul. Hell on one's image, though."

Sometimes maintenance can be a pleasure. Like when Morris is involved. He's a welder a ways down Vancouver Island who specializes in woodstove repair. Morris is extraordinary in his own way. He is a real human being who has a good heart, a smart brain and a deep interest in, of all things, woodstoves. And the people who love them. The man has been in the business for over twenty-five years and speaks of baffles and vents, chimneys and bricks, different gauges of steel and various techniques for welding with the enthusiasm of a sixteen year old boy with his first Playboy magazine.

We've never met.

When our stove needed a rebuild, I called a number on a business card and talked with Morris. I explained our situation and, of course, the challenge of having to drive by his place during the business day on our way south and of having similar time constraints when returning home. Both such times he would be at work.

"No problem. Drop it off at my house and pick it up a few days later on your way back. I'll leave it just outside my garage. It'll be safe."

We did. It was. And not only was it fixed, it was better than new. That was three years ago. The other day I called and left another message which he returned.

"Oh, you're the guy on the island, right? You have the Artisan model that I fixed by beefing up the side rails and a few other things."

We spent the next hour discussing stoves, possible improvements, my learning to weld, what type of welder to buy and I even received an offer of a few hours of lessons from him when I get one.

Sally said, "You spent more time on the phone talking to a guy you have never met about the insides of a stove than I do in a whole week of conversations with my friends!"

"Well, that says more about you and your friends than it does about the fascinating world of wood stoves."

Now, generators are a mixed blessing. They are noisy and go through fuel, but when the sun lets us down we are happy to have backup. The reliable old Honda 2000 had a frayed starter cord. I used to ignore those things. "No sense fixin' it if it ain't broke, eh," I'd say, just oozing that air of country wisdom. And I meant it, too. But that is just procrastination with charm, really. And then there's the old proverb that makes much more sense: A stitch in time saves nine.

I could have taken the generator into the Honda dealership in town but that would have entailed transporting it by boat and car and then picking it up again a few months later. Worse, I'd be a couple of hundred dollars lighter at the very least. I have long opted to go it alone on this sort of thing. Anyway, how hard can it be to replace a starter cord?

A Honda 2000 looks like a big red bar of soap. But it has screws and bolts, tabs and slots, clips and cinches, just like the rest of us. I've been getting past clips and cinches since I was sixteen. Nothing to it.

But I checked it out on the internet just to be sure. And of course it isn't as easy as it looks. I had to print out a page of instructions. I won't bore you with the sequence of events but suffice to say, Sally and I worked on that little genset all afternoon and we didn't waste a move. Well, maybe one or two, like when Sal dropped a bolt under the deck. But, basically, we just followed the steps, put the parts in a little container, replaced the cord with a piece we found from our odds and sods and then reversed the steps to put it back together. Piece of cake.

But there were dozens of steps! Honest to gawd, I could remove your appendix with fewer steps. Fewer tools, too. You see, the whole generator has to come apart. Obviously gensets don't get made into neat little bar of soap-like packages and still allow you easy access to them. We took off the feet, the sides, the ends and the fuel tank and moved all the wiring. Then we took off the pull cord assembly. Plus of course we had to do this with bolts and pins that were rusted.

One bolt, the little blighter, was so tough I had to drill right through it, use an easy-out to bring out the remains of the bolt and then find another metric (wouldn't you know) bolt to replace it. No big deal but not a twenty minute task. But it impressed Sal. That's pretty good after forty plus years.

Living off the grid means using what you have on hand, making do or doing without. It doesn't mean dealerships. It doesn't even always mean getting parts from the parts supply. And it sure as hell doesn't mean knowing what you are doing. It *is* kinda fun—especially when it works out.

Parsley, basil, mint, rosemary and other garden herbs

-27-

Healthcare or Self Care

When I was younger the doctor I was seeing asked me about my family history. Illnesses, hereditary conditions, that sort of thing.

So I asked my mom, “Do we have any history of heart disease in the family?”

“No dear.” she smiled.

But then I got to thinking. “What was it that Aunt Hilda died from?”

“Well, she had a heart attack, dear.”

“And Auntie Joan?”

“Well, that was a heart attack.”

“Uncle Sammy? Gwyneth? Grandpa?”

“They were heart attacks, too, dear.”

“What do you *mean*, we have no history of heart disease?”

“We don’t, sweetie. There was no history. It was just bam! They dropped dead on the spot!”

And so it goes in my family. Which brings me to my actual point. A lot of people ask, “Geez, what if you need a doctor out there in the boonies? Or you have an emergency?”

I *have* needed emergency care several times in my life. Playing sports, feeling invulnerable and driving fast will sometimes do that to you. I can’t remember a time when I got prompt service in the city. I cut off one of my toes during a motorcycle race at about ten in the morning, and it was sewn back on that same day at midnight. I sat in the emergency ward for over twelve hours. Almost had enough time to grow another toe.

When I got run over by the outboard out in the boonies, at one o’clock in the afternoon, I was transported to the local hospital by helicopter, arriving less than two hours after the accident occurred. I was patched up and caught the ferry back home early that same evening.

But I don't think the subject of health care begins at the hospital. Frankly, I am beginning to think it is more likely to end there, but that's another topic. I think health care begins at home. And we eat right, exercise all day long and watch a lot of documentary films and no television. That's got to be healthy, right?

I guess what I'm saying is that health is not a major issue for us, despite having the basic malfunctions of average sixty plus year olds. We try to make it that way by thinking that way. Of course, sometimes an issue has to be faced and it is likely that will arise with more frequency as we age. That's life. But Sal and I have chosen to deal with concerns when they arise, not to live in anticipation of their arrival. That may just be a form of denial but I think healthy living is often attitudinal and living with the right attitude, we think, is half the battle.

We all assume that living in the country means living simpler, minimalist and hardier lifestyles. Tanned faces, harder muscles, a better diet with less junk food, that sort of thing. We believe it *is* healthier. And so it has seemingly been proven these past few years as I have weathered visibly, rediscovered the odd muscle and hardly bought a stitch of new clothing. I have come to think of myself, in comparative terms anyway, as being physically better than I was because I am now craggy where before I was saggy. Admittedly, I am also raggedy but there are few who notice.

But I am beginning to have second thoughts about the health benefits of so much hard work. I am so much more active that I ache all over. My back has been sore for months. And, worse, dirt seems to be accumulating in the newly formed crags. There is no question I am pushing the building envelope (mine) and some parts are beginning to protest. For instance, I have inexplicably become selectively hard of hearing whenever hard work is mentioned. "Huh? You talking to me? Can't hear you!"

Having said all that healthy stuff, we still go see the doctor every so often. Dentist, too. More and more the optometrist and, when I can afford it, the massage therapist. It all helps to keep the old rig on the road. But all that maintenance can be done by appointment and we simply make such appointments for town days. Or try to.

"Mr. Cox, what is your address?"

"You want to come over?"

"*No*! No, thank you. It is just that I have never even heard of this place. Where is it?"

"Remote island up the coast. Ferries, logging roads, small boats. Isolated, lonely, dangerous. Adventure, bears, wolves. Hunting deer to survive..."

"Wow, really? You live in the forest?"

"Yup. The truth is that it is a bit more civilized than I just made out. We do have satellite internet and a cell phone. There *are* wolves, though, and bears. But we buy groceries at the grocery store, so it's not that wild. And I'm sorry, but I have a wife already."

"What…? Well, that's good for you, I'm sure! She must be some kind of woman! That lifestyle is pretty cool, I guess. My boyfriend would like it, but me, I like going to restaurants, shopping and my spin class and stuff. It sounds too rough for me. Now…can you come in one day next week at nine in the morning?"

"Well, I can if I have to. But you see…as I live remote it takes hours just to get to town. It works best for me if I can get an appointment around noon. Can we do that?"

"Oh, gee. The doctor has lunch at noon. How about later in the day at around four? I can fit you in at ten past four on the seventeenth? The examination takes an hour and a half. You'll be the last patient."

"Well, I can do that, if it's all you have. But you see I would like to get home while there is still light. It's much safer than boating in the dark. Could I see the doctor after lunch? I don't care how far in the future we have to go to get a one o'clock appointment but that would work best for me, if it's possible."

"Wow! How do you get anything done in town?"

"That's why I have a wife! Oh, relax! I am only kidding. The key is not to try to get too much done—shopping is about all. No visiting. No browsing. Or we *can* do all that if we stay the night. But it's best for us to minimize our expectations and maximize our pace. We try to hit the ground running. Summertime is easier. The light evenings allow us to get home later. But the window for safe travel in winter is small. Plus we have dogs to feed."

"Ooh! Doggies! I love dogs. What breed are they?"

Receptionists. What's not to like?

Let me tell you. I wanted to make an appointment with another doctor on a day I had to be in town for other reasons.

"I'm sorry but on that day the doctor does walk-ins only. No appointments. You'll have to come in and wait."

"Well, I can do that for a couple of hours but I live remote and, if the appointment is late, I have to come home in the dark in a small boat. If I come in early, will I get in before say, three o'clock?"

"Sorry. Walk-in is walk-in. No appointments means no appointments." The conversation was over. So I didn't go.

A few weeks later we were in town on the same day of the week and so I went to the walk-in. I got there about noon and thought I had a good chance to see the doc before three.

"Sorry, your doctor is on appointments only today. Dr. Smith is doing walk-ins. Would you like to see Dr. Smith?"

"Well, I didn't get to see my doctor last time I was here because it was walk-in and now it's a different doctor. Do you have a rule book or something? Or is it just a crapshoot for health care you have going on here?"

That didn't sit well with the receptionist so she looked away and dialed the phone. Security, perhaps. I chose to leave. In fact, I have never returned. Fortunately for me, and many other outer islanders, Doctor Mary, new to the area from California, chose to provide service to us *on our island* every two weeks—amazing!

Another health care service provided on the island is flu vaccinations every fall. Two public health nurses come for a day and try to flog vaccines on a paranoid rural subset of humanity. They have encounters. I decided to be one of them. It's fun acting like a curmudgeon from the sticks.

"Wouldn't be doing this if it weren't for the wife. She's the big cheese. Still, I don't like what the government is offering. It's all a trick, you know. You gals have trouble sleeping at night knowing that you are injecting that nanorobot, mind control chip technology into people? Or did they inject you two first and now you think it's all good?"

"Uh, sir, you don't have to have the inoculation. It's a public service."

"So they say. But I hear tell them nano-things are in all of us nowadays. The only real reason to get another shot is to get your nano-things updated, like an update from Microsoft. Once you are in the system, you gotta keep up or else your programming will go all whacked. That's where Alzheimer's comes from. Old people forget to update. We're all programmed by Bill Gates!"

By this time their professionalism is kicking in and they are going with the flow.

"Yes, sir, but you are aware Bill and Melinda are into eradicating diseases, right? And so this may just be part of that plan. Now that would be good, wouldn't it?"

She says that with a lovely smile in an obvious effort to keep the patient calm and relatively relaxed while she and her assistant start doing their task with amazing speed. They are going to keep this encounter brief.

I take another tack.

"Can I have this shot in my butt? I get to drop my drawers and bend over? It's always more fun that way."

"*No!*" They say in unison, getting worried looks on their faces and working even faster.

Shelley, one of my neighbours, shows up just then.

"If you want one of them nano-probes here, Shelley, you gotta get neckid first. These here nurses want to see you in your altogether 'fore they'll stick you with the new technology. Don't you worry about me, I won't look."

The nurses fix me with cold stare and a sharp jab and tell Shelley that it is not necessary to disrobe and that I am just some sort of trouble maker.

"Can't I get the shot in my butt?" Shelley asks, "It's always more fun that way."

Welcome to the country.

Bergamot is an herb. It's named for a Spanish botanist, Nicholas Monardes. You'd think the plant would be called Monardes then, wouldn't you? And it is called Monarda when referenced formally. Like at black tie plant conferences. But usually it is called Bergamot and sometimes Bee Balm and it is used to make tea, attract butterflies and hummingbirds to the garden and otherwise add some colour to one's life. It is also used in solution to treat certain kinds of dermatitis.

Wormwood refers to various plants of the genus Artemisia but most commonly Artemisia absinthium. It seems to grow just about everywhere in the world and is used in many cultures. When brewed into a tea, it acts as a digestive tonic effective in dealing with everything from stomach ache to diarrhea.

There are many more herbs used as medicine, of course. I am sure many readers have personal experiences they could relate. And I could recite quite a few more. But the point of making mention of it is that both those herbs have been in recent use around here.

Sal and I both needed a bit of wormwood remedy during a stint in Central America. We found some in an open air market in Guatemala and used it to brew a foul tasting tea while we were there. It worked wonders.

Much to our surprise, one of our local friends, Judith, grows and processes the little tummy cleanser and she gave us a supply of homemade capsules (much more pleasant to ingest than the tea) when we got home. Our minor parasites were, in a sense, disemboweled and laid to waste.

Sal also recently developed a minor itch on her hands and so into the Bee Balm solution she dove. After one dip, much of the itch was eased. Resolution was achieved with a few more treatments.

A few years back, I was suffering from some muscle related pain and another local lady, Lise, came over with tincture of Arnica for a compress that worked a miracle on bruises and sore muscles.

Using herbs and wild things has been integrated into the health practices of this community for a considerable time. And some of us (well, us, not so much) are pretty good at it. I am always amazed at the various and effective herbal cures suggested and made available to me when the need is voiced.

Alternative medicine? Not really. Using herbs in the form of compresses, tinctures, balms, teas and even as ingredients in meals is as old as time. This so-called alternative medicine is really the tried and true, basic and initial medicine. But how many people still do it? I think the farther people live from conventional medicine the more they rely on such things.

Whenever we had an ailment in the city, we went to the doctor. We sat politely until well after our appointed time and then described our problem to the disinterested professional in thirty seconds or less. Then we left with a prescription for an industrialized, packaged and expensive drug. Or, on occasion, had an organ removed. I think that is now the common approach for most people.

But here's the thing. We can often treat ourselves better than a doctor who is challenged by time and interest. For minor ailments, such as stomach upsets, burns, cuts, aches and pains, I tend to know my own body better than they do. Oh, I know they have more Latin names for my parts but I know them by old familiar nicknames and, anyway, a nose by any other name is still a nose.

I guess what I am saying is this. There is an alternative to running to the doctor for everything. And there is an added bonus. I don't have to travel. I don't have to wait. And I don't pay the pharmacist. Okay, occasionally I have to sacrifice a goat during the full moon but, still, it is way better than sitting in a germ infested waiting room.

But life happens. And so do heart attacks and other horrors. Some of our neighbours have set a pretty high standard on how to deal with those unpleasant events. They basically just carry on. One fella had the equivalent of a bomb go off in his chest and, though his convalescence has been lengthy, it has been evident and progressive. He is still going like a train. Possibly a slower train, but chugging along, nevertheless. Cancer, kidney malfunctions, weird diseases, major trauma…we see it all…but usually folks come back home and keep on truckin'. That is a very good thing.

And I can't help but think that the circumstances that might otherwise finish many people off are kept at bay, somewhat, by living out here. Each day just feels healthier. And I think it is.

I guess what I am saying is something like this. Instead of taking two aspirins and calling your doctor in the morning, sometimes a weekend (or better yet, a life) in the forest is what should be prescribed.

Inlet Transporter bringing us fuel

-28-

Freedom's Not Just Another Word

It seems that Freedom is not so much "nothing left to lose" as it is a function of social constraints or, perhaps, just grey matter gone gooey. Get away from peer group pressure in the city, from neighbours who practically live on top of you and from the accepted and expected norms of behaviour and you will, unfortunately for your spouse and family, find your true nature. Being truly yourself can be a surprising thing. As my brother-in-law once put it, after a visit, "Rural people aren't nuts, they are just being themselves—to the max."

The people who live out here in the forest *are* free to be themselves and many of them have taken to it like a lemming does a cliff. They are certainly eccentric, if not over the edge. Some are complete loons. And, of course, in the spirit of being politically correct, there is nothing wrong with that.

Mind you, my opinion on what is goofy behaviour is also changing the longer I live out here. I guess I am becoming myself. Apologies to all. I have shifted from conventional Statistics Canada poster boy-type thinking to contemplating the alternative wild and crazy theories of life, diet, economics, politics, weather and the media, just to name the current top six. These topics are normally raised over a cheap bottle of plonk by my new friends and neighbours, without any unnecessary prodding. I think I am slowly being converted. I used to just laugh and laugh when they talked their nonsense to me. Now, I take notes.

There are a lot of eccentric behaviours exhibited in this community. For instance, you have no idea about fad diets until you have met some of our more outlandish citizens. They will eat anything it seems, except what you'd expect.

Phil the Fruitarian showed up at our place for a visit and announced that he was a fruitarian and had been for years.

"What's a fruitarian?" I asked.

"I only eat fish and berries—like the bears."

"Phil, bears are omnivorous, like humans. They'll eat anything. Anyway, I'm sorry to tell you that all we have to offer you is a ham sandwich, homemade apple pie and a cold coke."

"Oh! Well, that will be fine, thanks." He cleaned his plate and took a coke to go.

Will is a strict vegetarian but we were serving barbecued steaks when he dropped by. I had cooked eight of them for the six invited. No problem. Will ate both the "extra" steaks. Presumably he went back to being a vegetarian the next day. He was no freeloader, mind you. He contributed soymilk and a bottle of Omega Three essential oils to the dinner. A bar of carob-based "chocolate" was added to the dessert tray. A little known fact: vegetarians like Scotch!

Janice came for a weekend. She only eats raw. That's right…as in uncooked. She chowed down on fresh veggies and cheese. I didn't have the heart to tell her about pasteurization.

Circle Dave is beyond eccentric. Having said that, he is amongst the most pleasant of companions and is genuinely welcomed wherever and whenever he shows up. I like him. He's fun in a "where is this heading?" kind of way. One day he appeared at our place.

"Hey Circle Dave, good to see you. How did you get here without a boat?"

"Well," he said with a huge grin, "that depends. Where am I?"

"You are here! At Dave and Sal's. How could you get here without a boat?"

"Good question. My boat sank last week. I launched it at the boat ramp but I forgot to put the plug in and it just kept going down. It sank with all my stuff in it. I was so discouraged I left it there and went home."

"I'm really sorry to hear that, but how did you get here? You need a boat to get here. Work with me on this, Dave. Think hard. Got boat?"

"I must have!" he said laughing, "I think it's down at the dock. I must have walked over from there. Ha, ha! How could I get here without a boat?" He was looking at me as if I were mad.

We had some tea and a nice visit before he went back over the hill to the dock and to who knows what conveyance.

But the really eccentric notions are saved for politics and economics. On those topics, we reside in the Conspiracy Centre of the World. Well, as much as you can, given that there is already a conspiracy to keep all things centred somewhere else.

"It's all a plot, a conspiracy. You see, George Bush and the Queen are in on a secret pact with the Swiss banks (substitute Pope, Israelis, oil cartel, Bill Gates, the Rockefellers, Putin or Scientology for any of the three named above) and they are planning to take over the world!"

I try to understand.

"You may be right but we can't even keep the planes and trains on schedule and most kids under nineteen won't do as they are told under any circumstances. So, just how do you think these evil geniuses are going to pull all this off?"

"By way of genetically modified foods, TV programming and they spray us!"

"They spray us?"

"Yes. Don't tell me you haven't noticed the haze in the sky. That's residue from the regular spraying."

"What are they spraying us with?"

"Hormones, mostly, a little radiation, some chemical cocktail and, it is believed, vitamins."

"Vitamins?"

"Yeah, we have no idea what they are for."

"You know all this sounds a bit nutty, right?"

"Yes, it does. But you are one of us now, so try to follow along. It's why I am a vegetarian and I don't have a television. No genetically modified foods for me. And I stay indoors at night when they do the spraying. I suggest you do the same."

In the spirit of keeping comfortable while under the radar, one of my neighbours, Roger, knits hats from wool his wife Rachel spins. Wonderful hats. They are beautifully made and incredibly warm in the winter. They are the official hat of the islands. He makes one for each and every resident. If he likes you, he also offers to sew in an aluminum foil liner to keep the secret rays from the government microwave beams off your brain. He informed me that this only works if the foil is shiny side out.

The good thing about his skill is that the foil doesn't weigh anything and no one can see it inside the tasteful liner. It's quite comfortable, actually, and I do feel a bit more protected somehow.

We do have a phone book for the islands, published (well, photocopied) locally. Not every resident has a phone, but the alternative way to contact them is listed so the concept is there. Sometimes it's a call sign for a VHF radio or maybe an email address. Most of us don't live on roads, and if we do, the roads are really tracks that don't have names so longitude and latitude is listed in case of emergency so the Coast Guard can be given this information by our neighbours in order to find us.

Most interestingly, all the names listed are first names. No last names, but when there are duplicate names such as the Dougs, Daves and Mikes, initials are used for last names.

"People got upset when I asked to use their last name," said the publisher, who will remain nameless.

I could go on. We have the seasonally naked guy (all seasons, it seems), the two perpetually stoned quiet giants, the new age spiritualists, the dedicated missionaries, the reclusive millionaires…

It may seem odd to have this much oddness but it isn't. It's harmless but colourful, eccentric but entertaining, and the really good thing is that you have no doubts about everyone's true character. This is who we are and I couldn't make this stuff up.

There are definitely more bachelors than spinsters living feral. It's natural, I guess. Women tend to value relationship more than men do, I think, and so they are not alone as much. Often the older men get, the lonelier they become, and if they are rural and single, they are often isolated. And isolation makes you quirky. It's just the way it is.

I saw Len on the dock the other day and inquired as to his health. He has a bad back.

"Not bad, considering I just moved the old fridge out of my bedroom all by myself and I'm no worse for it."

"Fridge in the bedroom?"

"Been there since 1969. It was an old second hand fridge back then and needed venting so I put it upstairs in my bedroom so as to be closer to the roof. Shorter venting stack."

"Of course, who wouldn't?"

"Anyways, it's an old American built Servel. They stopped making 'em in 1957; mine's from the forties. It runs on propane. Built a nice little closet around it so that all the fumes would collect and vent. Worked real well for all these years."

"So? What happened? Interior decorator unhappy?"

"Who? What? Ha ha. No. Damn thing just wouldn't get cold on one side. Weird. Half the freezer was cold and the other half wasn't. Figured it was getting old so I just got a new one shipped over. Took the old one out. Not easy getting a fridge down a flight of stairs. Had to take the door off. Kinda ruined my door seal doing that. The original one went bad years ago but silicon goop did the job until now."

"Too bad, sounds like quite a nice little unit."

"Yeah, but here's the kicker. When I got it out I found out what went wrong. Seems half of the back vents were all clogged up. So there was no heat exchange going on for half the fridge."

"Clogged up?"

"Mouse nests. The little buggers had been building nests in there for decades! They were feet deep! Musta gone through more'n a few mouse generations! Ha ha ha."

"Who woulda thunk it? So, now what?"

"Well, I got the old gal down on the front porch, eh? And now that I see what's wrong, I am figuring to clean off the nests and crap with a leaf blower and attach another propane line. Once I get the old door back on, I'll fire it up. Just might work fine for keeping prawns."

Sometime when you are driving in the country or maybe watching an old rerun of *Deliverance*, you'll notice a dwelling with an appliance or two on the front porch. If you are like me you wonder, how the hell does an appliance end up on the front porch?

Now you know.

For the most part, our friends and neighbours out here are disengaged from the rhythms of the larger world. Not like hermits so much, but rather like ambivalent non-consumers, we often aren't in the game.

We don't buy much. We don't want for much, we lust for less, and we usually work only for the basics. This tends to distinguish us from the larger society which—on the surface anyway—seems more inclined to keep up with the Joneses.

Disengagement manifests in so many ways it is hard to see at first. There is, of course, the obvious eschewal of fashion. There is also the lack of consumer habits such as frequenting Starbucks or hooking up cable television, from air miles to car miles traveled. Regular working hours and regular upgrading of consumer items are definitely activities we just don't fit into our lives.

Ask an off-the-gridder about Justin Bieber and the answer is invariably, "Justin who?" Ask someone about the Canucks and lots of people will just shrug and say, "Who cares?"

But if you ask us about the mountain pine beetle, fish farming practices, monoculture reforestation, the Enbridge pipeline or even seaweed and ravens, well…the ensuing conversation may threaten your schedule for the summer.

People living up the coast know their stuff on that score and they care passionately about those subjects. And, for the most part, they practice what they preach. We compost, conserve, preserve and make do. We consume little, drive less, eat local and think globally—as in Gaia not the United Nations. Almost every single one of us is very engaged on a personal scale with the natural world. The societal one? Not so much.

A wonderful and somewhat quirky side benefit to this lack of involvement or dependency is a tendency to be innovative and creative. Our neighbours (and increasingly, us) do workarounds, invent things, solve problems and create magic from nothing. A lot of things are made from scrap. Really! A few years back Hugh, when his generator burned out a main bearing, machined one at home from scrap metal! That's right! The guy made a bearing! That is not easy.

Did you know you can make a woodstove out of an old propane tank? How about a barbecue made from a forty gallon drum cut in half lengthwise? When Cam and Claudia didn't have a fridge they piped water from their stream through an insulated box to keep food cool.

There is hardly any situation I can think of out here where people haven't shown independent, creative thought and actions. It shows up right in front of you everywhere you turn. It is pretty neat.

The other evening we were boating home and noticed a haze of smoke at the abandoned squatter's cabin across the channel from our house. The squatter's cabin isn't really a cabin. It's a shack with one wall missing and a list to one side at a fifteen degree tilt due to its log foundation settling on the sloping beach. Imagine a small garage with the front door missing and the wooden floor lacking the odd plank, the roof leaking, the walls with fist sized holes open to the outdoors and no amenities whatsoever.

Smoke usually means that Mike has dropped in for a respite from his hurly burly days in the city. Not this time. It was coming from a small beach fire which was being tended by a tall, thin woman in her mid fifties. Emaciated as a runway model, she was somewhat striking, if not skeletal and a little frightening.

She had obviously arrived by kayak. It was a bag lady kayak. Old, beaten up, faded and lacking all the normal accoutrements, it was spare and basic in the manner that old shopping carts are. Adding to that impression were shallow boxes strapped to the deck of the small vessel. These boxes held her possessions, possibly some food. A bag lady de l'eau.

We came in close to the beach with the engine at idle. She exchanged a few words with Sally and ended her part in the conversation with a broad smile and a curtsy, verging on flirtatious; all of that in response to us checking to make sure she was okay.

I confess to being touched by her warm and ready smile. She was possibly a little mad, but quite gracious and pleasant nevertheless. What struck me most, though, was that she was here in the first place. One has to work hard to get this far up the coast and the squatter's shack is amongst the least appealing places in the area being located in a dark, dank location on a rocky beach. The weather was socked in. Shelter was poor. Supplies were minimal and company was absent. What was the appeal?

That she was poorly equipped and really minimally prepared in every way was obvious in the extreme. But she was also independent and clearly choosing to remain so. Carried herself with pride, actually. We asked again after her needs and hearing of none, we bid her adieu and departed with a wave.

She was gone the next day.

-29-

Idyllic But Not Idle

There is an irony to living the so-called idyllic life off the grid. So beware of that marketing-based allure, it really is an illusion. Idyllic it may be, idle it is not. Doing little or nothing in the country is impossible. It's fulltime, intense and demanding. It's busy out here. No couch potatoes need apply.

I am so often asked, "Don't you get bored living on a remote island?" No, I am never bored. There is not enough time in the day to get everything done.

Firstly, there are chores to do. Every day is filled with what used to be taken for granted; heating the house, maintaining the water system, dealing with refuse, getting mail, tending the garden, that sort of thing.

Simply going for groceries involves a boat ride to the neighboring island and a long drive down a dirt road, as well as hiking up and down hills carrying boxes and equipment to get supplies home. And doing all that in any kind of weather.

And we are bombarded with new lessons and skills to be learned. Our neighbours out here know stuff; real stuff such as welding, carpentry, engine repair, reflexology, yoga, canning, seasonal foraging, home schooling, boat building, gardening, masonry and all the necessary maintenance skills such as plumbing and electrical work.

They don't wait for the gardener, the cleaning lady and especially not pizza delivery. (Although someone did order a pizza one time that came in on the mail plane.) For Sal and I "take out" is a frozen home cooked meal that we "take out" of our freezer. And we don't use the Yellow Pages because there is no one to call. People out here "just do it". Nike would be proud.

Socially, we are overwhelmed. We have more social obligations than the Queen. And no one lives next door. When we go visiting we are lucky if our hosts live on the same island! One long time resident couple knows this well and when they invite folks to dinner they come and get their guests in their own boat and then drive us inland to their house by way of an all terrain vehicle. Of course dinner has to start early so that everyone can get home safely before dark or catch the right tide. Many big parties end up as sleepovers. "Let's do lunch sometime" is not a throwaway line up here, it's a major undertaking.

Every community dinner is a potluck and usually includes at least half of the community. You need to bring a large entrée—preferably a side of beef, although that can get complicated with all the vegetarians. And a hostess gift is no trifling matter either. Flowers won't do. Country etiquette suggests something for the larder; a fish, a box of apples or a jar or two of preserves are de rigueur. Sometimes, when visiting, we might also take some surplus garden produce, wine, slippers, a flashlight, maybe a little something for the kids and, oh yes, the engine parts that we've picked up in town for the host. We've gone overseas with less luggage.

Here's some irony: burning free wood in the fireplace is likely the most labour intensive heat known to man. And the time involved! I once balked at getting up off the couch to turn the thermostat up or down. I now plan weeks in advance for my firewood chopping sessions. I have to. Sal thinks we could make the whole process easier by getting in firewood all year long. Think about that: work all year to make the chore easier? Does that make any sense?

Here's something else: I have to fix and maintain my tools. And I need tools with which to do that. I used to have tools for years. I never used them. And they were fine. Now I use them and I have to work on them as a result. Does no one else see the cruel irony of working on tools with more tools just so that I can do more work? Is it just me?

Now that we have theoretically reduced our schedule by semi-retiring (ha!), Sal finds she can't keep up. She goes to bed earlier and rises later. Maybe it's the logging, I don't know. She *is* a bit slow with the peavey. Perhaps we should cut down on the construction or the cement work. I've already postponed the really heavy steel work until next year.

The above is not to imply that I am stronger than she. On the contrary, I know what time she goes to bed because I am already there. And I see her leave in the morning from the same horizontal perspective.

But here's the *real* irony: even though we spend more time working physically, it feels a lot more like leisure. Maybe because it's real work. Maybe proximity to nature nourishes the soul. Maybe because there is a direct, immediate and personal connection between the work being done and the result. I dunno…I wish I could explain it. I guess you have to be here to really experience idyllic country living. And, if you do come, expect to be put to work!

When we lived in the city, we held down full-time jobs, raised two kids with all that entails, maintained a house, socialized and entertained, and participated in a myriad of activities. Where did we find the time?

Yesterday, as a random example of what we do now, we went and fixed our neighbor's plumbing. That was good. John has done so much for us that it was nice to be able to reciprocate a little while he was away. Sal then went over by boat to check on our other absent neighbors' cabins. Then we moved some logs, bathed the dogs, fixed a few things and did some computer work. After dinner we did some baking (yes, I helped!) and a few more chores…watering the garden, taking in the washing. We tried to watch a movie but incoming phone calls kept interrupting so we finally gave up and read instead.

Sal fell asleep while reading but she always does. She sits there with her head drooping and the book slowly falling until it hits her lap and then, with a start, the book is lifted and the eyes are open for a few seconds and the cycle repeats for as long as an hour. She is even worse if we watch a nature show featuring David Attenborough or some Discovery Channel thing. Before the initial credits have rolled, she is unconscious.

"I really like nature shows, I think. I just can't stay awake long enough to be sure!"

We are busy every day. Our plates are full. Our cups runneth over.

One chore we are having trouble finding time for is fixing Sally's boat. It is high and dry awaiting repairs. I *have* got to get on those repairs. I really do. It's been over a week now and Sally is getting more and more comfortable driving my boat. And it just doesn't feel right. Sort of like your wife driving your truck all the time. Or, if you're a cowboy, riding your horse. Just ain't proper.

And it's not my fault. Not really. We've been busy. A town day, guests, community volunteer work. And on any days that were not otherwise occupied it was pouring with rain. There just hasn't been a decent repair window. I blame the weather.

"Geez, Dave, what are you talking about? You guys are retired. You've got nothing to do all day. You just sit around and relax, right?"

Well, it might seem like that but, honest, we are busy. I swear. Okay, I don't get up early. I admit that. But I never have done. I used to only apply for jobs that did not require early attendance. I am not a morning person, okay?

And, of course, you can't do fiberglass boat repairs when it is dark, right? So, right there we have some major limits on the potential opportunity for working. I am just a victim frustrated by circumstances…

Still, that does leave a good six hour window on a nice day and, so far, we just haven't managed to find it. But we will. It will get done. You'll see.

Eventually a perfect day came along to do the boat repair. And I was ready to go. But Sal left for a spontaneous community work day and I need her hands to help me when I am doing well, anything, really. Anyway, she wasn't here for the planned boat repairs. So, I didn't do them. Worse, there were a bunch of vegetables and stuff all over the kitchen and I knew what her plans were for it so I decided to prepare dinner. I made a stew. I think. Not sure. Sally called it a stew of sorts. It smelled okay.

Look. There are people who build boats. And there are people who sail boats. They are rarely the same people, boat builders and sailors. That's the way it is. And it's the same way with cooking, isn't it? Only some cook. All eat. I am in the latter group. It's what we like to call a division of labour. Sal cooks. I eat. We're both happy. Mind your own business!

But—just so you know—I do cook once in awhile, like the sensitive, nonsexist, sweetheart that I am. Down deep. I help out in the kitchen now and again. I feed the dogs. I barbecue steaks. I assemble the pizza. I make some pretty mean sushi. And, well…popcorn…and I pour the wine…mind your own business!

But that is what I am writing about, actually. I was not minding my own damn business which was supposed to be boat repairs. I spent a couple of hours cooking instead, for gawd's sake! And all this while Sal was doing construction on a community project! How is that boat ever going to get fixed if the world has gone mad?

The next rainy day I cleaned up the workshop. It took all day. Things were all out of place. Screws in the nail containers, tools in the wrong boxes. Dirt everywhere. Sal has really been letting things slip!

"Shouldn't you be a bit more diligent in tidying up around here, Sal?"

"What are you talking about? It's *your* workshop!"

"I thought everything was *ours*? That's what you say about the dishes. Doesn't that mean these are *our* tools and that you own a share of the mess just as I own some of the dirty dishes?"

Funny how much pleasure I get from such exchanges. It makes the work go quicker. For me, anyway.

It took us a day to clean up a workshop that is only twelve feet long and four feet wide. You'd wonder how that was possible. I certainly do. Of course the dogs had to be played with. We had a couple of tea breaks and Sal went down to check the boats and tie up a loose log. That cut into the work somewhat.

Plus, I confess, I like to sharpen things as I find them before I put them away. So, every once in a while all cleaning stops while I fire up the grinder and ruin the edge of some tool. *And* add to the dust and mess, of course. One step forward, two steps back.

Learning to sharpen is really quite an art. I have a book on it. But it is really hard to do it right. *And* hard not to cut yourself when it works out—which it rarely seems to do. More than a few blood stains around my grinder, I can tell ya! Tip: never borrow a library book on sharpening without also checking out a book on first aid.

The worst part of cleaning up is the catchall box. It's the place I put small things such as extra nails, screws or small parts left over from repairing something. Everyone has one, right? It is temporary storage until I put them away properly. Later. Like today when I am faced with the daunting challenge of sorting through hundreds, if not thousands, of bits and pieces, none of which are valuable or are needed at the moment, but that I have learned are essential to keep for later on. Like, when I am repairing that same thing again. So I am sorting through pounds of bits. What a crazy making but necessary thing to do.

Then there's the part or something that I don't recognize but I know it belongs…somewhere. And so the search begins to find the right spot for it which, of course, means nothing, because fifteen minutes later I haven't a clue where I put it.

"Sal, did you see that little bronze thing with the hook and adjustable lever attached? Where is it?"

"Geez, I put it somewhere. Somewhere I wouldn't forget. Sheesh! Where is it? I just had it a second ago."

And so time passes as you both search for the thing you didn't know you had until you recently found it and that you have now lost once again.

"I must have had a series of mini strokes or something. I can't remember a bloody thing!"

"Oh, yeah, Sal, that reminds me. What was it that I asked you to remind me of earlier?"

"I can't remember. Was it getting out the dog food? Phoning someone? Putting something on the shopping list?"

"No. Oh yeah! I remember now!"

"What was it?"

"To clean up the workshop."

One memorable rainy day we were unloading a huge pile of supplies to bring to the island. We were using our inflatable boat that had to be inflated before we could load it. I was in a hurry to get it done before darkness set in. I backed the car and trailer down the boat ramp to the water and assembled the boat. I pumped it up. I launched it and filled it with all the stuff we had brought. In the meantime, my usually trusty and hard working partner had taken her sweet time to find her glove linings, put on some chap stick, fix her hair, find her hat, change her boots and powder her nose.

I was not pleased with the division of labour at that point.

When Sal deigned to show up, the job was virtually all done except for the one hundred and thirty pound outboard motor that still had to be lifted from the trailer, carried down the ramp and placed on the stern of the boat. I had left that to the last because it was a two person job with one of us (me) having to be in gumboots.

"Nice of you to show up." I said, not at all nicely.

"What are you saying?"

"I am saying that you look all comfy and cute but there is work to do out here and you left it all for me!"

With that, Sally bore a hole through my head with her glare, while walking towards the trailer. She didn't take her steely eyes off me. Then, with a mere flick of her upper body, she lifted the outboard and strode down the ramp and into the water with it. Defiantly, she slammed the machine onto the boat.

"Well, you just gonna stand there or are you gonna get in and fasten it to the transom?"

Sally weighs a bit less than the motor. Maybe more than a bit less! I just stood there, gobsmacked. How is that even possible?

Sometimes our city friends ask "What the hell do you two do all day out there?" I dunno…ask Sal.

Wood shed simultaneously being built *and* filled with wood

Woodshed and back of house in winter

-30-

Move Over Emily Post

When people in the city come to visit they bring a bottle of wine or, perhaps, a nice bouquet of flowers. It has become somewhat traditional in polite society, I gather. Sally covers those bases for me as a rule. I just have to show up—a duty I am increasingly failing at.

People behave much the same way in the country, of course, but the gifts vary a little more. We have had wine and flowers, of course, and at least half the wine is homemade. The flowers are usually in clusters and clumps and presented in pots or plastic bags. The point is to plant them, not just vase them. Vegetables sometimes come that way, too.

A dozen eggs would not be unusual. These would be your organic, free range, homegrown, wandering-in-the-orchard chickens we're talking about here. Real chickens. Real eggs.

Just as likely we'd get a few pounds of apples in the fall or a nice fish. Sometimes a salmon—had a few of those over the years. And Judith once gave the dogs a bag of deer bones with plenty of meat on them. They were most appreciative.

There is a lot of give and take and no matter how hard you try to keep it square, it is hard to keep up with all the giving going on. We have some very generous neighbours.

I have to say, though, that it would be hard to top our last hostess gift. It came from Doug. It was pecker poles, the long but skinny logs that are too small to mill. They float out there amongst the more rotund logs. Typically, they are no more than eight to ten inches in diameter at the butt. Pecker poles are used for posts when constructing small buildings like wood sheds and such. I mentioned to Doug that I had used my last two. He happened to say that he goes pecker pole hunting all the time. He suggested I join him some time. And that was that.

Today, Doug dropped by with a nice bouquet of pecker poles in tow. Four of them. Smelled bee-yoo-tee-full, they did. He stayed for coffee and a visit and we talked boats for awhile and then off he went. When was the last time someone dropped by with a nice bunch of logs for you?

As you might have guessed by now, country etiquette is a different thing altogether from city etiquette. It's not like your run-of-the-mill cul-de-sac or condo etiquette at all. It's primal, goofy and sometimes has a barbecue flavor. You know how happy we were with our bunch of logs. That creativity is really appreciated. Unlike its more sophisticated urban cousin, the rules of country etiquette have not been written down (until now) and it takes a bit of learnin'. Like the banjo.

First off, you can't dress too good. And, as you can deduce from the previous sentence, you shouldn't talk too good, either. It doesn't matter if you or your neighbour is a professor of English or a Justice of the Supreme Court, y'all gotta dress a little raggedy and use short sentences, preferably exhibiting humour, and always being self deprecating. Your conversation should be limited to wood cutting techniques, the weather and, of course, those darn city folk. Something like the following example should serve you well.

"We're heading into town this morning. Can we pick anything up for you?"

The proper answer is always, "No, thanks. We're good"

The purpose of that exchange is not just what it seems. Although it is part of country courtesy, it's also complicated social positioning. Firstly, the offer is genuine and de rigueur. They *have* to ask—they get points if they do and lose points if they don't. Anyone going into town should ask their neighbours if they need anything. Town is a long way off. What is left unsaid is that it must be anything less than five pounds in weight.

It mustn't weigh too much because everything has to be schlepped from stores to cars to boats to trails to stairs and over or through other significant physical obstacles.

You never say, "Hey, yeah, I could sure use a few bags of cement." You'd be eliminated from future offers on the spot.

If you request something it should be an item you need urgently, not Japanese mayonnaise or sausage casings. Well sausage casings would be okay if you'd just shot and hung a deer and needed to process it pronto.

That brings us to the other reason the offer is rife with the potential for a social faux pas. There is also a requirement to show how independent and self sufficient you are. The more Spartan your cabin, the less you should need and that fact should manifest itself by declining help and showing that you never really need anything. Self sufficiency is to country life as a Mercedes-Benz is to the elite of the city. Get with the script!

If you've just severed your left arm, haven't eaten in a week and your house is on fire, the proper etiquette is to say to any neighbour arriving, "Glad you're here. After I put out this fire, I was going to head into town for a band-aid. Of course I was going to stop by your place to see if I could get you anything."

There's more of course. If you are passing someone carrying things up or down a hill you grab something and carry too, but only once and only one way. To do more is to be labeled a fool. To do less is less than neighborly.

Always wax rhapsodic about someone's cabin, same for the garden and the workshop. It is impossible to say too many nice things. And the more outrageous the outfit they are wearing, the more compliments for either gender. As long as you can discern gender—be very careful there.

If anyone actually looks good, don't mention a thing or the state of your marriage will be the subject of local gossip for months. Wounds and major trauma can be noticed and discussed, but not early signs of pregnancy, skin disorders or contagious diseases.

Never talk politics. Ever! Firstly, no one in the forest cares anymore—they opted out. Secondly, no one ever changes their mind—they opted out of that, too. And thirdly, there is only one political statement that is expected, "I hate 'em all! Don't care anymore. I opted out of all that!"

The tragic consequence of even making that statement is that you will be deemed suitable for the local community organization and they will try to recruit you for committees.

You must always defer to the other guy when talking about one of his machines. And he has to defer to you when the talk shifts to *your* machines. Doesn't matter if the guy is a mechanic with Boeing, your chainsaw is different and only you know why it won't start. And he should know that.

Conversely, if you know that his chainsaw is out of fuel and the sparkplug lead is loose, don't say a word. Just listen to him describe the mystery and scratch your head. Look perplexed. It's just good manners.

Of course, when he goes in to call the local mechanic, you can pour in some gas and reconnect the lead and start it. But when he comes out shocked, you have to say, "Darned if I know. I just decided to pull on the starter a few times to get a feel for it and it started. Who woulda guessed?" Immediately start scratching your head again and look extra perplexed.

One of the more peculiar yet polite rural behaviours is the visitor calling to the house they are visiting from about three hundred feet away "HELLOOOOO…" This howling query is a substitute for phoning ahead and is intended by the visitor to warn the visitee of their arrival in time for them to get some clothing on. Why everyone assumes their neighbours spend their day in the buff is beyond me, especially with all the chain-sawing going on.

Mind you, on a few occasions I have approached the home of a neighbour without the required warning yell and regretted it. So have they. Some people do, in fact, wander about in the nude and, when they are also sporting a chainsaw, it is a discomfiting sight. We have now learned to call out loudly like everyone else.

You always take something when you visit, but store bought is not acceptable. Homemade jam, a basket of berries, home grown vegetables and homemade wine are fine. Even fresh road kill works for the truly bushed, as long as the hide is reasonably intact. A package of cookies, a purchased veggie platter or anything wrapped in plastic says a lot of bad things about you. Commercially produced wine and beer is always acceptable but is considered a bit showy by the purists. But, personally, just so you know, I'm okay with it.

Emily Post described good etiquette as common sense. But, if you are in a crazy situation with people unfettered by urban conventions, feeling the freedom of the wild and the absence of any rules, common sense becomes uncommon. In fact, a better operating maxim might be—proper rural etiquette is a science, the depths of which remain unplumbed. Be careful out here!

Our community holds a market day once a week at the local government wharf. Sometimes tourists drop in on the mail plane or by boat to frequent the impromptu cafe that is operated out of the freight shed. This floating restaurant is popular, so the tourists see twenty or so locals all eating lunch and such, sitting on a small dock in the middle of nowhere.

The usual group of neighbours on this occasion was augmented by the crews of a couple of touring boats who happened to drop in for lunch. People we hadn't seen before. And they sat at the tables!

We assembled in pockets off to the side like the standing-room-only crowd we were. A bit weird, but it wasn't that bad. Some of our folk eventually mingled with their folk and the market did boffo business that day. It was pretty nice, really.

I always find it fascinating to see tourists togged out in their new, shiny Gore-Tex jackets, sporting personal flotation devices with attached safety gear. Even the dog shows up in a PFD. Honest! The contrast is marked when they are hanging out with the locals. This is not to imply that we aren't dressed appropriately for the conditions. Mostly, we are. But island fashion etiquette demands the practicality of layering and "worn" doesn't mean worn out. We look more like cowbirds and the tourists, peacocks. Gawd, they are pretty in a Day-Glo sort of way!

The tourist boats are always clean and shiny and tiddley, too, in keeping with yacht club sensibilities. I used to be a yachtie. Yes, I was once one of them and my teak was oiled and my decks were scrubbed.

Island boats—even those belonging to the tidiest of owners—tend to have plastic totes, buckets, equipment and spare parts strewn about. They are for transportation, rather than trips, and for work rather than leisure. It shows. It takes nothing to identify a local boat. See an old, down at the heels boat with a well kept, newer outboard? It's a dead giveaway and totally representative of my own boat.

Funny, isn't it? Resistance is futile. I think I've been assimilated.

Sally's Whaler up on the marine ways improvised with logs

-31-

On the Grid

We have too many boats sprinkled about. There's the sailing dinghy that needs a new centerboard. We still have the old inflatable that served us well in earlier years but now has a few spots where the Hypalon has worn thin. It leaks very slowly and I know we're not likely to ever get around to repairing it, but we can still use it in a pinch. We have Sal's boat, the eleven foot Whaler, my boat, a sixteen foot Campion runabout called Wasabi (if you saw the colour the name would be an obvious choice) and my old Whaler-style Surf that I don't use any more but I can't bear to get rid of quite yet. That makes five, if you're not keeping track, and that doesn't include the three kayaks.

Go to anyone's place on the coast and you'll see their current bateau, its immediate predecessor half-filled with rain and missing its engine, an older one upturned on the beach, another one half-buried in the forest and maybe a few more here and there. It appears to be a weird, unconscious habit we all have.

"Hey, a friend of mine wants to get rid of a nice little runabout cheap. Maybe free. You want it?"

"No! A thousand times no! I've got boats up the yin yang. Nope, can't use it. Don't want it. Don't ask! But, ah…what kind of boat is it?"

And that is how it happens.

I had been cruising boats—on Craigslist this time. Of course when you look you sometimes find. And I saw a small fifteen horsepower Suzuki outboard. We weren't actually thinking of replacing Sal's outboard quite yet, but it was perfect for her. In addition, the fellow who was selling it lived on the way to my brother's place where we were headed for Boxing Day dinner.

The motor Sal had on her Whaler was a twenty year old 9.9 horsepower with a long shaft. She was adequately powered but had too much motor in the water which slowed her down and made the longer shaft and lower propeller more vulnerable to debris. Plus it is old. Plus it is a two-stroke. So we went to see the Suzi.

And…we bought it! "Merry Christmas, Sal!" She was surprised.

We travelled home a few days later. I was at the house getting the fire going and our systems up and running while Sal motored over to the next island to start unloading the luggage and food from the truck into her boat. She was able to get everything in except for her new motor which she left in the truck.

As she headed home I got a call on the walkie-talkie.

"I just pulled away from the dock when something went clunk. I looked over the side and saw the lower half of my engine dangling in the water." She had hit a deadhead and torn her motor almost entirely in half.

I went out to rescue her. I towed her back to where our truck was parked and we swapped engines. She buzzed home nonchalantly with her new Suzuki.

Moral of the story: timing is everything.

Speaking of timing, my outboard is not running properly—could be the timing. This is not good. Outboards are a challenge. Without them, we are greatly inconvenienced and usually it takes great gobs of cash to get them running again. Not to mention the heavy lifting involved.

They are not like car engines that deliver miles and miles of service between cranky spells. These things deliver miles and miles of cranky spells before needing servicing. When they stop it's usually in the dark, often in the rain and always when it is totally the worst possible time. There is nothing like an outboard not starting to measure the maturity and equilibrium of a person.

I shared my outboard dilemma with some friends.

"Oh geez, I had that once. The head was all Swiss cheese, it was. Electrolysis, eh? Just ate that head practically right off the engine. Could be you're hooped on this one, bud!"

"Yeah, that happened to me, too. Head was just gooey muck, really. Amazing it ran as long as it did. You are doomed, man."

Frankly, I now think it is just a bit of water in the carburetors but one is obliged to suffer the horror stories offered by everyone when you ask their advice. They never tell you of the time they simply forgot to open the gas line or didn't notice that the kill switch was in the off position. No, that would be too easy a fix. No doom—no humour. But it turns out that there are enough different ways that outboards can fail to provide a challenging learning curve for years to come.

Seems props spin out. I didn't know that. I was zooming along on the way to Rob's one time and it felt as if the clutch was slipping but, of course, there is no clutch.

"Oh, you probably spun the prop," said Rob when I got to his dock and described the symptoms.

"Well, duh. Isn't that what one does with props…spin them?"

"No, this is different. The inside hub spins off the outside hub that holds the blades so that your engine power is not transferred to them."

"Oh. What do I do?"

"You take it in to the propeller repair shop, of course."

"Uh, but the prop doesn't work to get me there…"

"Well you use your spare prop, don't you?"

Spare prop? I am starting to learn some lessons out here, no question. But the learning seems to take place in the middle of the problem—not while reading about it in the comfort of my chair in front of the fire.

Outboards have other idiosyncrasies, too. Sal was flying along in her little boat one day when the motor just up and jumped off the transom! There she was doing fifteen knots with the tiller in her hand and only the spinning of the prop keeping the engine anywhere near the boat. It was free!

Now, the old Pudding isn't the type to let an outboard motor escape on her watch. So, with one hand on the tiller, she reached around with her other and managed to push the kill switch. This caused the motor to start to sink but, before it could do that, she had wrestled it to the boat while slewing to and fro and, in a swift and acrobatic manner, repositioned the engine back on the transom. Carefully tightening the clamps extra hard, she fired it up and carried on. Total elapsed down time about three minutes!

"You won't believe what happened to me on the way home," she told a friend later and proceeded to explain. Brenda looked at her like she was making a big to-do about nothing.

"Oh, that's happened to me. It happens to all of us. That's why you're supposed to bolt the engine onto the boat's transom. Those clamps they come with are not good enough, even for a small engine. Anything bigger than yours and it's gone in an instant. Sinks right before your eyes. One second you're motoring along and the next—no motor."

You only learn about outboard motors hopping off your transom when one does just that. You only learn about spinning the hub of your propeller when it happens. There is no easy way.

But there *is* a kind of magic that happens out here which is hard to explain. It seems whenever we need a little help, it appears.

Diagnosing the problem I was having with *my* outboard motor prompted me to change the fuel filter before setting out to run some errands. Despite all the predictions of doom and gloom running through my head, it ran fine during the first half of the day. I thought I had solved the problem. Seems I was wrong.

I got in my boat and headed home. That did not go well. The engine started missing. And it continued that hesitant staccato noise that missing engines make all the way home. It was horrible. And, of course, I was imagining the worst.

Frankly, I had very few tricks left up my sleeve. If the fuel filter wasn't the problem, and it obviously wasn't, then what accounted for the missing? I dreaded the thought that it might be electronics. I hoped it was just the carburetors as I had previously thought.

I hiccupped my boat to the dock and was just about to tie up when a familiar green boat pulled alongside.

"Hey, Dave! How ya doin'?"

"Hi Doug! You snuck up on me. Didn't even see you coming! I'm good, but my motor is missing. Yes I know, it's right in front of me, but it isn't running right."

"Oh. Okay. Let's drain the carbs. Always drain the carbs first. It's often that. And if that's not it, then we'll take the cover off and cover each of the carbs with a hand to see which one is not working. Or I could go to my place and get my carb synchronizer and we can recalibrate them."

"Great. But I don't have my tools. I'll do it tomorrow."

He reached into his pocket and pulled out a Swiss Army knife and opened it up to the screwdriver blade.

"There you go. Let's do the carbs now!" And so we did.

And it seemed to run fine!

"Are you coming up for a beer?"

"Nope, just came to say hello. I'm off home to make dinner. See ya!"

So—get this—there I am in the middle of pretty much nowhere. All alone for all I know, with no one in sight. And the carbs act up. I limp home and just as I get there, a ghost angel outdoorsy mechanic type guy just appears. And, if we needed carb synchronizers, we could have got them. Whatever the hell carb synchronizers are. It's magic, I'm telling you. And it is a magic we seem to encounter everywhere. Bloody amazing it is.

It *was* truly amazing, but tragically the motor continued to act up the next time I took the boat out. So I ended up taking it in to an authorized marine dealer. My usual outboard repair guy works full-time and does repairs part-time and he was just too swamped so I went conventional and took it in to the marine mafia. These guys are made men in the marine world. The Corleones. The Sopranos. And it wasn't going to be any different this time.

"Oh yeah, Mr. Cox." Guido pulled the hood off and had a look ($100) and then pulled the sparkplugs. They were fine but a bit old so he put them to sleep and put in new plugs ($100). Then he visually inspected the carbs ($100) but needed Big Al and the Rat to lend a little influence, ya know?

After they had lunch down at the Bada Bing, he looked at the carbs again and decided to pull 'em. Big Tony okayed it. That's a big job ($100) and he then left them overnight in the cleaning solution ($100). Ha ha ha. No one wants to be left in the cleaning solution, ya know wad I am sayin' here?

Next morning, he blew them dry and replaced them, using new gaskets.

"We had them in stock. What a surprise, eh? Usually takes three weeks to get that stuff in! We're all still shaking our heads over that! Must be the new kid. And that seemed to do it ($100). So, all fixed! With taxes, that'll be $700."

And, with the submission of the bill, the clerk's face turned hard and he put his hand inside his jacket like he was packin' heat. I responded by emptying my wallet and all my pockets.

"So, is there an extra charge for putting the outboard in the back of the truck? Is there an automatic gratuity or should I just add a tip? Are your or Guido's kids pursuing another university degree after the one I just helped pay for? Or are they practicing law already? And, by the way, do you have a good local source of caviar? We just can't seem to find any of the good stuff."

"Huh? Unh…I don't think Guido eats caviar, Mr. Cox. You want I should ask?"

A new seventy horsepower outboard will set you back (with taxes and all) about ten thousand dollars. You can buy a new, dinky Kia sedan for that. The Kia has seats, a roof, a radio and everything—including a bigger motor, more complicated transmission and brakes. You won't find any of that extra stuff on an outboard. The syndicate controls the drug trade, gambling, extortion, murder for hire, and outboard motors.

But back to the crime scene they call a shop. Guido could have been working hard watching the cleaning solution or analyzing complicated data from his diagnostic machines. Maybe he, Big Al and the Rat were deep in discussions over my Honda challenge. I dunno. That's where they have you at a disadvantage. You just don't know.

Maybe he just put the hood back on and called it a day. That happens. So there is the very real possibility of getting the motor back home, putting it on the boat and ten minutes later, it does the same thing as it did before. Trust me—that *has* happened before.

"Geez, Mr. Cox, sorry about that. Just bring her back in. No trouble. We'll have another look. Guess it was more than just the carbs, eh?"

"Oh, okay I know where you are because I was just there. Do you know where I live? Perhaps Guido would like to come pick it up? No, on second thought, forget I said that. Just kidding, eh? Okay? I'll bring it in. What was I thinking? When's convenient for you?"

"Oh, anytime is okay, Mr. Cox. We always enjoy our little get-togethers. But Guido is pretty busy, ya know? And we'll have to run the diagnostics again. No idea how long this will all take. Ha ha ha. Could be expensive!"

The part of boat maintenance that Sal and I *are* good at is the manual labour that doesn't require any particular expertise, such as cleaning and painting. My boat was slowing down due to the garden of sea life growing on its hull and it was time to get it out of the water to clean it.

We wanted to get it on the grid. Never satisfied, eh? On the grid. Off the grid. There's *no* pleasing these two. In this case it is a homemade tidal grid, however, located in our lagoon and designed to hold a boat about two feet off the sea floor. "Getting it on the hard" is the proper expression but political correctness has diminished that term's common usage. So, now we are just trying to "get it on", utilizing an old hippy phrase that has legs, so to speak.

If I position the boat in the water above the grid and do it too early, I have to sit there waiting for the tide to go out. But this man waits for no tide. So, I planned it perfectly. I would wait until the water was just a smidge higher than required for the boat to rest on the grid, position it carefully and then wait for a mere three or four minutes while it settled as the water retreated. Efficient, eh what?

Like so many of my lazy bone plans, I missed the right level by a minute or two. Timing is everything, as we've already concluded. But I had missed the incoming tide by so little time that I thought I could still make it. So I revved up the motor and, with the bow lifting under the thrust, I tried to force my way onto the horizontal bars of the barely submerged grid. The boat got stuck half way on, of course—bow in the air, transom sinking and me not knowing what to do next, an all too familiar feeling. I watched in horror as the precious seawater drained away. Sal, of course, was nice and dry in her boat nearby, giving me advice and admonishing me for being a doofus.

She is always there at times like these. It's uncanny. If she didn't forewarn me and have "I told you so" at her disposal, she is there at the time of the calamity and has "what a doofus" to use instead. It's comforting, in a way to have someone there to witness your humiliation *and* to console you. Makes you feel better.

So, I did what any man would do—admitted my error and jumped into the water. With my weight out of the boat and a few well placed shoulder heaves it slipped back off the grid to its floating position and the boat, I sensed, was not just a little amused at our reversal of roles. We were both wet from the Plimsoll line down.

"Never mind," I said to my dry and grinning nautical critic in the boat nearby. "I'll do it tomorrow. Should be a piece of cake then. This was just a practice run, really."

"Practicing wading, are we?" she said. Sally's not that good at consoling.

When it was Sal's boat's turn on the grid we discovered it had a hole in it. We started work on a beautiful day to patch the hole. We ground, we sanded and we did what one is supposed to do in preparation for a fiberglass repair. We think.

"You ever worked with fiberglass before?" she asked.

I'm not stupid. I know what that question really means in fem-speak. It means if I haven't ever done it before she will be taking over. And furthermore, the first step will be to stop everything and look up instructions on the internet.

It's a question very similar to the ones posed when driving to an unfamiliar place. Do you know how to get there? Do you have the directions? Like most guys, I drive by feel. And fiberglassing is exactly the same.

"Yeah, of course I've done it before. Been there lots of times. Plenty." Adding "plenty" was a verbal mistake. I should have stayed with a simple, terse "yes". She senses weakness if I protest too much.

"Like when?"

"Well there was a time long ago—long before I met you—when an old girlfriend and I did some fiberglassing together."

"That's not true! You and I developed an interest in boats after we got together. You didn't know the pointy end from the blunt one back then."

This was not going well. She was getting stronger. I could see the next few hours slipping away getting advice from how-to sites on the net.

"Well, there was that time I watched Brian make his deck box. And I helped him do it."

"Doing what? Cracking stupid jokes?"

"Well, it was pretty funny. You should have been there. Everything got stuck. Ha ha. But then there was the time Brian and I replaced the deck on our old boat."

"What did *you* do?"

"Lots. I did lots."

"Okay, then. What do we do next?"

That conversational change of pace almost tripped me up but I am pretty quick on my feet, verbally speaking, and I had a fallback position, a fail-safe thought in waiting, at my fingertips. It's my go-to answer when she gets me off balance like that.

"Well, we start by cleaning. Gotta clean away all the dust. Then we gotta clean it some more. And then again with Xylene and do that a whole bunch of times. Clean, clean, clean."

Sal's a sucker for the cleaning fallback tactic. She is a clean-up-after-every-step-and-sometimes-in-the-middle-of-the-step sort of person. When in doubt about what to do next, if I just say we have to clean, then that usually buys me enough time to make up the next step.

So, Sally cleaned and wiped and cleaned and wiped while I, in the meantime, read up on the mixing ratio of resin to catalyst. I also read that I shouldn't mix it if the temperature was less than ten degrees Centigrade. But we were way too far into the job to bother with that right now!

The guys who write these instructions are geniuses. Seems I was to use five milliliters or 15 drops per ounce. Think about that. One measurement is in metric (milliliters) and the other is in Imperial (ounces). And the third is in "drops" for gawd's sake! I figured to do sixty drops in four ounces and asked Sal to check it. I handed her the bottle.

She stared at it. And then stared at it some more.

"Sixty drops in four ounces, Sal. Waddya think?"

"Not using milliliters?"

"It's too hard to measure five milliliters. That's just sixty drops. What do you use, a thimble?"

"You sure this is right?"

"That's the way I read it. You read it any different?"

"No."

"Okay. Let's do this thing!"

And so we did. But the stuff hardened up pretty quick. So much for the temperature restrictions. Made me think maybe thirty drops would have been enough. So that is what I'll try tomorrow when we do it again.

That's right—do it again! You see, we somehow let a bubble get trapped in the goo and so I will have an air pocket about the size of a Ritz cracker to grind out when it is set up. And then I'll do that part again.

Two steps forward, one step back. *Only* one, I hope.

The next day I ground out the Ritz cracker and went about glassing up that pesky little spot. At that point I wasn't *hoping* things would work out well, I was *sure* they would. Sal was waxing and polishing the hull. Waxing and polishing are closely associated with cleaning. They're like cousins in the obsessive-compulsive world of perfectionists. Things were starting to look good.

"Hey! Look here, David. There's a drip of water coming out of the hull. How is that possible?"

I took a close look and, sure enough, the hull seemed to be weeping a bit. I poked it. It burst into tears. Not good.

"It looks as if we've got ourselves some kind of barely visible leak, sweetie. I'm going have to grind that area out and see what's going on."

"Noooo…I just waxed there! Can't we just let it go? I mean, is it really bad or just a little bad?"

I picked up the grinder and took a few passes. The hull, all of thirty years old, was remarkably thin at that location and it took nothing to cut through. Under the skin was wet foam. No question: we had a leak there and it was likely due to a simple manufacturing defect decades ago as there was no indication of any damage. The skin was just very thin. And so the cha cha cha continued.

I confidently assured Sal that it was a fluke.

"Don't worry, this sort of thing doesn't generally happen in Whalers, sweetie. They are usually very heavily laid up. This was just an anomaly."

"Geez", she said. "I guess I better tell you about that second little drip then…"

On the other side, there was also a little teardrop or two. And a few extra began to flow from me. Sob. I ground out that next little spot. Wet foam again. And so a third patch was underway. Cha cha cha.

We quit working just after five, to the extreme consternation of the dogs. They like to be fed at five and, if we are at home they don't tolerate tardiness lightly. There were a lot of intense looks and leaping about. So, we fed the dogs, had a glass of wine and contemplated our navel…er…navy.

"Good thing you have fifteen horsepower on that boat now, Sal, instead of the old ten. At this rate, you'll need the extra five to compensate for all the extra water you are carrying."

We calculated that, with the foam occupying most of the space between the double hulls, Sal's boat might carry an extra five gallons of water which adds up to about fifty pounds. Not good, but still functional. For a while, anyway.

All of this got me thinking…where do old boats go to die?

Mankind has been building boats for eons. Why aren't we up to our knees in old hulks? Yes, I know a bunch sink. And the steel ones get cut up and recycled. But that still leaves a lot of wood, fiberglass and other types of boats. Where are they?

Oh yes, they are sprinkled about people's yards.

Sally shingling the new studio—one of our projects

Bench constructed from flotsam

-32-

Life is a DIY Project

In the country we have projects. I initially understood projects to be chores with a longer time span, but apparently I was wrong. Projects have a beginning and an end. Chores are the things you do over and over again. A project can be as simple as cutting a round of wood to make a trivet or as complicated and time consuming as building a workshop.

The other thing that distinguishes a project from a chore is that a project is supposed to be fun. For example, gardening is a chore, although it can also be a pleasure, so that's not a great example. Cleaning up is a chore, for sure.

Some chores, you say, have a beginning and an end. What if you re-route a pipe, change the oil on the outboard, or replace a rotten board on a deck? Well, even though these endeavors, individually, are not ongoing, they are part of maintenance and maintenance itself never ends and is usually not defined as fun. So maintenance is not the same as projects, either. Get it?

Doing projects usually means having several on the go at once. It is not necessarily a good work habit, to be sure, to be able to wander from one incomplete task to another, maybe several times a day, but it is the way to do it here.

I always run out of parts at some point, or damage one of my own fleshy parts. Either way, the project is interrupted. And I can't zip down to the hardware store and get back in twenty minutes. So I move to the next half finished undertaking on the list and try and make some headway on it. That is simply the way it is. I don't fight it. I go with it. It's a Zen thing. "First I work on one project, zen I work on another!"

One of the things that always sneaks up on me is cleanup. If I have four or more chores on the go at all times, what is the point of cleaning up?

May as well go from one work site to another without putting everything away, especially when I know I'll be back tomorrow. Makes sense.

Not to Sal. Sal is tidy. She likes things to look nice. Looking nice means putting things away. She used to be obsessive about it but now she is better. Actually, she's just sneakier. Now she only puts the crucial tools away when I'm not looking. Usually when I have gone in to get a drink of water or made the mistake of taking my eyes off her for a second, whoosh! The crescent wrench is back in the tool box and I didn't even see it go!

So, like an idiot, I assume I misplaced it and go back to the sink where I got the water to see if I left the wrench there. In the meantime all the bolts, screws and measuring devices are gone! Put away nicely, as Sal says. Of course that is the giveaway. When she tries to put too much stuff away, I catch her.

"Sweetie, did you see my wrench? I thought it was right here."

"Oh, that? I put it away."

"But I was using it!"

"Well, you've been using it for the last five weeks! I figured whatever had to be done was done by now!"

"Hmmm…are we still dealing with your desire to tidy things up or are you trying to say something else?"

"I have no idea what you mean, but I'm sorry to have interrupted you. Clearly you still have plenty to do and I suggest you get on with it!"

Sally uses the threat of cleaning up as a management tool. And she wonders why it takes me so long to finish a project?

Sometimes doing projects can be a malaise, even a type of sickness. It is weird, actually, because it seems healthy but I'm not sure it is. It makes you stronger in a way, but it could kill you. I call it Obsessive Project Syndrome or OPS. (If the project is special I am on special ops.) While it is not contagious in the city, it is remarkably common out here and it has annually recurring symptoms. Like malaria in the jungle.

To be fair, I don't believe the disorder originated here. I think the sufferers brought it with them to the rural environment. The disease likely incubates in the urban centers and festers for a time, but it is held in check by other obligations in the early stages. It breaks out when there is less resistance or demands from others.

Those under great stress suffer from a similar syndrome—they keep it together until the pressure is off and then they allow themselves to let go, giving in to their feelings. Typically they go nuts. In that way it's a bit like post traumatic stress disorder, only the symptoms center on projects.

Early signs of onset include tool gathering, workshop building, junk collecting and a growing collection of how-to books. And out here the ground is very fertile for the confluence of just the right chemistry as the disease takes hold, the symptoms grow unchecked, the disorder expands and, eventually the sufferer is consumed by it. Mind you, a lot of stuff gets built during the virulent phase.

I, thank gawd, am largely immune. I was born that way. Some people are just lucky. Call it laziness, attention deficit or just plain lethargy…whatever. I am blessed with a natural resistance to hard, physically demanding projects. And, even if I were to succumb, trust me, there is no sign of self discipline or even continuity, let alone obsession. I struggle to finish projects and I am aiming for smaller and fewer, not more.

OPS is the irresistible desire to undertake yet another project. In severe cases, this desire becomes an obsession and the victim's life is consumed by larger and more challenging projects as the sufferer, of course, ages and the needs for such projects diminish.

Typically, physical suffering does not seem to be experienced (as if the brain is numb) and the afflicted simply die with a hammer in their hand. It is tragic in a sense but, by and large, it is as good a way as any to go.

But it is not actual death we have to lament or fear. It is the consumption of time, energy and the depletion of the bank account that causes the most suffering. For the spouse, anyway. The afflicted seem to be enjoying themselves in some sort of demented state of bliss. And the more the sufferer delights, the more his partner suffers.

You think I exaggerate? You should get out here sometime. My nearest neighbour is building a perfect little float house for his grandchildren, complete with miniature kitchen and bathroom, all in a delightfully rustic style, complete with a handmade woodstove and other impressive touches. My other neighbour is building a ramp and dock that will easily accommodate a cruise ship. Old guys in their sixties whacking and chopping, bolting and cutting, drilling and sweating out in the sun all day. They start just after sunrise, sometimes work in the dark. Sheesh…they've got it bad!

I got a little carried away after watching the sufferers of Obsessive Project Syndrome in my vicinity. I caught a hint of it. I thought it would be super cool to have my own mill and make my own lumber for my projects. Sally, in her infinite wisdom, suggested I spend some time with Derek.

My friend Derek has a portable sawmill. But, of course, there is nothing portable about it. It's about thirty feet long with a twenty foot bed and sports a pretty big engine turning a six foot or longer horizontal band saw. It weighs about the same as a two ton truck. He bought it. Had it shipped to the island. Carried each piece and assembled the whole damn thing in the middle of the forest. Then he cut all the wood he needed for his homestead and for that of his cousin. That is a lot of lumber. And that is a lot of work. The milling alone is an amazing feat.

Even though Derek has some standing trees on his property he occasionally purchases logs from the local logging outfit. He had about a dozen twenty foot lengths of logs at his work site and none was less than twenty inches in diameter. Each was only a quarter or a fifth of a tree but they were still very big and heavy.

Derek had agreed to mill some siding and some beams for a community project and had requested a bit of assistance. We headed out in his beat-up pickup in the rain to make macho in the woods. Like a typical lumberjack guy, he wore his red plaid heavy flannel logging shirt and a filthy cap. I was dressed in a clean hoodie. I have so much to learn!

The first thing I learned is that it is pretty bloody hard to move logs around a muddy field. So real men use real trucks and real ropes and they drag them into approximate place. Some of those real men stand around and watch. Those ones pull up their hoodies. Then the real men use peaveys to roll the log onto the bed of the mill. And then we begin to cut boards.

It is truly a fascinating concept, actually. We, as a species, have decided to carve out square sticks from big round ones. Or, more accurately put, we make rectilinear boards from round trees. Waste is prodigious and inevitable.

"Hey, Derek, now that I see how this is done, wouldn't it be more efficient to make *octagonal* beams from round trees?"

I heard him say quietly, "The other guys warned me about this." And then loudly, "Just push the log and you can work out the philosophy of it all later, okay? And while you do, ask yourself how you would fasten octagonal ends."

So that shut me up for a while.

When we finished milling we stacked all our freshly cut lumber on the truck kitty-corner across the bed. Had to. The wood was all longer than the bed of the truck. It stuck out six feet on either side. That is not so much a problem when you are going down a two lane paved road. Scrambling a mile or so over a heavily rutted dirt road with strong saplings growing right into the roadway was like negotiating a weird forest slalom. And to keep the wood relatively in place and because the passenger side door would now not open, I sat atop the load.

Next time I will scootch across the driver's side and sit inside. I kept seeing saplings just miss the load as we whizzed by. Catch a sapling and I would be sent airborne. Been there. Don't need to learn *that* lesson again.

But, just as the skies opened, we arrived at the work site and unloaded the milled lumber.

"Geez, man," I said, lying through my teeth, "that was great. What a great day! Great experience! Yeah, just great. Have to do that again sometime…but, well, I think I'll go home now. We done?"

All the time I was saying that, I was also vowing to pay whatever the price was for milled wood without ever even thinking of complaining about the cost again. And I have shelved my plans for getting my own mill. Sally was pretty smug about the outcome, but I credit my natural resistance to Obsessive Project Syndrome.

Now, neither Sal nor I are artists. We like to think we have a sense of aesthetics, a smidge of good taste and, of course, we know what we like. At best, we are decorators with an eclectic bent. At worst, we live in a schmozzle.

But one really should try to make one's surroundings pleasant, shouldn't one? That is the sentiment we subscribe to. To that end, we gild the occasional lily and paint over the rust now and again. We try to have standards, even if they do slip. We try to keep up appearances, whatever that means.

Out here a popular motif is "found" art or, put another way, salvage-with-paint. Basically, we decorate with junk...sorry, junque. To a practiced eye with a foot in fantasyland, some of it might pass for art but, by and large, much of the artistic expression is really in the placement of said junque.

Hmmm...what to do with that old hunk of tractor in the ditch?

"I know, I know! Drag it out, spray it clean and I'll paint flowers all over it. You can weld our mailbox on the hood. It'll be folk art!"

And that sort of thing catches on. I've seen old boats used as planters, painted boulders sporting dragons and such. Old trucks in the middle of gardens is a staple of landscape architecture. There are tires and drums used as yard ornaments which would be considered butt ugly if it weren't for the painted images of squirrels and seagulls gracing them.

It seems to be accepted as art if someone can figure out a way to paint flowers on something, rather than truck it to the dump. Face it, that in itself is creative. Mind you, to be fair, some of the stuff *is* damn good. I don't know that it qualifies as art, but it can be exceptionally pleasing to the eye and enhance the surroundings in which it is found. I think I am being slowly converted to found art.

One of my projects was some cute painted wooden hummingbirds to add a little cachet to the generator shed walls. I think I would have to describe *them* as folk art. A bit embarrassing, perhaps, to be in the same category as the reproductions of dairy containers or galvanized washtubs sold at places such as Barn Depot and Farm Furnishings. But having said that, the style has grown on me in a kitschy, funky, cliché sort of way. So after the hummingbirds I painted a scene on an old saw. A few paddles came next. It's now like an itch. Every once in awhile I have to scratch it.

Sal's got it, too. But her stuff is actually original! Which is a polite way of saying completely whacked. She has taken found art to a higher level. First, she found an old frame-like structure floating in the sea. It is made of wood and comprises irregular shaped squares. She hung it on the wall and put some rusty crap in the various squares.

I didn't like it. Not at first. Just didn't fit my notion of art.

"Hey, Sal, what's all that crap doing hanging on the wall like, well, a crap hanging?"

"Never mind. Just be quiet and paint your paddles. Don't bug me."

Temperamental, eh? Just like an artist. So, I backed off. And over the past few years she has continued to add to her wall crap…oops…mural of found objects.

I must be getting more local all the time. I kind of like it now.

Sal likes rustic furniture. So do I. So she fishes worn boards and sea scrubbed branches from the ocean now and then and drags them all up the beach to dry out. Then—when her energy is high—she suggests a new project for me.

When we are working out in the garden on the raised beds, we are, of course, mostly standing, but lately we have been taking a thermos of tea and having more frequent breaks than before. But there is nowhere to sit, so the next piece of furniture rustica is supposed to be a bench.

"Can we have arms this time? I'd like to have arm rests for the tea."

"Arms? Sweetie, I can barely make the legs reach the ground. I can't imagine adding arms. You sure?"

"Yeah. Arms. And a nice back. Something to lean against. Maybe a curved back drift woody thing…"

"Sure. Why not? I just hope the sea coughs up the right materials in the right dimensions and some of it is curved just right. If not, you might have to be satisfied with rustic. And the charm of rustic is that it is, well, crude and clunky and make-do."

"Yeah, I know. I just want nice *comfortable* rustic. Something like you'd see from those other rustic furniture guys."

"I'm too rustic for you? You're shopping around?"

"Well, arms *would* be nice."

So, there you have it, the ugly side of rustic furniture making. The keeping up with the Hatfields and the McCoys and their logs and branches, flotsam and jetsam boards. The competition is fierce.

Everybody changes and yet, they remain the same. I am no exception. Or am I? I'm the same guy who lived and worked a modern life in the big city but I live and work up the coast now. And I live and work differently here. I talk and think differently, too. And it isn't modern, that is for sure. So, am I really the same guy?

In Vancouver, I made my living by talking, thinking and addressing unusual challenges, from working with delinquent youth to helping to assimilate refugees, from building a boutique market for kids to running a medical clinic in skid row. In Vancouver, I talked and planned, convinced, cajoled and tried to manage different types of people. Work was incredibly complicated.

Out here, there are fewer people to talk to, let alone any who would allow me to manage and cajole. And, anyway, the single sentence conversation is the rule. If the conversation goes on for too long, the person you are talking to wanders off. No time for a gabfest.

I don't have time for long conversations either. Not anymore. Now it is "yup" and "nope". But the work is significantly simpler, too. Well, simple in concept at least.

"Hey Dave, heard you needed some wood now that you're not going to mill your own."

"Yeah, starting a new project—building a deck."

"How much ya need?"

"About seven hundred and fifty board feet."

"Cedar or fir?"

"Both. Fir structure, cedar deck."

"I got enough. Ya want it?"

"How much?"

"Same as always."

"Okay, deal. When can you deliver it?"

"I'll figure it out. Let ya know."

"Okay. See ya."

"Yeah, see ya."

Elapsed time? Four to five minutes. Actual conversational time? Twenty seconds. The balance of the time was spent looking off into the distance, shuffling a foot, my conversational partner lighting a cigarette, and both of us pondering it all. So, with all the other stuff going on, obviously we have to keep the conversation short!

Any further details will be covered off with a few well phrased grunts on Wednesday's community day. Sometime in the next month a boat will pull up at high tide with the requisite amount of wood to be deposited on the beach above the high water mark. I'll come down with an envelope and help unload. We'll exchange a few pleasantries before he leaves.

"So, Dave, gonna get on this deck job right away?"

"Well, you know me. Right away could mean next spring."

"Ha ha ha. Okay, see ya!"

"Yeah, see ya!"

So, I dunno…am I the same? Or am I different? *Feels* different.

Dinner with students

Parking at the end of the road can be risky due to falling trees

-33-

Mayday

Is it just me or is the term "Emergency Preparedness" an oxymoron of sorts? I mean, if you are, as *they* wish you to be, prepared for all the various, but still anticipated emergencies, is that not enough to cancel out the definition of emergency? If you are prepared for whatever happens, can you actually have an emergency? Wouldn't the incident experienced be downgraded to simply an inconvenience?

Of course, another way of thinking about this is also true—if you have an emergency in the form of, God forbid, an accident, then by definition you were not prepared. Duh.

But, it's probably just me, picking nits. It's simply that this current preoccupation with safety and planning for every eventuality seems counterproductive somehow. The only thing I have observed directly from all the security and safety measures preached ad nauseam is that less gets done.

I am not suggesting living dangerously—no, not at all. What I am suggesting is that some, if not all activities, pose some risk. That is life, after all. In fact, I likely cut myself at least once every day while building the house. I still sport bruises, aches, pains and the odd laceration from just getting through the day. WorkSafe's declaration that "there is no such thing as an accident" means, in my opinion, they are in denial. And that can't be safe, now can it?

Imagine my surprise when the regional Emergency Preparedness Committee came for a visit to our island and declared for all to hear that we are all "living in a state of emergency"! To be honest, I had already partly dozed off before the introductions were complete so, at first, I wasn't sure I had heard correctly. Then, realizing the dire warning, I rose to the occasion and began shrieking and crying for help until my wife settled me down again with a well placed elbow to the diaphragm.

"We usually tell communities to have one week of food and water stored along with batteries and flashlights for emergencies. Extra blankets, a radio and a secure box for your valuables are also good. But, you folks can obviously survive comfortably for a much greater length of time and are pretty independent as far as your systems go. Can you even have a power failure?"

"Uh, Gerry's old generator is pretty unreliable but everyone else's is okay and he kinda lives in the dark a lot anyway."

"Do you have water?"

"Lived in British Columbia long, have you?"

The people out here can live comfortably for as long as six months without ever visiting a store. They can, and do, fix most everything that breaks, and make parts when they need to. These people aren't sissies.

As a consequence of the profound observation that we are living in emergency conditions, we are now designated the safe haven for the people living on the northern half of the adjacent island—they're *on* the grid. Obviously *not* a great place to be in the event of an emergency.

I need to make a point—living off the grid is not the same as preparing for doomsday. I am not a doomsday prepper. I would like to think that doomsday would be much more pleasantly experienced out here than in the city, but that is not and never was the reason for moving to the country.

And, anyway, those prepper folks seem to miss the point of doomsday. You don't live through doomsday. If it is doomsday, then by definition, one is doomed. Like a dead Polly.

Anyway, friends come to visit. They ask questions. They ask about our lifestyle. Some of them ask odd questions. But it is all very nice and makes for good conversation. Lately, however, I have noticed that there is an implied survivalist label hung on us. "So, ya got that alternative energy thing happening, eh? Figure to ride it out, eh?"

"Yeah…ride out what?"

"You know…the end of days…the end of life as we know it. So…what kind of firepower you sportin', sport?"

"Uh, we don't have firepower. Not really. An old shotgun somewhere. Don't really need anything. I mean, for the savage psycho hordes to get to us they have to get a boat, spend a bunch of money on fuel and then drive around a lot and what are they gonna get? Our tomatoes? Our homemade wine? We're too much trouble for your basic urban zombie psycho crowd I think."

"Yeah, I guess. Still, I recommend you pick yourself up a few tactical assault rifles. Ya never know."

"Hmmm…maybe I will…you got any?"

"Oh yeah, armed to the teeth, I am. Got a gazillion rounds of ammo, too. Take the whole Muslim nation to get to me."

"I thought you lived in a downtown condo?"

"I do. But, man, are we ready! They have to get past the security in the lobby first. Then we'd have the elevators shut down so they'd have to climb the stairs. Man, it'd be like picking off pigeons. They wouldn't have a chance!"

"Well, that's true, I'm sure. But do you have enough food? What about water? Got an axe to chop some wood? Do you have a fireplace? If you really think it's all going to implode, shouldn't you get out of the condo?"

"Are you kidding, man? Ya get out of the condo market and like, you can never get back in."

"Yeah, good thinking. But, like, wouldn't condo prices be lower after the doom thing has happened?"

"Whatever, man. All I know is that I am prepared. Like, for anything. I even have a bug out vehicle!"

"What's that?"

"The vehicle you need to escape with, dude. And ya need a bug out bag. That's the survival gear ya bug out with. You gotta do some research, man!"

"Sheesh. What's your bug out vehicle? What's in your bug out pack?"

"My Prius, man. Think about it. Complete stealth, eh? No one would guess I was buggin' out in a baby blue Prius. And my pack has a pile of granola and energy bars, Gatorade for the electrolytes, flashlights for actual light and, of course, my wind-up radio and a first aid kit. 'Course, I'll be packin' heat and lots of rounds when I bug out. Should be good."

"Yeah, I guess. Thanks for the heads up."

"No problem man. When the doom hits the fan, I am buggin' out and like, don't worry, man. I'll get up here. I'll make it. Bring you a rifle, too. Don't worry about a thing!"

Oddly, I am not worried. Not a bit. Not even about my bugged out friend. I don't think there's too much to worry about, really. You see, I get the concept. Should doom come to a neighborhood near me, I will respond appropriately and do the right thing. I plan to expire. Call me crazy.

Got up, got out of bed, dragged a comb across my head…but before I could get a nice cup of tea the phone rang. Sally answered and I hear her brief response to whoever is calling.

"Yes! I'll get him rousted and outfitted. He'll be there as soon as possible."

I turn to her expectantly.

"There's a fire up at the lodge. The smokehouse started burning and got away on Mike and Gabby. Clark and Carl are up there now but they think they need another pump to get it under control. Jen asked if you could get up there with one."

I got dressed and raced down to the genset shed for fuel while Sally called John on the walkie-talkie.

"Sally calling John, Sally calling John."

"Good morning Sally. What's up?"

"I just got a call from the lodge. They have a fire out of control. Can you grab your pump and join David? He's getting stuff together and he'll be ready in ten minutes. I have to go to work at the Post Office so it's just him."

"I'll get my pump. We'll take my boat. It's faster. I'll pick him up out front on your beach in ten minutes."

John, Jorge and I sped up the channel at about twenty knots. The lodge was at least fifteen nautical miles away. We'd take almost half an hour going as quickly as we could. There was a light chop and we pounded a bit in John's nineteen foot aluminum boat. Not much was said. We were worried.

There hadn't been any rain for over three weeks—unusual here, even in summer. It was very dry. A fire out of control in these conditions is a danger to a very large area. In this instance we were looking at a potential threat to thirty or so homes over an area of about twelve to sixteen square miles.

If Mike, Gabby, Clark and Carl were on site, then Max and Judith, their immediate neighbours, were also likely there. The best possible first response team was already fighting the fire. If they were still worried and looking for more pumps, we didn't like the way this was shaping up.

Fire is a big threat to those living remote. There are no immediate fire-fighting resources in the conventional sense. Of course, there are neighbours but part of the definition of "remote" is that they are few and far between. The Coast Guard would have been called and they have a fast boat but they are a good hour away. We'd get there ahead of them and they are not properly equipped to deal with wild fires anyway. The government's Wildfire Management office for our area is way down the coast in Powell River. They cooperate with the Campbell River office which is much closer to us. We had no idea what their response time would be.

The only real protection anyone has is a quick reaction time combined with the right equipment. Not everyone has the pumps and hoses necessary. Worse, many of us have not set up a pump and tried it out.

I was glad that both John and I fell into the category of those who have equipment, know how to run it and had done so at least once. But our problem was that we did it a year or so ago. It had just been a trial run. Now we were wondering about our abilities and our equipment. Can I remember what I practiced? Was the gas fresh? Did I have all the lengths of hose I'd need? Will the damn thing prime easily so that I can quickly pump seawater to the fire?

We arrived to a crew of about ten working pretty efficiently. Mike and Gabby had made more calls and other neighbours had arrived. Ours were the third and fourth pumps on site.

The topography of all the coastal islands in this area is pretty much the same—the land slants up sharply from the sea. Sloping up by as much as sixty degrees and averaging at least twenty degrees, each line of trees stands higher than the trees in front of it. That stacking pattern allows fires to spread very quickly up a slope. This was no exception. What started as a little flame in a small aluminum smoker, within an outhouse-sized cedar shed, quickly expanded to a twenty foot conflagration climbing the nearby slope of trees. The lodge itself was, thankfully, about thirty feet away and not in immediate danger. If the fire had gone undiscovered for much longer it could have reached the lodge and that would have been all the fuel it needed to get completely out of control.

When we first arrived I climbed up the hill pulling the hose while others put the pump together and got it working. Fighting the actual fire wasn't as hard as schlepping the equipment around and setting it up. Typically a good sized pump weighs around forty to fifty pounds and the hoses, fuel, nozzle and such might double that. In two or three trips that gear is pretty manageable on the deck back at home. But clambering up a rock face from an unfamiliar beach adds a bit of a challenge and laying out the hose up a hill that's on fire adds considerably to one's efforts.

Later, I spelled off a hose handler and simply stood squirting away like everyone else. Standing there with the fully discharging fire hose spreading water is the easy part.

All the real anxiety, worry and fear resided with Mike and Gabby. From the moment the fire was spotted they were in a high state of anxiety as they worked hard to respond appropriately. Fighting the fire themselves, before others arrived to help, must have been hell.

Given all that, Mike and Gabby did extremely well. First off, they got their own pump working while one of them placed calls for help. Then they began the fight as others showed up to assist and add equipment to the battle. After a couple of hours, it was mostly under control but their adrenaline levels continued unabated. Stress like that tires you out and they were visibly exhausted.

Even though the trees are fuel, they are at least visible to the fire fighter's eyes. A tree on fire is dramatically identifiable and attention getting. A strong volume of water will put a stop to that pretty quickly, at least on the surface. But the fire is also below ground where it is invisible. Now the fire fighter has a real challenge to hunt and root out the fire. Pun intended, because the fire *is* in the roots. You can douse the whole tree only to see a small cloud of smoke pouring out from some rock outcropping many yards from where the original flames were. If the fire has had any chance to burn, it has gone to ground and disappeared. Even if the obvious flames are doused, you are not even half done.

By the time the Coast Guard arrived we had five pumps and around twenty people working, three or four of them trained fire fighters who came from nearby where they were working for a local contractor. The fire was more or less under control. We had managed to get ninety-five percent of the fire out in a few hours. Everyone was feeling great about the progress.

Eventually a helicopter hovered in close and soon after three Wildfire Management firefighters appeared. These guys knew what they were doing and went about doing it. We had already done the bulk of the initial work but it was nice to be able to hand the ball over. They checked what we had done, sent the Coast Guard out to continue guarding the coast and, after a bit, shut down the pumps for a while so that smoldering root fires would be easier to detect.

The largest job after the fire for Mike and Gabby would be the continued vigilance required to monitor any flare-ups. I have no idea of the proper protocol but I do know that fires have erupted long after they were thought to be out. Mike and Gabby kept all our pumps for a few days so they could keep water continually dousing the whole area. I felt sorry for them because the long cautionary vigil was still on their agenda. Mike was going to have to check the burn site every few hours for at least the next twenty-four.

Once the professionals arrived, however, John, Jorge and I took it as our cue to leave.

Requests for assistance don't always come by way of a phone call. We had guests for lunch one day and had just finished eating when we heard the drone of heavy engines overhead. Ross and Fern operate one of the very best adventure tour operations on the coast and Ross had also been a helicopter pilot in his previous vocation. They were both familiar with the sound.

"It's a search and rescue plane. Must be something going on."

We turned on the VHF radio to Channel 16 and listened to the Coast Guard talking to a boat that was assisting another boat that was taking on water way too rapidly for comfort.

"This is Comox radio Coast Guard. Please provide your exact location. Do you need assistance?"

"Yes. We need assistance. Vessel *Lady B* is taking water. We are the *Sportfish* and will take the vessel *Lady B* to the nearest dock. Our location is (they read out their GPS coordinates). We really could use a pump!"

"Pump arriving by way of Coast Guard fast boat and another vessel in the vicinity. Estimated arrival time for both vessels is approximately one hour."

We were only about twenty minutes away. But I had just put my boat up on the beach for maintenance. I called the *Sportfish* and asked if they required quicker service. They answered yes. Then, as always, I called John.

"Hey! Feel like being a hero? Some guy is sinking and he needs one of our pumps but we'll also need to use your boat. Mine is on the hard."

"Let's go!"

We quickly loaded his boat and headed north to where the VHF conversation we overheard had described the scene. They had described a pretty small area and without referring to the GPS we figured we could zero in on them. Should be easy to find, we thought, even though the afternoon light was limited.

As we were getting closer to the area it was not at all clear where they might be. We could see no lights. We didn't see a boat under tow. We didn't see the *Sportfish*.

"You've gone too far! Stop! Go left."

Go left? Whoever was saying that could see us. I recognized the voice coming over the VHF. It was Renate, a neighbour who lived about half a mile from our current location. I guessed that she had seen the activity, listened in on the radio call and was watching from her window. When she saw us in danger of missing the boat, she decided to direct us. She sent us up a channel that we had not considered and we began to search in a place completely different from what we thought had been described.

The sinking boat was heavy aluminum, dark grey in colour. The name of the vessel was printed in large black letters on the half submerged stern. The fellows on board were urchin divers and were clad in black wetsuits. No lights were on and the area was in shadow. Against the grey rocky shore they were all but invisible and dropping further out of sight as they slowly sank deeper. We saw them when we were less than a hundred feet away. We never would have found them without Renate's directions.

We pulled alongside. I slung the pump over to one of the crew and then followed that with the pick-up hose while John nestled his boat alongside. We attached the outflow hose and started the pump. The water was already over the engine. The entire engine compartment was swamped. A lot of expensive machinery was being ruined by the sea.

One guy had been in the compartment with a ten gallon pail bailing for all he was worth. He was not winning the battle when we showed up. But the little Honda pump we brought worked well and the water level began to drop very slowly. It took about twenty minutes for the engine to break the surface. And that was only a small portion of the water in the boat.

By then the Coast Guard boat showed up and another pump was put to work. After an hour the aft (back) section was relatively dry and the hole that had been ripped open in the hull when the outboard leg had been damaged was now evident. The ocean was doing its best to fill up what we had just pumped out. We had to get the stern higher or the boat would continue to sink.

Urchin divers pick sea urchins. No surprise. And they put the urchins they collect in large net bags. Each bag holds hundreds of urchins and weighs about a hundred pounds. And each bag looks like a giant pincushion with thousands of spines sticking out. There were already about fifteen bags on the dock and we threw out the remaining ten or so to lighten the load and get the hole above water.

Of course after throwing out the bags we just stood there looking at the hole and wondering why our efforts hadn't worked as well as we'd hoped until it dawned on us to get out of the boat ourselves.

The Coast Guard provided the crew with some emergency stuffing which resembles thick cotton batten, specially designed for a breach in a hull. The crew stuffed it in the hole and, though it continued to leak, the flow was now pretty much under control. It was time to go. We gave our contact information and left them to it, just as two more Coast Guard vessels came on the scene.

A couple of hours later one of the Coast Guard boats returned John's pump to his dock. The holed vessel was under tow back to Campbell River. We listened on the VHF as they made their way in the dark and against the current. The guy who was to haul them out at the local shipyard had already been called. They'd likely have the boat on the hard before midnight.

All in a day's work for the Coast Guard, I guess, and not an infrequent occurrence in the commercial fishing industry. It can get a bit dicey out here at times but luck was with them. They stayed afloat. Saved the vessel and got to go home the same day. They even kept their catch. We thought.

But it didn't end there. Out here, good manners always show up by way of some sort of consideration. For instance, the next time the urchin-pickers were in the area they might drop off a salmon, just as Mike had done when he returned my pump after the fire. But this never happened. And I always wondered why. Turned out John did too.

"Well, I wondered, too, Dave. It seemed odd. I found out that, while the boat was up on land being repaired, the Department of Fisheries showed up. Seems the urchin pickers had taken their catch from the nearby marine park. Seems they took way too much as well. They broke more than a few things that day besides the boat. Somehow I don't think we're on their Christmas card list, even though we helped save them from sinking."

Good Samaritans helping environmental lawbreakers. You gotta wonder.

The dinner party had been fun. The guests were about to depart. It was dark and late. The temperature was dropping. There was a knock at the door.

That isn't easy. How does anyone get to our remote location, accessible only by water, so late at night and hike up to the house to knock at the door without so much as the dogs noticing?

It was Lise. Her outboard motor had conked out and had left her drifting in the channel. She had made a huge effort to row her boat against the current to make it to the beach in front of our place, guided by our house lights. Dressed in pure black she could have passed for a Navy Seal on a mission impossible of some kind. Only her pale, white face gave her true mission away. She was in desperation mode.

Our guests rode to the rescue and towed her home. But not before she had a piece of chocolate cheesecake and a stiff Scotch.

"I'm going have to break down more often. Right about here!"

We all laughed.

After everyone had left Sal and I got to thinking. It was black as pitch out there with the tide running. No lights. No radio. Had this occurred in the dead of winter Lise could have been in danger if she hadn't made it to shore. There is little to no boat traffic at night and not a great chance that anyone passing would see her anyway.

This is a harsh place at times. Errors are tolerated but not always forgiven. More than a few grizzled, seasoned, capable mariners have met their end simply because of one small error in judgment. Once again we were reminded of why we carry all the safety gear and do our utmost to be home before nightfall. Plus, on my boat, I carry a small, spare engine. It's my insurance to ensure that we get home. But even with the best preparation, accidents can still happen.

And of course we take risks all the time—every day. But we respect the sea with a reverence that hopefully keeps our maritime risks to an absolute minimum.

So, what's my point? I don't have one. Not really, just the obvious. I guess I just looked into the face of an accident that could have happened and it was a stark reminder. Going off the grid is more than just not having help and assistance, services and institutions, resources and supports. It is also, at times, a walk on the wild side. Accidents live closer to home. Danger is a constant and present neighbour with whom you have frequent contact. And relations are *not* warm and fuzzy.

No wonder we all feel more alive out here!

Doug taking the students for a boat ride

-34-

Fountain of Youth

A city friend, who will remain unnamed to protect the guilty, gave me a magazine. It was the *Special Housing Edition* of *Senior Living Magazine*, self-described as featuring active seniors on Vancouver Island. *Oh my gawd.*

First off, it seems its definition of a senior is a fifty-year-old and their definition of active is brunch! There are numerous pictures of so-called seniors reading, walking, petting dogs, drinking coffee with other seniors and getting in and out of special bathtubs. Whew! How do they keep it up?

Then there is a picture of a blond woman in pretty good shape reading on a beach and thinking, I wish that I'd moved in sooner. She appears to be about sixty and is referring to a retirement village that arranges her activities and makes her meals. The sixty year old women I know are climbing the local mountains, learning Mandarin in Shenzhen or working with polio victims in India. I swear this is true. So who are these people in the magazine?

Ten pages are dedicated to listing assisted living residences. Some of the features: walker-friendly, raised gardens, emergency call service and a bus. For a real exciting time there are escorted walks, group shopping and supervised gardening.

I guess what I am saying is this: there seems to be a current view of dependence and helplessness that prevails in respect to "seniors" and the word, in itself, is a mindset. I am in my sixties. I think I am just starting to sneak up on the "s" word. Not quite there, but close. Knees are there. Lower back is there. But the rest of me is still middle aged. Okay, maybe my waistline is on the cusp. But, generally speaking, I am *not* a senior. Oh, realistically I am a senior, but in denial. But these magazine types are getting special bathtubs in their fifties! Or, at least, special bathtubs are being marketed to fifty year olds.

One thing is for sure. Out here you are young if you are in your fifties. You're still a sex symbol (if you ever were one). Fifty-year-olds are still wet behind the ears and not in the least because they are still flying about in boats in all kinds of weather.

Sixty-year-olds are feeling their joints but are otherwise in the prime of their life and still learning, socializing and traveling to Mexico or Hong Kong or even, (gasp!) El Salvador.

The seventy-year-olds are the main contingent, the backbone of the community. They have the power. They have the wisdom. And they still have the ability to exercise it.

The eighty year olds are the ones whose health we inquire about but they still get in their own wood, do their own shopping and kill their own bears and skin 'em. Even the ninety years olds are a feisty bunch.

No customers *here* for those walk-in bathtubs anytime soon.

Of course all of that hardiness doesn't apply so much to me and Sal. Ever since we lived on boats for a decade we have had an exaggerated appreciation of the basic shower. We seem to be able to go with the flow, handle what comes up and roll with most of the punches, but afterwards, we increasingly need a shower.

I think this shower requirement was the first of the "old geezer" items we simply had to have. You know how people are as they age and get more set in their ways—what used to be a pleasure is now a requirement. "Oh, I just can't start my morning without a cup of coffee." Or, "Don't expect me to go out there. I'd catch my death." Or "I couldn't possibly walk that far. Call a cab." The "softy" list grows longer with the teeth.

The implication of these declarations of weakness, of course, is that these people are helpless without Jamaican coffee, high thread count cotton sheets or a temperature comfortable to within one degree of their preference. Self limitation, it seems, is being used as a statement of taste rather than what it is—self limitation. And the older some of us get, the more refined our taste until we can't seem to do anything. Sadly, it is a club I could potentially have seen myself joining at one time. The saving grace was moving here.

Sal and I used to shake our heads at these self imposed personal requirements for life. Six billion people around the world don't need their special pillow in order to sleep and are able to walk without Rockports. They carry on in the old, well, "carry on" tradition. And so did we.

We didn't use to have special requirements. Not Sal, anyway. She is simply too tough and had an English mother with the archetypal stiff upper lip as a role model. Me? Well, mostly I suppressed my special needs for the sake of trying to appear as macho as Sal (or her mother).

But then the need for showers started to creep in. And then the need for wine before dinner. Dinner could be a ten peso fish taco but we would simply *have* to have a cerveza at the very least. Rot began to set in.

Eventually, of course, I did let my inner whinger out but I did it quietly and rather later in life. Then, as the mewling increased to embarrassing levels, I moved to the woods.

Complaining out here is verboten. It is de rigueur to brush off the most horrific hardships with casual aplomb. If you accidentally cut the tips off a couple of fingers with your table saw you explain, "It was my left hand, so no biggie." You manage to run your boat at top speed onto a rock and your comment is, "Well, my boat needs a new hull and engine, but I can fix it easily once that bone in my arm mends."

Of course, relatively speaking, Sally and I are wusses and I have the silhouette to prove it. We simply must have our showers, don't you know? Sal needs her chocolate, and me, my Scotch. Internet has crept into the picture, too, damn it! And, in the interest of full disclosure, I've even traveled with my own pillow. It would've been just a matter of time before we started drinking imported bottled water and serving only organic Brie, had we stayed in the city. And really, just what sort of a meal would it be without sorbet between courses and finger bowls to follow?

But, mind you, I now dress like a homeless person. So maybe it all balances out in the end anyway. I'm counting on our country peer group to provide the reality check to keep it real.

I have a dead tree looming over my wood shed. It's old, ugly, brittle and ready to fall down at any time. I am sympathetic.

I have an old neighbour. He, too, is old, ugly, brittle and, by living up here, is also vulnerable to—and often in the position of—falling down. I am empathetic. I introduced the two of them.

"That puppy has to come down. It's dead and it's going to fall right on your shed if you leave it. I'll get my stuff and come over on a sunny day and we'll take it down."

"Well, I agree with everything you said, but for the "we" part, Kemosabe. What makes you think I am going to let an old coot like you get in harm's way?"

"Well, I was a logger when I was young. You weren't. You don't know how to do this. I do. I'm going to climb up that other tree nearby and swing like a pendulum until I can grab the old, dead one and then I am gonna strap myself in on it and take it down in pieces."

Yeah, right!

When he left I went about roping the old tree to other trees nearby. I basically hamstrung the dead, gnarly snag and put tension on the two lines so that, when I cut it, it would fall and swing away from the shed. Seemed like a good plan.

And then I left it for other things.

Yesterday, the old coot comes by while I am napping and, before I can get up and out there, he climbs the tree beside the dead one and drags a bit of equipment with him. I show up to see him thirty feet up a tree tangled in ropes.

"Is this how loggers do it?"

"Loggers don't do this! In the forest the trees are not near sheds, you big doofus. Here, you have to get creative! Now stop being so useless and send me up my equipment!"

Turns out the first thing I send up is his climbing harness. He's already up the tree and *now* I am sending up the climbing harness? The tree looked tricky to climb—I assumed he had his climbing spurs on.

We eventually got a third rope around the dead tree—higher up for better purchase—and then he came down. As I watched, I realized that he did not have spurs. This old guy had climbed the tree in sneakers!

C'mon! That's impressive. I don't care who you are, except a coconut picker in the tropics, perhaps. An old guy over sixty-five and stiff enough to have trouble tying his shoes goes up a straight, minimally limbed tree thirty plus feet without aids of any kind! Who are these people?

"She's down. We did well. Gotta go, see ya."

"Well, thanks for that. I was going to offer you a beer but perhaps you'd prefer a coconut or a bunch of bananas?"

"Heading home? Mind giving me a lift?"

"Hop in!"

Heather climbed into my small boat. She had been working on one of the community buildings, putting in a new back door. Seems she's been in construction all her life, running crews around the world. Tools come easily to hand with her and the kibitzing was classic work site stuff. She could "yup" and "nope" with the best of us.

For her, the back door refit was "nothing, honey" and she decided to build a back deck while she was at it. She said it made it easier to install the door, having a place to stand. Heather is a big, strong woman in her fifties. (I'm guessing, here. Hope I'm right.) A grandmother. She did more in her four hours of work than I accomplish in twenty.

I swung my little boat into her bay. I had never been there before. She pointed to the shore.

"See those rocks there, by the big cedar? There's enough water for the boat to get in close. You can drop me there."

I did as I was told. And she got out with her bundles of mail, books and an extra prop for her outboard that she had scored from a neighbour. As she pushed the boat off, I noticed that she was standing in water up to her ankles. Her socks and shoes were soaked.

"Geez, Heather. Sorry you got your feet wet."

"No problem. I'm just happy not to have to hike home the long way carrying all this stuff. The shoes will dry. Trust me. This is the way I get home when I'm lucky!"

She scrambled across the rocky beach carrying twenty five awkward pounds and headed up to her cabin in the bush. I'll see her next week when she shows up for another project.

Tough? Yeah. She's tough. Real tough. But she's not alone. There are other tough single women out here. The women with partners are tough, too. Generally speaking, all the women are tough in an outdoorsy way. But the single women simply have to do more for themselves. Or pay. Some of the single women keep it together by paying for some of the heavy work to get done, but that is a difficult way to cope. Money is not the great equalizer out here. People who have to pay to get things done sometimes don't always get things done.

So why do we live here? Why don't we go back to the city, get a job or something? Wouldn't it be easier, at the very least?

A few have tried. But they usually come back. Once you are out of the city, it is hard to get back in, especially when you are older. But the main reason is trade-off. It is better to scramble across a beach in wet shoes than re-insert yourself (or try to) into the "normal" way of living in the city. To a person, it isn't worth the effort. Life here is good. Shoes and socks dry quickly enough.

-35-

I Like Here

Foreigners, generally white, are referred to as gweilos in Cantonese slang. It is not always a racially benign term but, for the most part, it is simply just a descriptive designation. Apparently it once meant foreign devil or ghost man. Of course, depending on the context, it can take on a heavier or lighter weight. The word can also be used as an adjective to refer to western ways, behaviours, styles or habits.

Just as we tend to think of the word "Chinese" as a collective term, the Chinese tend to use the word "gweilo". But when I describe *myself* as a gweilo my Chinese friends laugh. So who knows what it really means?

My friend Dennis had an idea. He wanted me to share my "gweilo thoughts" with students from the school his grandfather had founded in Hong Kong. With a little more discussion we cooked up the idea of him sponsoring groups of four students to stay with me and Sal for a week each summer.

He said to me, "You know how you are a little weird? Well, share some of that weirdness with the students, would you? I think a little "weird" is good for them. I don't agree with all your crazy gweilo ways, but I do think the kids benefit from hearing viewpoints different from the Chinese way of seeing things. Can you do that?"

"Yeah, sure, any topic in particular?"

"Well, I do think that the gweilo way of being a bit independent of society is good. Not as far as you go, but I'd like them to hear about thinking independently."

"So you think I'm an independent thinker?"

"Not really. I think you're a bit crazy, but you are as close as I can get without it being dangerous!"

"I think that is the nicest thing you have ever said to me, Den!"

"Don't let it go to your head!"

"Why do you want to do this?"

"These students, especially the girls, are likely to sacrifice their own dreams for their family's needs. It's a common path for women in our culture. That means, because they are Chinese, female and poor, they may not take some great opportunities offered to them through education. These are smart kids. They can go to university and do a lot. I don't want them to disregard their families. Not at all. I just want them to give themselves a choice. I want them to see some alternatives to the Chinese way. You may not have much to offer but, whatever it is, it is definitely not the Chinese way."

"Okay, I can hardly wait. Wahoo! Little unformed brains to mess with. This could be fun!"

"That settles it. I'm sending their teacher, Miss Wong, with them, just to be on the safe side!"

Four hundred forest fires burned out of control just a few hundred kilometers northeast of us. And the wind was blowing our way. We were in no danger, but the last month of beautiful blue skies accompanying our usual clean crisp air had been replaced with a thick smelly haze that hinted of campfire. It was not pleasant.

Visibility was down to about one mile and the City of Vancouver, one hundred and thirty miles further away, was on an air quality alert. Seems they were at five on a scale of ten, enough to advise the elderly and those with breathing difficulties to stay indoors. This all happened the day our Hong Kong students arrived.

I greeted them at the airport, appalled at what they must think. They had just landed on the commuter flight out of the Vancouver International Airport and the sky must have been a thick grey all the way up. As we greeted one another, I asked "What does it look like up there?"

"What does what look like?"

"You know, all the smoke from the forest fires?"

"Wow! Forest fires! What forest fires?"

It turns out the air was much the same as they are used to in Hong Kong. For them, nothing was out of the ordinary! We drove through the usually picturesque town of Campbell River and I purposefully followed a route that showed suburbs, townhouses and the like to give a sense of what housing in Canada is like. They oohed and aahed at the large homes and were amazed at the lack of traffic and the absence of pedestrians. But the ominous grey haze that dominated the overall impression was still not a factor for them. Being able to see only a mile or so was normal.

They were exhausted after twenty hours in transit. And it was going to take another two and half hours to get home due to a long wait for the ferry. I had four students and Miss Wong, their teacher, sleeping in the car. When we reached the logging road they were lolling about like rag dolls as I drove them sliding and lurching down the rough and dusty twenty miles.

As they got out of the car at the end of the dirt road, deep in the forest, and saw the last steep hill they had to walk down to the water and the waiting boat, they were a little freaked out. I got the gang into the boat and we headed out to our island and, with the weather being a little rough, they got a bit wet from the spray. That woke them up!

We arrived at the distant and rocky shore and were greeted on the beach by Sally and our two dogs in what must have seemed like, to the students, the middle of nowhere. But, so far they were okay. They were coping. Mind you, in their world dogs are things to be very, very wary of and the concern showed on their faces and through their body language. They kept their luggage between them and the dogs.

It is the scramble up the barnacle and kelp covered rocks with their baggage in tow that is the next test. Sal tries to ease them in to it but, really, she, too, is on the beach with a suitcase or two and her feet are slipping. How much easing can she do?

By the time I get back from taking the boat around to the dock, the students have been introduced to the Boathouse and the tent that will be their homes for the week. They put on a good face but I can sense the shock setting in.

And then Sal feeds them. A good meal, coupled with a total of almost twenty-four hours of travel, would make even the most freaked out guest relax. The kids managed a second wind after dinner as they dutifully checked in with parents and friends via Skype or email to confirm their arrival. The house finally quieted at midnight.

Everyone had record sleeps. We didn't see hide nor hair of them until ten thirty in the morning. Big success! The previous night at dinner I had asked the kids how much sleep they usually got. Eddy said four to five hours: "So much to do!" Tracey, five to six hours. Hazel slept well at six to seven hours and Ivy usually had nine straight hours! Everyone was shocked. "Ivy! How you do it? How you sleep so much?"

All four students were originally from mainland China, although they were now living in Hong Kong. They all grew up in small villages where they learned to speak in their local dialect. When they went to primary school in China they had to learn Putonghua (Mandarin Chinese). And, when they advanced to middle school in Hong Kong, they had to learn English and Cantonese. Even though Cantonese and Putonghua use the same script the two languages are mutually unintelligible verbally. By the time these kids are reaching puberty they have had four separate languages to master.

Admittedly, they are masters of only one (and I have no idea which one it might be) and are unfettered manglers of English. We are often challenged to understand what they mean. That first night at dinner, Tracey remarked that she loved all the smiles. We all did. So we dutifully smiled at her. And so she smiled at us, too. But, after a pause, it seemed to her that we didn't understand so she told us again that she loved the smiles. And, feeling admired and praised, Sally and I smiled some more. And Tracey politely smiled again in return. And we looked at each other—as if the other was mad! Finally, Tracey sniffed rather vehemently and said, "I love the smiles!"

"You mean *smells*!" said Miss Wong. We all laughed.

When the kids first come, it is always a bit awkward. They are nice. We are nice. Everyone is nice. It's probably the way of all people and it is good, but it is also not quite real. It takes a little while for people to let their hair down and then things seem to be better. And that little bit of magic had started.

It is hard to describe, measure, predict or even address purposefully, but you know what I mean. Breaking the ice, but at a deeper level, I guess.

All of a sudden a look of understanding, a sense of familiarity, a quick laugh at someone's faux pas. Those small signs that indicate our common humanity are what I like so much. It makes it all so much fun.

We arranged activities for the students each day they were with us. One day it was kayaking. Sal led them. Imagine a mother duck with ducklings, only real ducklings are a lot better at what they do than this group. These guys were all over the place! Sally had the kids practice paddling on the dock before they even got into a kayak.

This didn't prevent Eddy from paddling backwards, and only backwards, once he was out on the water. For the life of him, he couldn't reverse his arm action to propel himself forward. He'd stop, look at the paddle, look at the water and then, while everyone shouted instructions, stroke backwards! He did this for five minutes straight as he backed up in a circle towards the beach he left from. It was hilarious! Well, maybe you had to be there.

Eventually, everyone got sorted out and proceeded in an ungainly fashion around the point and over to the bluff at the same pace as Fiddich and Megan, who were swimming alongside. The pace was not quick or straight. But they got there.

Then Meg decided she had had enough and directed the "help me" look to Sally who responded as instructed and put the sopping wet princess on her lap as she and the Asian gaggle slowly turned for home. As adventures go, this wasn't one. But the kids had a lot of fun and now they could add kayaking to their resume. I may have to refuse to be a reference, though.

We were discussing the next day's agenda at breakfast. Our friend and neighbour, Doug, was going to pick up the kids for a boat tour of the area. Eddy asked if we could also squeeze in chopping wood. Eddy's English is poor and it took a while for him to get the question out. But, when I understood what he was asking, I agreed to do it at the end of the day. I was about to continue with something else when Eddy interrupted me.

"I am sorry, David, but I have another question."

"Sorry. Go ahead."

He looked me in the eye very earnestly and said slowly, enunciating clearly, "How much wood would a woodchuck chuck if a woodchuck could chuck wood?"

I was speechless. That doesn't happen often.

Doug, the student`s tour guide for the day, is the quintessential loner. A gunslinger without a gun. A hermit but with friends. A bachelor who lives on his sailboat. Gregarious in his own quiet, tall drink of water sort of way, he maintains a mostly peripheral role in the community. Not in. Not out. Sometimes you see him. Most times you don't. If there is a gathering of more than three people, Doug is not often there. Which is fine. I am getting a bit more that way myself.

But some things draw him in. He likes young people and he likes meeting people from other countries. He comes by, picks the students up at the dock and says goodbye to us from the boat. That is about the only time we play a part in this—waving goodbye. We don't even know the schedule or the duration of the activity he has planned. A smidge unsettling for Miss Wong. Not for me. I took a nap.

They explored some beaches, visited a local family and Doug even threw in a bit of fishing. Plus they got to drive his boat! The kids were thrilled.

The next day Sally left early with the kids to motor a short way down the coast. They were scheduled for an hour or so with our local laid back yogi who is within weeks of being seventy. He walks with the fluidity of a teenager on sleeping pills. Rieko is as lithe and willowy as the slim hippy he once was forty odd years ago. He can bend in ways unknown outside of Cirque de Soleil. He is a walking testament to the wisdom of physically tying yourself in knots.

Rieko, his partner in lithe, Brenda, their house, and their life will be yet another experience of Canadians for the kids. Talk about skewing the data, eh? One would be hard pressed to find lifestyles as diverse as Doug's, ours and Brenda and Rieko's at the best of times. These kids will get it all in two days.

Later, when the students were talking about their different experiences, one of the kids said, "Oh, Canadians make the impossible possible!"

Naturally, I assumed they were talking about us and I beamed and puffed out my chest a bit. I thought we must be putting on a good show, as it were. Looking for a bit more praise, I asked coyly, "Well, that is a nice thing to say. What do you mean exactly?"

"Doug! He built his boat by himself from wood he got from the forest and he puts his motorcycle in it as well! And it is all so beautiful. I would have thought that was impossible! I have no idea how he did that! He makes the impossible possible. I will *always* remember this."

The three girls are in the kitchen with Sally cooking pancakes. Breakfast is still a ways off. Eddy is standing to one side looking a bit bored. He's disinterested in cooking. Likes to save his energy for eating! I went outside and cut a few rounds with the chainsaw and left them by the chopping block.

"What were you doing, sweetie?" asked Sal.

"Oh, just cutting a few rounds in case anyone wanted to take a few whacks."

Eddy slipped out, put on his shoes and the next thing I hear is whack-thunk, whack-thunk. It was like a duck taking to water. He couldn't help himself.

I went back outside. "Do you remember what you learned yesterday? Do you need any more instruction, Ed?"

"No. I think I can do it!" Whack-thunk, whack-thunk, whack-thunk. No splitting. Just thunking.

"Not a lot of strength is required, Ed. Remember, it's all in the rhythm. Swing those hips!"

Ed looks at me. Sweat is pouring down from his forehead. The little round of wood, the size of a Presto log, is undamaged except for a dent or two.

"Sooo hard!"

"Nah, little girls can do it. One handed. Blindfolded! You just need to practice."

"Oh, little girls with blinds? They can do this? One hand?"

"Yup, piece of cake. *All* of them. No problem!"

Ed wipes his brow, picks up the splitting maul and whack-thunks his way through that first piece. He is well on his way to lumberjack status. I walk away grinning from ear to ear.

The students wanted to do a project and they decided on building a simple outdoor table. There is a language barrier and the natural chaos that ensues from five people working on one table. It is kinda crazy. But it is also fun and, even better, it is the reason the Chinese students are here.

No, *not* to learn table making. I am in no position to teach any real carpentry, but they are here to exercise gweilo thinking and, especially, independent thinking. Having to work things out for yourself is very uncommon in Chinese society. Usually there is a teacher and the teacher shows you the way. It is a recipe, always a recipe. It is very rigid. All they have to do is learn by rote and they pass the test. Memory? Yes. Understanding? Not so much. Table making with Dave is a course of a different colour.

Even a simple table requires thought, planning, measuring and imagining the end result in your head so that you can first build it virtually without cutting the wood. As we go through each step, they are impressed with the complexity.

"Oh David, this is so much mess!"

"Excuse me?"

"So much mess!"

While it is true that I tend to work in a disorganized manner and mess is an inevitable outcome for me, at the time I was thinking that everything was quite orderly. In fact, I was pretending hard to be organized so that the kids might learn good work habits. So, I pursued it. Seems Hazel had no idea that so much *math* was involved in carpentry and so she was remarking on all the mess…er…math.

And so we continue to get to know each other.

"So, guys, we are going to make a table. What size table should it be?"

The question is met with four blank stares. I repeat the question. And we all wait while the wheels in their little heads try to come up to speed. Size suggestions are hesitatingly offered up. Each is refused by the crazy as a hoot owl teacher. Confusion reigns. I smile. They look perplexed. Finally one kid says, "What are you going to use the table for?"

"*Yes*! That's the right question. Let's think about use. Let's talk about use. What kind of questions come up for that?" And so it goes.

I taught the students how to use the chop saw, with lots of instruction and coaching. They were very careful and very good when learning how to operate it. Miss Wong, however, was having a heart attack. I explained to her that a scar is the best way to remember an adventure. She just looked horrified.

By the time we were half way through making the table frame, I reached for the tape measure to mark a piece of wood to cut. I couldn't find it. Two of the kids had already thought about the next step, referred to the sketch, found the wood, marked it and cut it. Yes, you read that right. They had done it!

This "just do it" attitude was very, very different from the way they usually behaved, especially at school. This time they anticipated! This time they took the initiative!

"So, you think I'm going to need two pieces this long, eh? What makes you think that?"

And they explain, pointing to the sketch.

"Right! Now, did you measure correctly? Can we fasten the wood without checking it? Are you sure?"

"Yes! We are sure. Screw the wood!"

And so we did.

At this particular juncture, they all feel as if they are well on their way to becoming accomplished carpenters...if only the tools weren't so heavy! Some female Chinese students are so slight that, try as they might, they cannot hold the drill level. Putting in a screw is virtually impossible. They just don't have the heft that such a task requires. Having said that, they keep trying even if it is nigh on impossible. It is both admirable and pathetic at the same time. Sadly, sometimes size matters.

But the best part of the day was the whales. Yup! A large pod of a dozen or so came up and cavorted about right in front of our house. Tails flapping, bodies rolling, snorts, half leaps. Orcas are pretty big! They leap high about as often as I do. Most of it is a lot of, well, cavorting. Whales gamboling and playing around. It was great and the kids were thrilled. Later in the day, the whales came back for a brief encore. They were politely announced by Fiddich who heard them coming and ran to tell us, otherwise they might have gotten away while we were all inside. Whales are impressive but a dog trained to be a whale watcher is no small thing either. Yeah, east meets west and the fun is just beginning.

The students were making dinner for us, a ritual that was to be continued in future years. Tracey's in charge.

"Is it Chinese?" I ask.

"Of course! I am Chinese so whatever I cook is Chinese!"

Can't argue with that logic.

We had red snapper on the menu and the students decided to gather oysters and clams as well. They marveled at the cleanliness and abundance of "free" dinner.

But oh my gawd! The dishes! And the time! These guys worked very hard to make a great meal but no wonder McDonald's is popular in China. I had no idea Chinese cooking is so labour intensive. We must have all folded dumplings for half an hour at least. That's seven dumpling folders for thirty minutes or over three person hours of intense dumpling folding—*not* counting making the pastry and the filling. Think about that. China is poised to become the world's largest economy and it's only the meal preparation time that is holding them back. Another few thousand more McDonald's and KFCs and the world is theirs!

By this time our skies had finally cleared of smoke from the wildfires and the students were able to go out after dinner to look at the stars—something they never see in Hong Kong as there is so much ambient light and pollution. They lounged on the deck chatting and playing with the dogs. One of the kids said, "This is not real. Hong Kong is real. I don't like reality. I like here!"

Once again, the refrain: "This is not real. Tomorrow we go back to Campbell River and then by bus to Victoria and enter the real world again. No more sitting. No more relaxing. No more extra sleep or fun with dogs.

Soon we go back to Hong Kong and the real world of so much study and so much hard work!"

"That is true if you choose it to be true. But think about it. When you go back home, where is Sally? Where am I? Where are the dogs? If this is not real, do we disappear?"

"You live dream life! We students have to go back to ugly world. It would be nice to stay here!"

"I admit that it would be nice. And that is why we do it. If you think it is nice, too, why don't you do it? Why not let the others go back and you stay?"

"Impossible! I have to go back!"

"Why?"

At that point the question hits home. Hazel wonders why. And there is no answer forthcoming. She just looks at me confused. The usual answers don't seem to work. A tear rolls down her cheek. She turns her face away and wipes it dry. Still no answer.

I know that Hazel can't stay and she knows it, too. But she really does have choices in her life and it is that realization that hits home. Maybe she doesn't have to do what everyone expects her to do. Or does she? And that is the question she now ponders. To what extent is she freely making choices and to what extent is she a prisoner of circumstance?

Of course, we all think about that at some point. I know that as soon as I am free of an obligation or a previous relationship or even just a project, the freedom feels a bit like emptiness and is soon filled with something else. Often it is a similar burden to the one just released. We tend to repeat our choices. But, really, we don't have to. Much of it is habit.

For the Chinese kids all of it seems done by rote. They seem to have less freedom to choose in just about every area of their lives. They are programmed more deeply than we are. It is this type of conversation that Dennis wants us to have with them. He is still unsure if it is a good thing, though.

After all, he is a pillar of the society that values obedience, harmony and productivity. He doesn't feel as if he has had a lot of choices, either. His calendar is filled. And he doesn't really want a lot of renegades running amok. It is so unharmonious. Still, something prompts him to send these kids.

He thinks we are a safe first step to seeing choices. We can raise the questions but we don't offer the opportunity for anyone to actually jump ship. They are going to have to think a great deal more like this if they are to get off the Hong Kong Highway to Harmony and Obedience.

And, of course, if you get off, what exit do you take? Where do you end up? For these kids, we are just showing them that there is a map with different routes on it. Ninety-nine percent will end up where they expected.

But Hazel is in Liberal Studies at the university. It is a new faculty intended to foster a bit more radical (but still safe) thinking. This is what she came for. Who knows where this all may lead?

-36-

Joining the Country Club

One hundred years ago (give or take) a lot of people lived in our area. The town of Campbell River hardly existed back then. The island we live on once had three times the population it has now and supported two stores. Now we have none.

The reasons for this, of course, are obvious and can be summarized nicely by the term urbanization. The implication is clear. We are evolving, improving and living better. Go urban or devolve. Put more bluntly, there is a death threat being broadcast to all small communities.

Already the vast majority of the Canadian population lives in cities and this migration from country to city is playing out all over the world. The trend is likely to continue. Progress, eh?

But that trend didn't influence those who stayed here, those who came back and those who came here from elsewhere. It doesn't seem to include those planning and preparing to come here in the future. Why not? What is it that makes people buck the trend and choose to live hardier lives with fewer, rather than more, modern conveniences? Are we just nuts?

The Reverend Alan Greene of the Columbia Coast Mission wondered that same thing about the islanders he encountered back in the 1930's and concluded in his journal at the time that "it was their need for independence".

I'm not sure that's it. Not entirely, anyway. I think man is mostly a social animal and isolation and separation is not our chosen path to happiness and fulfillment. I think even the most eccentric amongst us wants to belong a bit. Once in a while. Somewhere. I think we all crave a little community now and then. And, more than that, we want to be members of that community, not guests or visiting strangers.

Community building is a tough job. Too hard for me. And community building in an area populated by individualists is an even tougher task than usual. The outer islands attract independent individualist like rock concerts attract Bic lighters. It is an area united by the principle of "let's not unite".

Lately, our neighboring island has been up in arms over the moving of the library into a new building. Fur has flown over that. We on our island are not exempt from tempests in our local teapots. We have our own community issues. But, because we are a smaller group and meetings are mercifully rare, things usually work out. The key is to let issues flare out.

The trouble with these issues is that you never know which one is going to go super nova on you. I am always surprised. Danger lurks everywhere and no less so than at the local dock.

"So, Dave, we sure could use a new voice on the community board. Would you run?"

"Well, thanks for the invitation but I'd rather suck on nuclear waste."

"Ha, ha, ha. That's good. Ha, ha. No, seriously. You are a mediator and we seem to disagree a lot and well, we could use a little help."

"No. You see, being a mediator means being neutral. If I sat on the council then I would be perceived as pro-council by those who don't agree with it. I'd be perceived as anti-council by those on council whom I would come to alienate. And I'd be disliked by everyone else. This is not good for a mediator's career. I am going to remain neutral. Call it disinterest. Call it paranoia. I choose to call it professional neutrality."

"Well, geez, Dave, I should warn you, then…"

"Of what?"

"We don't accept neutrality up here. Hereabouts you have to stand for something. Doesn't matter what it is, really. You just have to have an opinion on stuff. If you don't have an opinion on things, no one will trust you."

"But I haven't been here that long. I don't know enough to have an opinion on things. What kind of things are we talking about, anyway?"

"Well, there's the big brouhaha that blew over a while back but there are a lot of hard feelings still. The community is pretty divided over that one. Got ugly, real ugly. Seen things you never expected to see—things you never want to see again."

"Wow, pretty touchy, eh? But it's over?"

"Well, the cow died so the question is moo."

"Moot, Bob. M-O-O-T."

"Yeah, I know that. But we all like to say "moo", anyway. You know what I mean."

"Yes, I do know. You guys are a riot. Now I know that I'm going to regret this, but what was the big issue?"

"Well, are you for free range or against it?"

"Free range? You mean like in chickens?"

"No, Dave, keep up with me here! Cows and horses. Are you in favour of free ranging cows and horses or are you against it?"

"Oh, man, I don't care. Really. On that topic, I truly am neutral."

Well, Bob's eyes narrowed as if he was seeing me clearly for the first time. He dropped his voice an octave and, showing barely repressed passion for the topic, he asked me one more time.

"Dave, I told you. Not having an opinion is *not* an option. Now I like you fine so far and all, but you are really pushing the envelope here. I have no choice. I need to know. *Are you for or against free ranging cattle*?"

I was trapped. No way out. I had to answer but, like most traps, the answer was not going to spring me from every part of this dilemma. So I stalled.

"Yeah, well, of course I have an opinion on that. Big issues involved there. And I can see that it is an opinion that counts. In this day and age, most personal opinions don't count much anymore and I applaud you for taking my point of view so seriously…I'll be thinking this one over real hard. When can I get back to you?"

"Nice try, Dave. No stalling. What's it gonna be, free or not so free?"

"Sheesh. Well, now…I need to know a bit more before I come down hard on one side of the fence, so to speak…like…uh…how big is this island again?"

"Almost one hundred square miles."

"How many people live here?"

"Fifty."

"How many critters?"

"Well, before the cow died, there were was one cow and one horse."

"I see…", taking a deep breath and letting it out slowly so as to convey considerable thought, "Well, in that case, given the existence of only the single horse, I will cast my vote on humanitarian grounds for the remaining, and likely grieving, lonely old horse to roam freely."

"Good on ya, Dave. Good on ya."

I was pleasantly surprised. Another bullet dodged in the rural jihad.

Some of the guys have been working on the community kitchen together. Half a dozen or so of us putting up drywall, mudding, talking, and having lunch. It is fun and a nice way to spend the day. Stories told, some jokes, a few laughs. Some might think we were bonding.

That is, in essence, what working on the community buildings is all about. My friend John calls this "fellowship". Another fellow calls it "community". I think of it as kinda goofy but, regardless, we all enjoy it.

My wife is big on bonding, though, for me, anyway. "Why don't you go up to the workshop and find some guys and do that bonding thing? You know, like guys do?"

"Sal, I don't bond! Okay? I talk. I socialize. I may even "like" or "enjoy". I do not bond. That is just bloody weird. Paramecium bond. Men don't bond. Guys who think they bond freak me out!"

"Well guys standing around, hands in their pockets, talking guns or engines or whatever. Isn't that bonding?"

"No, sweetie, that is not bonding. That is called talking. Bonding is when glue is involved. All that male bonding stuff seems highly overrated to me. Actors in movies claim to bond. No one else does. Maybe if you fought in a war together and saved each other's lives and married twin sisters and bought a business together you'd bond. But it would take more than that for me. I'd need glue. Epoxy. So, stop with the bonding, okay?"

As we wrapped up this conversation, John called me on the walkie-talkie.

"Hey, Dave, wanna go out and get some logs, old buddy? Do a little bonding? Waddya say?"

"Yeah, sounds good. I'll just get my boots."

I look at Sal. She gives me one of her beautiful smiles.

"Don't forget the glue, sweetie."

"Hey, Darcy, you going up to work on the kitchen on Wednesday?"

"Nah, too frustrating. There's no plan. No direction. I like to have a specific task assigned and the materials and a set of plans nearby and then I'll just get on with it. But this project is too loosey-goosey. I don't know what I am supposed to be doing."

"Yeah, I know. But that's the only way it works. No one will work if anyone is in charge. And all the plans are changed by the one doing whatever it is they choose to do. It's all very organic. You just gotta go with the flow. The good thing is that things are getting done. It's coming along nicely."

People show up as their schedules, hormones and whims dictate. Once on site, they decide to stay or leave as their mood determines. Sometimes the mood is affected by who else is there or who isn't. You never really know who the crew will be.

And then they do what they do, depending on what tools have been brought, if someone was kind enough to bring some lunch, or whether the work is going according to their personal standards. Not only is it hard to know the composition of the crew at any given time but it is just as hard to determine what they will do next. It is all totally fluid.

Plans change, too. Our community has a very dedicated designer who always provides an overall plan on paper which is what the schedule, budget and decision to proceed is based on. However, who is available or willing to take on a certain part of the job is a potential game changer. Materials and tools are huge variables. The availability of certain materials might change the plans.

For instance we just might have five gallons of leftover paint—which right there could decide the colour we are going to use. Other times, we have someone buy the paint when they are in town. That commitment is sufficient to delegate the decision making process to the purchaser. When a paint store donated returned paint *they* decided the colour.

Other times we could have a lumber supply of certain dimensions and that might influence things. The kitchen we are working on currently has walls clad in drywall, in no small part due to a member of the community bringing in more than they needed for their own building and willing to part with the extra. And the stove is a generous contribution from another neighbour—style and size decided by the price!

Tools are a real bugaboo, though, when we're working. Some people bring them, some don't. But everyone working usually needs a tool of some kind so that means we are often in a tool shortage situation. But somehow we make do.

When you see a school of fish, such as herring, zipping in unison one way and then another, each movement a brilliant display of instant choreography, you might think they are pretty marvelous. I do. What coordination! What unity! What communicative and cooperative genius!

We're not like that. We're more like a hockey riot. Except we seem to get things built rather than destroyed. It's a miracle.

On another work day John, Gerry and I head up to the community buildings to install the new entry doors and finish some outside sheathing. It's your classic island crew. John is hard of hearing (deaf as a long dead duck) and Gerry mumbles semi-coherent half jokes mixed in with requests and instructions as he thinks aloud. He often keeps his glasses in his teeth as he speaks. If he is wearing his glasses, he has a pencil in his mouth instead.

"Nowunderthecomooty…lostfaithinyedaveyuolgit! Passammereh? Angityr handsoutothebluddyway, eh! Got it? Wegonnatakituprighthere ehandyoolot blanceitferasec. Anyonegottasmoke?"

The exact translation of the above is: "No wonder the community has lost faith in you, Dave, you old git. Pass the hammer, eh? And get your hands out of the bloody way, eh? Got it? We're going to tack it up right here and you lot balance it for a second. Anyone got a smoke?"

My interpretation of it: "Let's get started. Pass the hammer. You two hold the doors in place while I put a nail in."

He knows we don't smoke.

And so it goes all morning as I slowly get better at interpreting the monotone, polysyllabic, carpenter's pidgin that passes for Gerry's communication.

John really can't hear a thing. With the background noise of the construction site complete with a generator, he doesn't have a chance. And I don't repeat Gerry's semi-gibberish because I am trying to mentally translate it, interpret it and process it.

John is pretty smart. He participates fully by reading Gerry's or my body language and anticipating the next step. Not easy. He just waits for a movement from me or Gerry and jumps to it. If I make a move to hold the doors, John grabs his side of the frame. If I move past the doors for the plywood on the floor, he scarcely misses a beat and picks up his side of that. We are like an ugly Russian ballet. And we are mute.

I have to learn gibberish-with-pencil-in-mouth and John has to learn two body languages. We get better at it as the day goes along.

Gerry knows his stuff. He's been a carpenter all his life. He has the ability to build outside the formula and still make it work. I'm trying to anticipate his moves but I can't.

"Sheesh, man, I'm glad you're doing this. I would've thought we'd have built tilt-up walls and then added a stud or two but I never would have built it like this. No criticism, none. I just wouldn't have known how to do it this way."

"Seeanystuds, dya? Iswadyado if yadongot anybloodywood, eh. Anitsbetter, anyway. Bloodyel we gotnomaterials, dowe."

Translation: "See any studs do you? It's what you do if don't have any bloody wood, eh. And it's better anyway. Bloody hell, we got no materials, do we?"

My interpretation: "Dave, we don't have the wood or materials for that. And the normal way is stupid, anyway. This is better. Different. But stronger. Don't worry about the rules. They were made for people who don't understand physics. Once you have the principle of the concept handled, you can be more creative and we have to be because we don't have the lumber!"

I don't think John spoke a word all day. He just worked. I occasionally tried for clarification or asked a question of Gerry, none of which elicited a comprehensible response, what with the glasses and pencils and all. So we worked in a state of guesswork and anxiety trying not to misinterpret a gesture, a mumble or a twitch. John and I were constantly doing double takes as we searched for signs or hints. Or danger. We moved like squirrels. It can get stressful.

John left early. He had to go home, anyway, but I know that the tension of trying to guess his way through a creative construction process was getting to him. He bid us adieu around one.

"NizeguyJohn, eh!"

I thought he'd said, "noskajakay" and was wondering what the hell that meant and so I just looked at him like I was an idiot. And Gerry looked at me like I was an idiot, too. We were at an impasse. After a few seconds of that, he just shook his head, mumbled something to himself and we moved on. I finally figured it out.

My interpretation: "Nice guy. I like him. Good to work with. I'd work with him again."

We got most of the work done by four and so I was packing up my tools.

"Ifyadonneedemleaveemanl'llfinishmyselflader."

Translation: "If you don't need them, leave them and I'll finish it myself, later."

My interpretation: "You were only useful for bringing your tools. Leave them with me and I'll finish up here on my own, maybe tomorrow. Let's go home. I'll fix you a cup of tea."

It's a wonder. It really is.

Community work day again. Nice, bright, late fall day. Still some orange in the trees. I am standing in the community workshop looking out the window and I see a herd of goats wandering down the road. Coming up behind are the two local women whose herd it is. A few of the goats stop now and then to nibble on trees and things as they pass down the hill. It is all very, very picturesque. But I do spend a moment wondering why a herd of goats is headed for the dock.

Forty-five minutes later I decide to head home and I, too, begin to head toward the dock. I am half way down the hill when I see the goat ladies tethering three goats and leading them from the field of one of the local landowners. Seems the herd had found some nice forage there and they had all stopped to snack. The goat ladies had other plans and a schedule that they now deemed pressing enough to put leads on a few goats and start moving them down the hill.

I stopped to admire the scene. A group of twenty or so goats were living large off the land of whoever had the greenest grass and two goatherds were trying to keep to a human agenda. It was entertaining.

"Why are you taking those goats to the dock?"

"They're going for a ride!"

"That's a lot of goats for your small boat!"

"Only three are going—new home."

"Oh. And the rest of the herd is just along to say good bye?"

"Yeah, they know. It's happened before. They like to come this far, anyway."

And then the women pull on the chosen three and the rest of the herd reluctantly begins to follow. We all walked down the stretch to the public wharf. Twenty little goat bums ahead of me.

When we got to the end of the approach, the ladies hauled the three down the ramp. The rest of the herd gathered at the head of the ramp but they didn't follow. They just looked on as numbers one, two and three were readied for the boat ride. Then, after waiting for a respectful minute or so, they all turned on their heels and headed back up the hill to the neighbor's pasture. The goat ladies just carried on with loading and preparing. It was a study in natural management.

The goat herd has a home. It has acreage. But the goat ladies think that goats should walk in herds to feel fulfilled and so they take them up and down the logging roads now and then for their ambulatory repast. The goats eat on the go, as it were. And then they eat on the come, as they return home. It seems to work out just fine. The animals are extremely healthy, quite beautiful in a goat sort of way and obviously content in their surroundings—nice to see.

And that, in a nutshell, is part of the draw of our community. There is always something of interest going on. Sometimes it is a new boat at the dock, the mail plane coming in, or maybe an encounter with a long unseen neighbour. It's hard to know—it's always changing. Sometimes it's just seeing a herd of largely unfettered goats on the dock saying their goodbyes to a few buddies.

Interior of our home

-37-

Hick is Hip

In case you didn't know, going country is now hip. It's the latest thing. Eschew the Ferrari for the cottage. Forget nouveau cuisine and instead grow your own asparagus and yams. Raise some chic chickens and pick salal berries. Of course there are new standards to aspire to, but the trend to natural is definitely catching on. Better hurry, but be careful. There *is* manure out there.

Personally, I think my wife and I have gone too far down this road to trendy. We've gone country to the point of madness. We are so intensely local we're practically loco. We buy only local produce and fair trade coffee (whatever that is). We're even looking for the guy on Vancouver Island who grows his own bananas! It's probably too late for us. We've been absorbed by what has become a phenomenon—a natural phenomenon—and we have become au courant in the process.

Worse, we are fully committed to the oxymoron of alternative living. Quelle surprise! Alternative has gone main stream. I really should have known. It's all part of being one of those damn baby boomers. Scratch a boomer and there's another one right behind him itching to take his place, forming a crowd, defining a trend. Boomers make and follow trends and, if we need any assistance, instructions will soon follow on the cover of the Lifestyle section of the local paper.

And boomer trends show up in the weirdest ways. We have the now de rigueur Portuguese Water Dogs. Sal collects feathers, rocks, shells, dried mushrooms and twigs for decorative purposes. She is putting fresh cut kale in flower vases! She's knitting, too. She's planning a quilt, for gawd's sake, and baking up a storm. This summer she planted herbs. Turns out there is a whole world based on this stuff. I thought it was only Martha.

As I write this, there is a large pot of chicken carcass, vegetables and herbs on the woodstove slowly converting to stock. It should be the cover shot of some country cooking magazine.

I confess to inexplicable urges, myself. I've already made some rustic furniture that we all know is eventually destined for the fireplace. Birdhouses are next—same destiny. I've had thoughts of gardening but, so far, successfully suppressed them. But this much I know for sure, I will succumb to hickdom, preferably in a hip kind of way.

I've also thought of making mead and we already make our own almost undrinkable wine—Chateau Swill. We both wear thick plaid shirts and rubber boots. And I talk chainsaws and falling. Turns out our life in the country is a cornucopia of clichés, a traipsing of the trite. We are, without doubt, knee deep in the newest popular lifestyle. We're fashionable again. Who knew?

I swear I had no idea. Honest. I thought I was running away from it all, breaking new ground, seeing the forest through the parked cars. Going to seed felt like a revolutionary idea, something radical. Instead, it's all so radically chic. Gardening and woodwork are all the rage everywhere. It's unbelievable.

And there is seemingly no end to these country living manifestations. Our local community has gardeners, furniture makers, restorers of old tractors, quilters and knitters and gender is not a factor. Well, maybe it is a factor but usually you can't tell by looking. We all look like potatoes in country garb.

We also have groups of foraging experts, fungi finders, stream keepers, tree huggers, wolf enthusiasts, marmot protectors, bird watchers and every known form of unconventional health practitioner. Unconventional health practices are, naturally (pardon the pun), the convention out here. Of course the yoga instructor is king!

Don't get me wrong. This newish trend to all natural is not all bad. In fact, the food is better and the stresses are less. But it is a bit startling to discover that the groups dedicated to saving old apple seeds, old farm machinery, old fences (woven willow and dry stack) and even old varieties of chickens, turkeys and cattle, are now cutting edge.

The irony is that the impetus for all this new age country zeal comes from repatriated city folks. Yes, like us! They (we) are the market on which the country business thrives. The long-in-the-tooth who are the experts on mushrooms, kelp, bee keeping, and milling their own lumber are now the new consultants. Back-to-the-land is a growth business in every way. Of course, the bumpkins are now buying big screen televisions, sports utility vehicles and vacationing in exotic locales. I guess it is payback time. Some are even incorporating which reminds me, I really should register a new website, countrybumpkin.com. Oops, I just checked—I'm too late.

I'm not kidding about all this. Rumor has it that all sorts of celebrities are up here stripping bark from cedar trees to make baskets, trimming the tops off nettles for dinner and picking mushrooms—with trained nature interpreters, of course. They have been paying the locals to gather oysters, dig clams and pick berries, too. Hiring locals is called treading lightly on the planet by the rich. According to the local grapevine Oprah likes First Nations art and Michelle Pfeiffer wears rubber boots.

So now that hick is hip I'm just going to have to live with the fact that I'm no longer eccentric. Trust me, I can handle it. I can do mainstream. I'm a refugee from the suburbs, after all. Ordinary is my game. Country cachet will pass. I figure I just have to wait it out. Natural, simple and organic in every way will, unfortunately, someday be passé and Michelle and Oprah will be jetting to other parts of the globe. All I'll have to do then is hang out and enjoy life in the country—and the mead.

Going hand in hand with country chic is minimalism. It's all the latest whether you live in a high rise or subscribe to Mother Earth News. Mission style furniture, the Volkswagen Beetle, hiking, even funky junque made from yard sale finds; it's all about appreciating the simple things in life. Minimalism, in theory anyway, is about taking time to stop and smell the flowers. But simple isn't all that it's cracked up to be. For one thing, it's complicated. And, for another, it's pretty darn expensive.

Minimalism is also a dichotomy. Less, they are trying to say, is more. Minimalism, as it is currently promoted, emphasizes simple over complicated, but also expensive over cheap. Think mountain bikes, Starbucks and Gore-Tex. Only the well-off can afford to do less with that stuff, right? To be a thoroughly modern minimalist one should walk, but walk in Rockports, ride, but ride in a hybrid Prius and generally try to make life appear simple through exclusive and expensive means. That's not easy. And when simple isn't easy, something is wrong, I say.

I aspire to simple but I can't cut it. Too stupid and cheap, I suppose. Ugly, too, if you must know. I look like a giant athletic bag in Gore-Tex. And I have a lot of trouble buying more expensive *walking* shoes as opposed to the normal shoes I usually find myself walking in.

I am beginning to think minimalism refers to the amount of satisfaction one gets, rather than to the lifestyle. It may also refer to your eventual bank account or, possibly, lifespan. But it does not refer to the amount of effort or money expended. Trust me. Minimalism is not for the lazy or the budget conscious.

Being a minimalist is a major commitment, not a fickle lifestyle whim such as beanbag furniture or Pilates. Once you go simple, there is no turning back. Go minimal or go home (in an air-conditioned SUV), I always say.

Minimalism also requires study. For one thing, it seems to require an unnatural commitment to learning about product content and business practices. One has to buy from countries that pay fair wages and don't pollute. All employees involved have to be content with life and be happily married; preferably non-smokers and their kids must be breast fed. How can anyone know this?

Minimalists, it seems, choose goods made by smaller rather than larger companies, but really prefer to buy handmade from the natives of Nepal. Minimalism requires a heavy investment in hand cranking devices and non-power tools, too. One needs lots of such tools to be a simple minimalist. Where a phone and a phone book once sufficed to effect repairs, the minimalist now needs a workshop full of tools and a happily breast fed, non-exploited assistant to feed and manage the draft horse.

One also has to boycott the grid. Being plugged in, it seems, is bad. Sitting in the dark, ergo, must be good in an alternative culture sort of way. And you should stay only as clean as you must to gain admittance to a theatre. Don't overdo water consumption despite the fact that a gallon or so falls on your head every day if you live in British Columbia. Use less, even if there's plenty. In this way, we help the fish. I think.

Did I mention pooping? Don't try to move your bowels without a considerable investment in biotechnology and composting, and the willingness to maintain a politically correct system of transport and storage for your poop, something you were simply trying to get rid of. It's no longer bowel moving, it's now bowel moving and storage.

And don't try to read a book without first rediscovering the principles of generating light from scratch. And, for gawd's sake, don't eat anything without determining that it's organic and that the farmer loves and names the chickens. There also has to be a plan to sustain production, recycle the containers the product is transported in and replenish the fuels required to cook it. It would also help if you could do all this without wasting any water washing the dishes or using any refrigerant or fossil fuels. Nothing comes easy in a simple life.

I was initially attracted to minimalism. I liked the idea of simple. City living was getting me down and, quite frankly, I understood less and less of what was going on. I aspire to little, want for nothing and desire even less. Minimalism sounded like my cup of tea. But I have reluctantly concluded I don't have the money or the brains required to be simple. I guess that I am destined to remain a complicated man. It's easier.

City friends continue to wonder how it is that Sal and I can live remote, isolated and seemingly without all the comforts of the city. The answer is amazingly simple (that word again!). We don't feel in the least remote nor isolated and we want for no comforts whatsoever. Admittedly, we lack a few conveniences but, with a bit of planning and a smidge extra work, we can stay comfortable enough to meet our own standards quite nicely, thank you. So can anyone.

We don't have five hundred television channels. The mail is not delivered every day and frequent shopping is impossible. I definitely do more of my own maintenance work (most, actually) and we don't get the restaurant experience much anymore.

Boo hoo.

Constantly encountering people I know is also greatly reduced. But I can live with that and I think some of the people involved are relieved as well, so it's a win-win, socially speaking.

In exchange for those minor alterations in lifestyle I live in a virtual paradise of flora and fauna. I am also healthier, if for no other reason than the air is pure and the work is more physical. And Sal's food is better than any restaurant. The seafood is definitely fresher.

There are no rules. There are no sirens. There is no traffic and I have no stress. We need less. We want less. And, thank gawd, there *is* less! Fewer bills, too. And, in this sense, truly, less *is* more. More satisfying, relaxing, affordable, livable and healthier. It really does not get much better.

When I look back on the years of our transition from mainstream cul-de-sac rat race living to being surrounded by forests and ocean I see more than just a shift in lifestyle. I see more than just downsizing or retiring. I now see a new lease on life. For me, the change has been wholesale, massive, life altering if not life saving. It has been huge.

I now know that there is something more to country living than just rest and relaxation. And it is much more than just going out to pasture when you get to retirement. It is now feeling like an alternative lifestyle but in a much more significant way than that phrase has ever meant before. I am starting to feel like a survivor of an increasingly stressful and toxic urban way of life.

One of the weird differences between living in the woods and the city is one's increased ability to be more present in the moment. This altered state of being may just be due to aging and failing memory but I prefer to think of it as the beginning of some sort of better late than never enlightenment. I am no philosopher, but going to the woods at least increases awareness of the senses and probably, by extension, one's sense of being.

Heaven knows I am overdue for some consciousness-raising. For the most part I have lived my life in the dark recesses of thought, worry, planning and cursing the myriad and inevitable screw ups associated with those activities. Plus I commuted. I didn't spend very much time smelling the roses on my way to or from work.

Chopping wood takes time but not so much focused thinking. Once you get the hang of it, it is difficult to screw up, the surprise of occasional bloodletting notwithstanding. Ergo, more physical time, less worry time, with just a bit of first aid practice now and then to keep your mind on its (and your) toes.

And that's a good thing. It is a much healthier state of living. Or it can be. I distinctly recall being so much in my own mind that I could drive twenty miles to an urban appointment without recalling anything I drove past while on the way. I was so deeply committed to thinking about the meeting coming up or what had just happened in the news that I failed to notice what was around me as I was driving in the present.

The easiest way of achieving conscious presence is simply being outside and having all the physical senses wide awake and the usual thoughts turned off. Walking in the woods is a sure fire way of leaving your cares and worries behind. It's a magical thing.

Each step deeper into the forest is like an entry to an empty stage with a huge but quiet and reverential audience. The space is broken only by your own intrusion. You are special only because you are there—no other reason. And you become very aware of your own existence. Very profound stuff if you think about it. Which, of course, you shouldn't do since it defeats the whole effect.

I noticed an example of this phenomenon of capturing the moment the other day when we had scheduled a small work party for a project. Some people were on site, others were arriving by boat and I was hiking along the beach. Orcas were sighted. There was a call on the walkie-talkies. Everything stopped. Everyone turned to look out. Orcas have an incredible presence and, if you are lucky enough to see them in the wild, they bring you to their space. They took centre stage. And they kept it.

And it is not just those magical moments that do it. Weather, too, is a big factor in awareness. In modern lifestyles, we can mostly ignore it and get along to the mall or the office regardless of how much Mother Nature protests. We deny the weather. Not so in the wilds. Out here you can't ignore her moods. She is simply too present. And, like a whale visit, she brings you with her.

It's impossible to ignore the present when you are in the woods. *Now* is big out here. It embraces you. Living even partly feral requires an intimate and immediate awareness of your environment. Fortunately, the surroundings are attractive and beautiful. The present moment is often so enchanting, so totally occupying, you are ravished by it. It is a momentous love affair with life.

I really have no idea if life is more meaningful or if my existence is any more enlightened. I haven't swapped my jeans for a toga, lost weight, gone bald or acquired a cult or anything really neat like that. Nor can I get into the lotus position or even a beatific mood. I am pretty happy just to be able to get out of a chair on my own. I have no demonstrably hard evidence of achieving even the outskirts of nirvana except for my desire to be here—and nowhere else.

I suspect I am doing well, however, if only because my mind is not so cluttered, my being not so burdened by trivial pursuits and Sally hasn't left me. It could, of course, just be a country convert's appreciation for this life running somewhat amok with enthusiasm and excitement. But, if that is what it is, that's not so bad either.

What is is, after all.

Acknowledgements

My sincerest gratitude is extended—

To those who read my blog. You guys keep me writing. You know who you are. Mostly I don't.

To my beta readers who spent an amazing amount of time giving thoughtful and comprehensive feedback without hurting my feelings too much: Benjamin Cox, Rosamund and Peter Davies, Rachel and Roger Mattice, Sid Midtdal and Eileen Sowerby.

To Emily and Brian Robertson for providing much needed assistance with so many things.

To Simon Davies for his invaluable advice and support.

To my friends and neighbours John Robilliard and Jorge Little who have always been there for us and without whom we would never have made our way in the wilds.

And especially to my wife, partner and much better half, Sally, without whom this book and all the happiness in my life would simply not exist.

Last, but not least, to the off the grid characters on the Mother Earth News forum and the free, wild and wonderful people of Discovery Sound, all of whom were and are an inspiration for living off the grid.

Sally, David, Fiddich and Megan

About the Author

David is a sixty-something father of two and husband to Sally for forty-plus years. He likes tea, puppies (although he'll deny it), cheap B flicks, and Scotch. Dave has done everything from running a medical clinic, racing motorcycles professionally to a stint as a banker. Prior to moving up the coast he was a mediator, arbitrator and business consultant for twenty years. None of this gave him any skills whatsoever for living off the grid.

Printed in the USA
CPSIA information can be obtained
at www.ICGtesting.com
LVHW021800240923
759181LV00005B/736